Faces  of Inequality

Faces of Inequality

Social Diversity in

American Politics

RODNEY E. HERO

New York   Oxford

Oxford University Press

1998

Oxford University Press

Oxford   New York

Athens   Auckland   Bangkok   Bogotá   Buenos Aires   Calcutta
Cape Town   Chennai   Dar es Salaam   Delhi   Florence   Hong Kong   Istanbul
Karachi   Kuala Lumpur   Madrid   Melbourne   Mexico City   Mumbai
Nairobi   Paris   São Paulo   Singapore   Taipei   Tokyo   Toronto   Warsaw

and associated companies in
Berlin   Ibadan

Copyright © 1998 by Oxford University Press, Inc.

First published in 1998 by Oxford University Press, Inc.
198 Madison Avenue, New York, New York 10016

First issued as an Oxford University Press paperback, 2000

Oxford is a registered trademark of Oxford University Press

Library of Congress Cataloging-in-Publication Data
Hero, Rodney E., 1953–
Faces of inequality : social diversity in American politics /
Rodney E. Hero.
p.   cm.
Includes bibliographical references and index.
ISBN 0-19-511714-X
ISBN 0-19-513788-4 (pbk.)
1. Multiculturalism—United States—States.   2. Political culture—
United States—States.   3. State governments—United States.
I. Title.
E184.A1H469   1998
306.2'0973—dc21   97-36985

1 3 5 7 9 8 6 4 2

Printed in the United States of America
on acid-free paper

Preface

This book is written with great interest in, yet some frustration with, the study of state politics in the United States. I believe that understanding state politics is important in itself and essential to a fuller understanding of the U.S. political system. It is unfortunate that state politics is sometimes viewed as less significant compared to "national" politics in the U.S. political system. That view is problematic in at least two ways. First, a national-state distinction is something of a false dichotomy given the nature of the U.S. federal system. Second, state politics is, in fact, very significant as this book consistently demonstrates.

At the same time, I have considerable frustration with how state politics is often studied. I share the views of Brace and of Jewell who have contended (see especially chapters 1 and 2 herein) that the study of state politics is overly "compartmentalized" and has lacked unifying theory. Moreover, it seems that our approaches to studying the topics have too often sacrificed the richness and variety of state politics to an ostensible statistical rigor. My own view is that more scholarly attention needs to focus on the "big picture" of state politics, and states need to be seen as central to the "big picture" of U.S. politics. I hope that this book helps nudge the literature in those directions. A goal of this book is to develop an interpretation, a unifying perspective, that is rooted in a major "dilemma," and prominent component of U.S. history—racial/ethnic diversity—as evident in and as it affects various contexts of state politics.

Perhaps ironically (given some of the arguments made later) the genesis of this book began from an attraction to Elazar's "political culture" argument. I, like many teachers of state politics, have commonly presented class lectures about political culture and found it to be an interesting, compelling thesis. And I co-authored an article often seen as supporting the political culture interpretation.[1] However, beginning more than a decade ago and emerging over time, I felt increasing dissatisfaction with it.

The interpretation seems(ed) to normatively and otherwise "privilege" certain populations and groups, and state political cultural systems. And, by defining political cultures almost exclusively in terms of the leading or dominant groups within states, without adequate attention (in my view) to the presence of "other" groups, the political culture perspective seems somewhat limited and largely a-contextual. Of related and equal importance, political culture seems to mask or gloss over some important elements, particularly ethnic/racial issues, as a set of pivotal phenomena in state and U.S. politics. These misgivings led me to perceive that underlying political culture might be some other social phenomenon, namely, social diversity.

The political culture view is not alone among interpretations of state politics that downplay the role of race/ethnicity, however. It seems to me that the contemporary state politics literature has been less attentive to issues of race/ethnicity than other subfields of American politics research. (And, arguably, other subfields have not given adequate attention to these questions. Perhaps not coincidentally, it appears that very few "minority" scholars are directly or extensively engaged in the study of state politics/policy.)

This book represents an effort to provide a framework for thinking about state politics and policy. I, like a number of scholars before me, perceived that race/ethnicity has been a defining characteristic of U.S. history. If race/ethnicity is indeed that important, theories and approaches should reflect that directly. This interpretation seeks to make our understanding of state politics more complete by not only more clearly acknowledging, but by systematically incorporating, social diversity. I certainly don't mean to suggest that diversity is the only important aspect of state politics, nor that other perspectives have nothing to offer. Also, there are aspects of state politics/policy where social diversity may provide only limited insight. However, this study demonstrates that diversity is very important, and probably at least as important as many other factors commonly considered.

Some orienting questions in my approach to studying state and U.S. politics, here and elsewhere, have been: What do "minorities" mean in, and for, U.S. democracy; and, what does U.S. democracy mean for and to "minorities"? That is, a more fundamental and adequate theoretical understanding can be gained, I think, by acknowledging and studying these questions because they bring attention to the "second" and "other" faces of politics. Thus, I see this book as an effort to shed light on previously underappreciated and understudied dimensions of U.S. state politics, with race/ethnicity at the core of the analysis.

With the general attention given to race/ethnicity in the United States, and its patent importance, I found (and find) it surprising that an interpretation like social diversity had not been put forth some time ago. Nonetheless, I suspect the argument will be controversial on several grounds. It already has been, "behind the scenes."

One (article) reviewer said the social diversity idea was (or is), simply, accusing other scholars of being "politically incorrect" and, in turn, is simply putting forth a "politically correct" argument. Another reviewer claimed that the argument was but a "cheap shot" at the political culture framework. A grant reviewer (for the National Science Foundation) suggested that what I should "really" do is undertake "DNA testing" of people (and that I should do so on my own, i.e., without funding). Needless to say, I view the social diversity perspective much differently, as a serious effort to critically assess and (re)interpret state politics.

The study incorporates considerable quantitative analysis, although I have consciously tried not to make that the centerpiece of the discussion. Rather, I have tried to make the social diversity thesis, as such, central, and to provide appropriate evidence, including scatterplots, tables, and figures, without having "data" obscure or overwhelm the critical points. Readers who have strong behavioralist/quantitative orientations may nonetheless view the book as not providing sufficient data. Again, I wish to emphasize the "forest" over the "trees," despite the presentation of much evidence.

The book therefore develops a perspective and explores it relative to many of the prominent issues or questions commonly raised in the state politics literature. One may notice that the chapter topics and titles tend to parallel those of "standard" (text)books on state politics. That is no accident. Applying a thesis to a succession of important issues within a subfield seems appropriate and necessary toward the goal of a "unifying" approach. It is also consistent with the guidance of recent works that suggest such a strategy.[2]

In some ways the thesis and findings echo V. O. Key's discussion of Southern politics in the 1940s. Race/ethnicity continues to be a political force in the U.S. political system—in significantly modified, subtler ways, and affecting other groups—including state (and local) political processes and policies. But I explore several dimensions that Key did not, such as various public policies and their aggregate and "differential" patterns, and I suggest that racial/ethnic factors may be of more consequence institutionally than previously acknowledged or understood.

However one perceives the issues and evidence presented in this study, I hope the social diversity thesis generates interest in state politics and policy, and how these are examined.

Acknowledgments

This book could not have been completed without a great deal of support, and tolerance, from my family, friends, and colleagues. All of them contributed in various ways to the project, and I am most grateful.

Among my faculty colleagues and friends who have talked with me about and commented on the ideas of the book, I'd like to thank Larry Dodd, Susan Clarke, Dennis Eckart, Michael Strine, Jeff Kopstein, Frank Beer, Simone Chambers, Mark Lichbach, and Anne Costain. I also very much appreciate the help of the American Politics Center and my colleagues there, and the Department of Political Science, University of Colorado at Boulder, more generally. The anonymous reviewers for Oxford University Press also provided a host of comments that improved the manuscript.

I have also benefited from the help and comments of graduate students at CU. Caroline Tolbert co-authored two articles and several papers with me on issues relevant to the book; I have also drawn on her dissertation. Robert Lopez, Mara Sidney, and Randall Partin have also commented on and/or worked with me on aspects of the study. John Halpin collected data and undertook much data analysis; he also helped with manuscript preparation and provided many helpful suggestions.

Patti Zike provided tremendous help in manuscript preparation and several related activities. Diana Stahl also contributed in this regard.

Finally, my family, especially Kathy and Lindsay, Chris and Jennifer, and my parents and sister, are and have been caring sources of support.

Again, I thank them all very much. Of course, any shortcomings in the book are my responsibility alone.

Contents

Faces of Inequality

1

Social Diversity and
the Study of State
Politics and Policy

The federal structure of the U.S. political system is important in numerous and varied ways. One major implication of federalism as an institutional feature is that states are permitted—indeed, expected—to be significant governments and policymakers (i.e., "polities") in the United States. States have historically been the primary domestic public policymakers, and despite tremendous changes in the U.S. political and social systems over time, they remain so.[1] By many accounts the policymaking importance of the states has grown over the last generation. In such major policy areas as education, welfare, health, crime and law enforcement, taxation, economic development, and transportation, the states and local governments are equally or more directly involved in policymaking and policy implementation than is the federal government. State governments wield a major portion of the "police power" of government—the power to make laws concerning the health, safety, morals, and well-being of the citizenry—in the United States because of the "reserved powers" clause of the 10th Amendment to the U.S. Constitution.

In a previous work, I argued that the political and social status of ethnic/ racial minority groups in the United States may be characterized as "two-tiered pluralism."[2] That is, despite the achievement of procedural or formal democracy, substantive democracy has not been attained by ethnic/racial minorities. This situation is attributed to historical, social, economic, and institutional reasons. In this book, I examine the importance of race/ethnicity in U.S. politics more specifically and fully at the level of state politics, the major arena for domestic policy.

The book argues—and provides extensive and systematic evidence in support of that argument—that the ethnic/racial compositions and configurations of the states have a major impact on state politics and policies. The importance of social diversity in this context is shown to be both broad and deep. Social diversity has a critical impact on state political processes and institutions, as well as on public policies, and it is also evident at the substate level (see chapter 7). Another claim is that social diversity's impacts are manifest in *all* the states and are thus an "American dilemma" in a somewhat different way than previously understood. Perhaps somewhat contrary to conventional wisdom, social diversity's impact is not confined regionally or to certain "political culture" types of states. The dilemma plays out differently, or has different "faces," relative to the social context.

The states are essentially alike regarding their legal or constitutional relationship with the federal government and to each other. However, internally they differ from one another in many, intriguing ways. For instance, the states differ in some rather obvious ways, including their physical size, population size, nature of their economy, and population composition in terms of age and racial/ethnic characteristics. Such differences have an impact on state politics and policies.[3] State political and governmental institutions also differ considerably. The power of interest group systems, the nature and strength of political parties and party systems, and the powers and capacity of governors and state legislatures help differentiate the states. In addition, "the political attitudes of Americans vary in important ways on the basis of where in the United States [i.e., in what state] they live."[4]

Its centrality to the U.S. political and governmental system, coupled with its differences, makes state politics significant and intriguing. Hence, a central issue is how to best *understand* state politics. What ideas, propositions, and theories help explain state politics accurately, adequately, and appropriately? As we will see (see especially chapter 2), there has been no shortage of efforts to address these issues, but much remains unexplained.

Issues and Challenges

Countless research articles and a fair number of books have examined state politics in the United States. While they are difficult to summarize, a major conclusion of the research is that it is very hard to draw any simple, clear-cut conclusions about state politics. This is partly because of the vastness of the research and partly because of the great complexity of questions and issues involved. Reviews and commentary on state-politics research emphasize and underscore these points, and they suggest further reasons for this lack of clarity.

A leading scholar claims that the study of state politics lacks a "unifying theoretical framework" that could integrate the many and varied studies of the subject.[5] Also, the absence of such a framework has made it difficult to reconcile research concerning macro-level findings with findings concerning micro-level behavior. That is, what has been found regarding the behavior of individuals within states is often not consistent with broader, more general findings of state politics. For instance, the "political culture" is found to be significant for some state-level outcomes,[6] but not necessarily for individual attitudes.[7] And states with a high proportion of citizens who consider themselves liberal often enact public policies that do not appear liberal.[8] California's rejection of a fair (open)-housing policy in the mid-1960s and its adoption of "Official English" in 1986 are but two examples.

Brace and Jewett claim that "studies in state politics are too often compartmentalized." Research efforts over the last decade or so have been marked by "discrete findings secured with better data and more sophisticated methodologies." But "without a unifying theoretical framework or set of questions," it seems that we "are learning more and more about less and less. The sum of the individually impressive" research in the field "does not add up to an equally impressive whole." The challenge, then, is to "develop a theoretical perspective that will help identify the forces that distinguish one state from another and explain how states change or resist the pressure for change. This challenge has gone unanswered," however.[9]

How might this challenge be engaged? Brace and Jewett suggest a contextually oriented theoretical framework that unifies major questions, and they speak favorably of earlier studies of state politics that "made creative and effective use of contextual analysis."[10] V. O. Key's landmark *Southern Politics* and other works "understood that people behaved differently in different contexts"; there was a clear and strong analytical perception that "context matters." "Individuals make choices among alternatives that are often shaped by their context."[11]

The central contextual component that Key focused on was the racial composition of counties and states—the southern states in particular. The present work suggests that broader issues and outcomes in state politics and policy may also be shaped by context. Thus, it is likely that state politics can be better understood by clarifying and emphasizing the nature and importance of different contexts. But what specific aspects or dimensions of the state context might or should be given attention?

Social Diversity

A number of scholars and theorists believe that race and ethnicity are major features of U.S. history. Indeed, a number of observers of U.S. politics—from Tocqueville to Myrdal and Key, to Burnham, and into the present—have viewed race and ethnicity as a historically central factor, as a major "dilemma," in the U.S. political and social systems. At the same time, the United States is often referred to as "a nation of immigrants." But it is generally acknowledged that not all groups of Americans immigrated under similar circumstances or during similar historical eras. In some instances, groups did not voluntarily immigrate. Nor did the areas from which they came have similar political relations or share various similarities with the United States. All of this has affected politics in the United States, including—and perhaps especially—state politics.[12]

Race and ethnicity are and have been pervasive influences in the political and social system.[13] However, racial and/or ethnic groups are not equally distributed across the country. Some states have relatively few "minorities" (blacks, Latinos/Hispanics, and so on) while other states have populations of 30 percent or more minority group members. Similarly, there are differences in the distribution of "white ethnics," as Italians and people from other southern or eastern European populations are classified. These patterns have produced a "politics of heterogeneity"[14] that differs a great deal across the states.

As this book will demonstrate, diversity is an important aspect of *all* state politics, although its importance takes different forms in different contexts. These contexts are associated with different faces of politics and policy, and diversity is a dilemma in some way in all the states, hence it is very much an "American dilemma." The situation needs to be fully appreciated and systematically incorporated into the theory and research on state politics. That is a major goal of this book.

This book is, thus, a call for a unifying, contextually based theoretical framework.[15] It seeks to address the challenge of developing a framework that is relevant to the major issues in state politics and, thus, to be comprehensive and unifying. And the framework is contextual. I delineate and develop a new argument—a *social diversity* interpretation—around which major questions, issues, and puzzles of U.S. state politics are considered. Specifically, I put forth and examine the claim that mixtures or cleavages of various minority and/or racial/ethnic groups within a state—the types and levels of social *diversity* or complexity—are critical in understanding the politics and policy in the states.

Key argued that race was the central characteristic of politics in the southern states; the significance of racial/ethnic diversity for state politics has also been suggested in numerous other works.[16] Despite considerable attention, however, racial/ethnic diversity has not been developed or consciously and extensively incorporated into a general interpretation of state politics and public policy. Yet racial/ethnic diversity may, and should, be seen as an "analytical construct" or "structural feature"[17] of U.S. state and national politics.

Social diversity as an interpretation, likewise, is consistent with Smith's[18] broader assertion that empirical theories of politics in the United States should be reconsidered because they have not adequately recognized or incorporated the inegalitarian ideologies and institutions that have defined the status of racial and ethnic minorities.[19] That is, inegalitarian views, not only liberal and republican traditions, are evident in American political thought and practice.

This book indicates that several traditions are relevant to state politics and are affected by context; they may be especially important given the narrower scope of conflict in state politics. Tocqueville argued that democracy in America was centrally linked to its "eminently democratic *social conditions*" (emphasis added). The social diversity interpretation argues that those conditions and related values relevant to state politics and policy are significantly affected by social diversity contexts. And the impact of context is more complex than commonly understood.

Typically, studies seem to imply that race/ethnicity is primarily relevant for explaining politics in the southern states and in other, selected circumstances. Studies often examine states by separating the South and nonsouth. However, the relevance of race/ethnicity beyond this is not always developed.[20] This book argues for and provides evidence to show that when state politics and policies are analyzed more closely, or are "disaggregated"— when state politics and policy are examined in both relative and in absolute terms—racial/ethnic factors become more apparent and their implications are more important. This study considers the processes and outcomes of state politics and policy in both general and specific dimensions, as developed later. A frequent finding is that states that do well in the former respect do poorly in the latter, and some states tend to be in between on both dimensions. This suggests that there are several faces to politics and inequality, most of which are substantially related to social diversity. Thus, racial/ethnic factors are important in understanding politics and policy in all of the states, not just in one region or set of states, or with respect to only a few issues.

Other approaches have been offered to explain politics and policy in the United States; those generally fall into two broad categories: socioeconomic and political.[21] Once seen as competing with each other, the political and economic explanations are now more often viewed as complementary.[22] Despite this synthesis and some rethinking of approaches, problems remain within each of the interpretations in terms of conceptualization and measurement.[23] Whatever utility existing approaches may have (and the approaches are summarized further in chapter 2), much remains to be explained about politics and policy in the states. Alternative explanations deserve consideration.

State Social (Racial/Ethnic) Diversity

A central characteristic of states is their racial and ethnic diversity, or relative lack thereof.[24] Racial/ethnic diversity, or what I also refer to more simply as *social diversity*, is important in itself. But it also may bridge economic, political, cultural, and institutional dimensions of state politics, as previous studies suggest[25] and as is indicated later (see chapter 2). The racial and ethnic diversity of the states includes, significantly, black (African-American), Latino or Hispanic, and other minority populations—groups that have come to be defined as "minority groups" or "protected classes" in implicit recognition of unique historical experiences in the United States.[26]

The unique experiences of blacks, Latinos, and other minorities are recognized at a general level in the literature on state politics. But regnant empirical theories of politics have largely ignored their significance. The social diversity perspective brings close theoretical attention to these groups and issues, placing ethnic/racial diversity at the center of the analysis.[27] This social diversity interpretation also differentiates between northern or western European populations and nonnorthern and nonwestern Europeans within a state, for reasons suggested later in this chapter (and further developed in chapter 2).[28]

To be sure, the historical experience of each minority and other group is quite complex. For instance, the group referred to as Latinos is a diverse one, differentiated by nationality (Mexican American, Puerto Rican, Cuban, etc.), time and circumstances of entry into the United States, as well as a number of other factors.[29] Similarly, blacks, Asians, white ethnics, and other groups in U.S. society have highly complex and different historical experiences. Yet the assumption here is that there is enough similarity within groups and enough differences across groups as delineated to support the designations and arguments made.[30]

State diversity patterns are measured with interval- or continuous-level data, and indicators derived from the data are used throughout the statistical analyses presented in this study. At the same time, state profiles or configurations are provided in figure 1.1, and I commonly refer to the states with respect to those broader patterns or characterizations.

Initially striking and theoretically intriguing is the observation that states appear to fall into several groups relative to their racial/ethnic patterns. Compared to overall U.S. patterns, some states can be characterized as racially and ethnically *homogeneous*. These states have populations that are primarily white or Anglo, that is, of northern and western European descent. They also have very small minority (black and Latino) populations and relatively few white ethnics (i.e., nonnorthern and nonwestern European whites).

In contrast, there are two types of "nonhomogeneous" states. First, some states have rather large white ethnic populations, as well as significant mi-

Racial/ethnic Groups	State "Types"		
	Homogeneous	Heterogeneous	Bifurcated
White (Northern and Western Eurpn)	High	Moderate	High
White Ethnic (Southern and Eastern Eurpn)	Low	High	Low
Minority (Black/Latino/Asian)	Low	Moderate	High

Figure 1.1 Summary of Racial/Ethnic Group Patterns Relative to Three Broad Types of States

nority populations and moderately large white populations; these can be called *heterogeneous*. Second, some states have *bifurcated* racial/ethnic structures, with large minority populations, primarily black and/or Latino, a large white (nonethnic) population, and a rather small proportion of white ethnics. Thus, states can be broadly delineated into three patterns or categories—homogeneous, heterogeneous, and bifurcated—according to the type and degree of racial/ethnic diversity.

Accordingly, these three types of states differ in their social complexity. Homogeneous states are the simplest, or most *uni*form. The *bi*furcated pattern has, as the very concept suggests, two major groups—white and minority (and small proportions of white ethnics). The heterogeneous environment is characterized by the presence of multiple groups and is something of an ethnic or racial *poly*glot.[31]

Social Diversity and Political Culture

Elazar's "political culture" idea[32] is perhaps the most influential single perspective, and among the most wide-ranging, in the study of state politics in the United States.[33] In some ways, the social diversity perspective parallels Elazar's framework; however, in a number of significant respects the social diversity interpretation differs from and fundamentally challenges that perspective. Indeed, it seems that the social diversity argument largely subsumes the political culture arguments. This will become clearer as I develop the social diversity view, and as it is examined and compared to other perspectives, in later chapters.

Elazar claims that state politics is significantly influenced by political subcultures, whether moralistic, individualistic, or traditionalistic. Elazar attributes political orientations, processes, and outcomes to dominant or predominant cultural values and related normative tenets. Those orientations or values, in turn, are said to derive from a state's dominant ethnic and religious groups. All the groups discussed in Elazar's earlier works are of European background; the political values and beliefs of racial minorities and non-European groups were not extensively considered in the political culture framework.[34] That limits the theoretical completeness or adequacy of that framework.

In contrast to Elazar, the social diversity perspective contends that much of state politics and policy, including political culture, is related to racial/ethnic diversity. At the same time, the political culture conceptualization is associated with, masks, and may even be a surrogate for state social diversity and other factors. Elazar's political cultural categories and those of the diversity typology tend to parallel each other. Most of the homogeneous states are "moralistic"; the heterogeneous states tend to be "individualistic"; and many of the bifurcated states fall into the "traditionalistic" category. However, there are important departures from these general patterns, as emphasized later in this (and other) chapters, and there are other important theoretical differences as well. My argument is that conceptually and empirically, the diversity categories of homogeneity, heterogeneity, and bifurcation are preferable to the political culture typology because they are clearer, are more precise, and better incorporate change. They are also more complete and more appropriate to the nature of contemporary state politics.[35]

Context is critical in explaining state politics and policy because social diversity takes on political meaning within social structures and constructions.[36] Racial/ethnic contexts shape the beliefs, attitudes, and ideologies of individuals and groups associated with the political culture thesis. The social diversity interpretation implies that the context within which individuals and/or groups are situated is as, if not more, important than the values or ideas that people "bring with them" or "have within." That is, context and culture should be understood as being "transsubjective" or "transindividual," as socially defined.[37] State politics and policies are products of the cooperation, competition and/or conflict between and among dominant and subordinate minority groups, not only of the dominant group within a state.[38] Thus, political processes and political and policy outcomes may be associated with specific political cultures. But to simply assume that this correlation is directly causal, to attribute so much of the processes and outcomes to political culture per se, may well be a misspecification.[39] This is because political culture is itself heavily shaped by state social diversity, as I demonstrate later in this chapter.

Various criticisms of the political culture view have appeared over the years, including its static and impressionistic nature. Important to stress here is that the focus of the political culture view on the dominant culture in each state necessarily excludes theoretically other populations, including minorities. The need for reconceptualizing state politics is underscored by the theoretical neglect of recent, as well as older, minority groups. The social diversity approach is thus more complete.

The presence and theoretical importance of non-European groups is relatively absent from the political culture framework or the large body of research that has emerged from that framework. For example, Elazar's "mapping" of state cultural designations does not consider the large increase in Latino and Asian populations since the 1960s.[40] Only in the most recent treatment of state political cultures are Latinos/Hispanics and Asians mentioned; even then the discussion is broad and brief.[41] The experiences of African Americans are also not treated as central to understanding the nature and evolution of state political cultures. African Americans appear to exist within, but not to significantly shape, state political cultures. In contrast, the social diversity interpretation contends that the long-term presence and growing number of racial/ethnic populations have affected, and are significantly affecting, politics and policy in the states, as well as nationally.[42] These populations have distinctive histories that are central to understanding state politics and policy. To a substantial degree, the political culture framework is, perhaps surprisingly, not especially attentive to context.

Evidence on Social Diversity in the States

A major task in this first chapter is to formulate and develop the diversity interpretation and assess evidence on racial/ethnic diversity in the states. Two major racial/ethnic groups or categories are used to create social diversity measures or indicators: (1) minority populations (blacks, Latinos, Asians) in relation to white populations are used to create an index of *minority diversity*;[43] and (2) white ethnics or European ethnics (particularly southern and eastern Europeans) are used to create an index of *white ethnic diversity*.[44] The residual conditions for each index—low racial and low white ethnic diversity—are indicative of homogeneity.

There is, of course, extensive inter-and intra-group complexity, and there also may be interminority political competition.[45] These issues are addressed in chapter 2 and elsewhere in this book, and I also suggest that such issues deserve further attention in future analyses.

Two indices are created to measure minority diversity and white ethnic diversity.[46] The racial/ethnic group categories follow from the logic of the interpretation and are more parsimonious than recent extensions and new measures of political culture.[47] These categories are generally consistent with much of the scholarship that has considered racial/ethnic group background, including Elazar's political culture view.[48] Fundamentally different, however, is the inclusion of minority groups (especially Latinos), as well as the significance given to group cleavages and group interrelationships.[49]

Figure 1.2 and table 1.1 provide interval-level data on the states, ordering them from lowest to highest in terms of minority diversity (black, Hispanic,

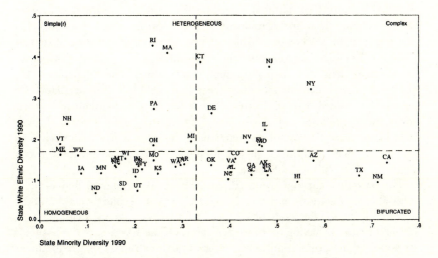

Figure I.2 State White Ethnic Diversity with State Minority Diversity

Asian), as well as white ethnic diversity; figure 1.2 places the states on a scatterplot relative to their types and levels of racial/ethnic diversity. The minority diversity index ranks the states from smallest to largest minority population, or from most homogeneous to most bifurcated (table 1.1). The white ethnic diversity index ranks the states based on white ethnic population. The general pattern moves from the most homogeneous to most heterogeneous states.

There is only a weak correlation ($r = .03$) between the index of minority diversity and white ethnic diversity, suggesting that the two dimensions are independent or orthogonal. Because the indices do not seem to suggest one underlying dimension, overall state diversity can be understood as the product of both minority and white ethnic diversity.

A number of points are notable in figure 1.2 and table 1.1. To begin, the racial/ethnic patterns are generally consistent with familiar regional patterns. The three states of upper New England (Maine, Vermont, and New Hampshire) are "near" each other on the scatterplot; the three states of lower New England (Rhode Island, Massachusetts, and Connecticut) are also fairly close to one another. Also, the Dakotas, among the most homogeneous states, are near each other, as are Minnesota and Iowa; and the latter two are not far from the Dakotas on the graph. Three geographically large and close western states—Montana, Idaho, and Utah—are also in this quadrant of the scatterplot. The states of the Old South tend to be in the bottom-right quadrant, although they are not necessarily among the highest in minority diversity in the 1990s; they were more so in earlier decades. Notably, several states with large Latino populations have emerged as being the highest in minority diversity—California, Texas, and New Mexico. Two states that border each other—New York and New Jersey—are distinct in being relatively high in both minority and white ethnic diversity.

Next, a number of patterns regarding the political culture classification are important.[50] In terms of minority diversity, of the *lowest* one-third (16) of the states, 38 percent ($n = 6$) are "pure" moralistic states (i.e., listed by Elazar [1984] as having this one culture as dominant); 75 percent (12) have moralism as their dominant or predominant culture, and 94 percent (15) have some component of moralism (based on the 1980 diversity data). Of the middle one-third of the states, 50 percent have individualism as their dominant or predominant culture and 75 percent (12) have some element of individualism. Finally, of the states with the most minority diversity, 38 percent are pure traditionalistic and almost 70 percent have traditionalism as their leading cultural influence.[51]

The pattern regarding white ethnic diversity also suggests that Elazar's cultural categorizations may well be related to racial/ethnic diversity. Of the states with the lowest levels of white ethnic diversity, the majority are classified by Elazar as having moralistic cultures. Of the 10 states with the smallest white ethnic population, *not one* has individualism as its predominant culture. Of the states above the mean, however, 47 percent (15) are purely individualistic and 73 percent (11 of 15) have individualism as their dominant or predominant culture. Indeed, 93 percent (14 of 15) states above the mean in white ethnic diversity have individualism as their primary or secondary culture. This suggests that political culture may in fact be a function of racial/ethnic diversity.[52]

Other analyses underscore the above findings. Evidence (eta-squared statistics) from an "analysis of variance" indicates that at least 40 percent, and as much as 66 percent, of political culture is linked to racial/ethnic diversity, depending on the type of racial/ethnic diversity and the political culture categories; that is, whether one examines minority or white ethnic diversity and whether only the states with "pure" cultures and/or those with "mixed" cultures are included.

Another striking feature of the minority diversity index is a strong monotonic pattern relative to political culture. As the percent minority diversity increases, the subcultural types delineated by Elazar move in virtual lockstep from moralistic to individualistic to traditionalistic.

The pattern regarding the index of white ethnic diversity suggests that Elazar's individualistic category may be largely a function of diversity. White ethnic diversity is significantly higher in the states categorized by Elazar as individualist, than in moralistic or traditionalistic states (eta-squared statistics of.42 to.46.)[53] Furthermore, inferential statistics reinforce the findings of these descriptive statistics.

State minority diversity accounts for 41 percent of the variation in the political culture continuum (as indicated by standard [OLS] regression, $p = .001$).[54] Because the political culture continuum is not linear, an appropriate form of analysis (logistic regression analysis) was used to estimate the impact of white ethnic diversity on states classified as having an individualistic culture (states classified as having a predominant individualistic political culture are coded 1; all others are coded 0). Knowing the level of white ethnic diversity, the model correctly classifies 78 percent of the states. In short, the analyses clearly demonstrate that racial/ethnic diversity explains much of the state variation in the political culture classifications.

The analysis also suggests, however, that the social diversity indices classify several states differently than does the political culture classification, as suggested in figure 1.3.[55] Particularly important is the divergent classification of two of the most populous states, California and Michigan. Two states with large Latino populations—California and Colorado—are also differently classified, suggesting that political culture may not adequately account for this increasingly large population.[56]

Most research addresses discrete components or dimensions of state politics.[57] Elazar's political culture is one of the few perspectives that is more comprehensive, seeking to explain a number of issues—that is one of its strengths. The diversity interpretation sometimes predicts aggregate or general outcomes that are similar to what the political culture view might anticipate. However, diversity views those phenomena as rooted in, as attributable to, different political and social forces and dynamics.

The states vary considerably in their differentiation, that is, their social

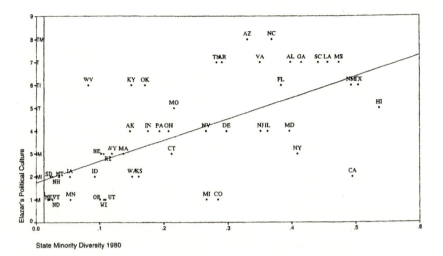

Figure 1.3 Elazar's Political Culture with State Minority Diversity

diversity. What is the significance of the diversity that does exist, what political patterns are associated with it, and how is it dealt with in state politics? The diversity perspective brings attention to these and related questions, and suggests answers based on a contextual framework. Other views tend to neglect such issues.

The remainder of this chapter briefly sets out general arguments or expectations of the social diversity perspective on major aspects of state politics and policy; specific arguments and expectations are more fully developed in later chapters. Beyond the arguments and initial evidence presented earlier, broader implications of the diversity perspective are noted here.

The Social Diversity Interpretation and Politics and Policy in the States: General Expectations

Types of Political Pluralism in the States

The diversity perspective suggests a number of corollary propositions. The degree and types of racial/ethnic diversity would be hypothesized to produce broad difference in the forms of political pluralism of the states. In homogeneous states, a *consensual pluralism* would be anticipated. While there may be high degrees of political competition,[58] including high political party competition, that competition is tempered by an underlying consensus arising from homogeneity, the diversity view suggests (see chapter 3). The moralistic culture is said to be characterized by a concern for the commonwealth, where "the people have an *undivided* interest, in which the citizens *cooperate* in an effort to create and maintain the best government in order to implement certain *shared* moral principles."[59] Elazar also argues that political competition and issues debates are quite intense in the moralistic cultures. The diversity perspective implies that shared or common interest is more likely where individuals are less racially or ethnically divided—in more homogeneous contexts; shared principles are more likely where there are shared racial/ethnic characteristics. However, research findings presented later suggest that the commonwealth outlook is not necessarily extended to those of different racial/ethnic backgrounds.[60]

In more heterogeneous states, a *competitive pluralism*, or competition between many groups including ethnic/racial groups, is fostered by greater white ethnic and moderate-to-high minority diversity, and probably is heightened by greater urbanization and factors such as population density. Where a predominant white (northern or western European) population coexists with substantial white ethnic and/or minority populations, social pluralism tends to increase political competition. This is probably why many political concerns—concerns dismissed by some scholars as mere patronage politics and not policy relevant—are viewed as salient issues in the heterogeneous context[61] (see chapter 3). This may take the form of "status" or "recognition" politics, but cannot be ignored as irrelevant. The bifurcated environment leads to a *hierarchical or limited pluralism*, historically manifested in various legal and political constraints.[62] Despite major social and political change during the last generation, this condition continues, albeit in modified form.

A result of these patterns is that what appear or are manifested as individualistic concerns or perspectives in heterogeneous contexts more readily coincide with communal, or "public," concerns in homogeneous states because of their very social homogeneity. Political competition and debate in the homogeneous environment is something like a "family feud," and family feuds can often be intense—hence the high levels of political party competition and policy-relevant or issue politics that scholars claim occurs in these states.[63] But as *family* feuds, they are circumscribed and underlain by substantial consensus and broad social similarity. Indeed, a major reason issues and policy can be so intensely debated is that major sources of political and social cleavage, such as deep-seated racial division, are largely absent. The diversity argument suggests, then, that equally or more important than the feud is the fact that political debates occur within the family—feuds occur within one's own group because of the state's homogeneity. In contrast, the political culture and several other approaches emphasize the feud, typically overlooking the context and parameters of the political and policy debates.

In homogeneous contexts, core values are shared, although intense debate may occur about interpretations and applications of values. But because the stakes are not as vivid or as redistributive in racial/ethnic terms, the nature of the discussion is different and appears more oriented to the commonwealth. This ostensible "issue emphasis" that occurs in the homogeneous setting is something of a luxury that is constrained in more socially diverse or complex contexts. In the heterogeneous environment, core values themselves are more open to debate because the stakes are more pronounced, racially and ethnically. As a result, many issues that may be viewed as relatively neutral or technocratic in the homogeneous environment become political issues in the heterogeneous environment, including who gets the government jobs.

In the bifurcated context, there is considerable agreement, at least among the white majority, on both issues—that is, "means," or instrumental values, and "ends," or basic and substantive values. Those basic values are grounded in beliefs of hierarchy, and the issue focus is on how to maintain or adjust that hierarchy. In the homogeneous context, there is agreement on basic values, and political, economic, and social equality are parts of and reinforce that basic value structure[64] (also see chapter 2). But there may be disagreement on issues—the means, or the interpretation and application of values. In the heterogeneous context, there is some disagreement on both means and ends.

These ideas are further summarized in figure 1.4, which places the types of states relative to their agreement or disagreement on issues and on values. Cumulatively, these patterns, linked to social diversity, may help explain state politics and policy orientations. To be sure, this oversimplifies matters, but the figure may be a useful heuristic device nonetheless.

Further Observations and Evidence

Support for the above arguments can be found elsewhere, including Elazar's work. Some examples are useful. Elazar claims that the clash between "Yankees," or whites in social diversity terms, and the Irish, or white ethnics, in Massachusetts was affected by the "sheer magnitude" of the Irish immigration and the "other immigrations" that occurred there. From the diversity perspective this is a clash of whites and white ethnics, although Elazar does not directly define it as such. Elazar contrasts the Massachusetts situation with the "relatively harmonious amalgamation of Yankees and Scandinavians in Minnesota, where the ethnic conflict was *confined* within the *same* political culture and became a competition for offices and status *within a common value system*."[65]

What Elazar attributes to culture may also be rooted in social diversity. Note that the groups discussed in these examples are white (and white ethnic) groups, and there are no "minorities" considered in the examples. Elazar adds:

> Where people *holding power* believe that those seeking to displace them *share their basic values*, they are less likely to fear political change. However, when such change promises to introduce *new people* who will alter the *very basis* of the political value system—that is, change the political *consensus* at is most crucial point—the *intensity* with which people hold onto their positions is immeasurably increased.[66]

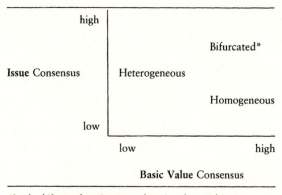

*In the bifurcated environment there is substantial consensus on both dimensions among the *dominant* (white) groups, although minorities clearly do not share in that consensus which has been grounded in dominant/subordinate relationships.

Figure 1.4 Social Diversity Contexts and Value and Issue Consensus/Dissensus Patterns

The diversity perspective would not necessarily challenge these claims, but would interpret the group dynamics differently. The diversity view would ask why—that is, what are the sources of these perceptions—and would suggest that ethnic/racial diversity contexts play a major role in perceptions of one's own group as well as of other groups, and affects cultural and value formation. Similarly, it would stress that perceptions are rooted in the different historical experiences that played a role in defining diversity and group relations to begin with.[67]

The Minnesota example suggests greater consensus among homogeneous (white) groups and the presence of issue competition—as Elazar says, competition for "offices" and "status." Note that, on the one hand, there is little indication of basic value disagreement and there is no direct suggestion of fundamental redistributive politics. On the other hand, the Massachusetts example suggests white versus white ethnic tension in the context of heterogeneity, but a context of few or no minorities. Not discussed in these examples is the bifurcated environment; there, white and minority relationships have been the most profoundly inegalitarian and potentially most intense. But relations have been strongly circumscribed legally, politically, socially, and institutionally, and ideologies based on race have supported hierarchy and bifurcation.

Social Diversity and Means to Social Order and Control

These arguments suggest the proposition that social context is related to structures or means to "social order," "social control," or "social production"[68] in society. Lichbach and others argue that there are several major approaches to achieving social order: contract/market, community, and hierarchy.[69] In the U.S. political system as a whole, contract/market, based on liberal and capitalist values, is certainly the dominant, but not only, means to social order. Numerous works have discussed how the U.S. Constitution was influenced by the liberal tradition and social contract thought, and how the Constitution was written to support a "commercial republic."[70] The social diversity argument accepts that contract/market orientations are critical influences in state politics. But this view also argues that that influence is modified by the social diversity context and other factors.[71] Some contexts reflect contract/market or liberal/pluralist politics most directly, such as heterogeneous states. Other contexts may go beyond that, complementing it with "community," the homogeneous states. And yet others have historically reflected liberal/contract or community/republican traditions to a lesser degree and had major elements of hierarchy, the bifurcated states.

The contract/market approach is found in its clearest form among states with the heterogeneous context because the social composition of those states permits—indeed, seems to require—rather close adherence to that model. In the face of high social and economic complexity, some entity is necessary to mediate that complexity and bring a modicum of political and social order. The contractual relationship between citizens and government is one side of the institutional response; markets are the other side, and in some respects the two are intertwined.[72]

To draw on recent commentary of Robert Dahl, in more homogeneous environments "egoism may [more readily] merge indistinguishably with altruism."[73] That environment tends to be hospitable to community because social commonality allows for simpler, somewhat less contractually driven political and social systems. The bifurcated states are where hierarchy is most commonly found. In line with the earlier discussion, and not inconsistent with the political culture view of Elazar, each of these social context environments appears to lead to different "regimes."

Previous work, including that of Elazar and other cultural theorists,[74] finds links between culture and a means to social order very similar to those just suggested here. Indeed, they directly use the concepts "community" (or commonwealth), "hierarchy," and "market" or "marketplace"[75] (also see chapter 2). But Elazar links these to the *culture* of (pre)dominant groups; there is, with some exceptions, little theoretical attention to the presence of other groups. Nor is there always adequate clarification as to whether the concepts refer to instrumental or substantive values, or some combination thereof. Other political culture theorists have criticized Elazar for failing to distinguish these.[76] But cultural theorists tend not to make a connection to social diversity, which I take to be the central factor. That is, social diversity contexts influence the likelihood that contract/market, community, or bifurcation will be a significant or major means to social order. This is not to suggest that the link between diversity and the means or orientation to social order is deterministic. There appear to be strong tendencies, however.

Institutions in the several environments are thus oriented to somewhat different goals. In the heterogeneous environment, there is a need to arbitrate or broker social heterogeneity and complexity. In the homogeneous setting, political and governmental institutions face a less daunting task, needing only to moderate or mediate issue disputes, but seldom facing major questions relevant to the "American dilemma" of race. And they can build upon a less complex social group configuration to augment the underlying consensus. In the bifurcated setting, government is expected to interfere little with the existing stratified conditions, themselves the product of institutions and social relations historically defined in racial/ethnic terms.[77]

Social Diversity—Perspectives and Expectations

Previous research on social diversity, which has focused mostly on public policy issues, indicates that there is compelling evidence for this interpretation.[78] The presence of and relationships between minorities, white ethnic, and white populations seem critical. Theory and analysis of several policies demonstrate that racial/ethnic diversity provides a parsimonious and useful theory of policy variation in the states. The framework accounts for substantial variation in major state policy, including policies or dimensions of policies that particularly affect minority groups. In the aggregate, greater minority diversity—that is, bifurcation—was associated with "worse" policy outcomes. When policies were disaggregated by race or ethnicity, policy outcomes for minorities were quite low in homogeneous contexts. The evidence suggests that heterogeneous environments are associated with mixed or in-between, if not positive, policy outcomes.[79] Hence, each contextual configuration seems associated with different faces of power or inequality.

There are a number of important, and unique, contributions of the social diversity interpretation, further developed in later chapters. First, social diversity contexts seem to shape general methods of social order or "regimes" and have significance for an array of issues in state politics and policy. Second, social diversity helps account for political and policy variation in the aggregate, as well as with respect to specific dimensions of policies.[80] Previous studies concerning public policy and race/ethnicity address the former, aggregate matter, but do not anticipate or explain the latter, especially the dynamics of race/ethnicity in homogeneous contexts. Social diversity's acknowledgment of and ability to address several dimensions of state policy are distinctive.

The previous analyses also underscored the need for greater conceptual and empirical care in the study of state politics and policy. The social diversity perspective adds to our understanding of state politics in part by being more theoretically inclusive and complete. Social diversity—including the concepts of homogeneity, heterogeneity, and bifurcation; related types of political pluralism (consensual, competitive, hierarchical); and several corollary ideas—provide new perspectives for reconceptualizing and reinvigorating the study of U.S. politics. That is what I develop in later chapters.

The Plan of the Book

This book examines the ideas of social diversity with respect to a variety of state policies and political issues. The issues and policies are those commonly addressed in standard books and textbooks and in the general literature on state politics. I examine social diversity relative to these issues to demonstrate its general significance and, thus, to provide a comprehensive, noncompartmentalized discussion.[81] The chapters proceed as follows.

Before turning to the application and assessment of the social diversity interpretation, it is first placed in perspective relative to other ideas and approaches regarding state politics. Drawing on and supplementing other works, I provide a summary and overview of perspectives on state politics and policy (chapter 2). Then, political institutions and processes are examined relative to social diversity (chapter 3). Existing measures of several aspects of politics and political processes are considered. Among the matters addressed are aspects of politics or of procedural democracy, such as the nature of party systems,[82] public opinion,[83] and interest group presence and influence.[84] Expectations relative to the social diversity interpretation are developed and examined. For instance, the social diversity perspective helps explain patterns of state public opinion and the policy relevance of state party systems.[85]

The nature and power of governmental institutions are examined in chapter 4. In general, social diversity predicts that heterogeneous states would tend to have more powerful and/or professionalized legislatures and governors because the complexity associated with heterogeneity necessitates government to manage that complexity and diversity. Homogeneous states are expected to have moderately strong institutions. Institutions need not be especially strong in this environment because of the broader social consensus; at the same time, some level of institutional strength is necessary to implement the policies that emerge from that consensus. Institutions in the bifurcated environment are expected to be weak because strong institutions might provide avenues for subordinant groups to challenge the dominant groups. Various measures of state government institutions and their strength, capacity, professionalism, and so on will be drawn upon.[86] Notably, few previous studies in state politics have attempted to or have had much success in explaining the power or nature of governmental institutions.

Extended analysis of a number of public policies is provided in chapters 5 and 6. Overall, the evidence strongly supports the claims that social diversity has significant implications for a variety of state policies, especially differential or disaggregated policies. But the analysis does not consider just social diversity; it also examines other variables thought to be important in explaining state policies. The evidence indicates that social diversity's significance is commonly greater than that of various alternative explanations.

Chapter 7 extends the analysis to the substate level and considers the implications of social diversity for several attitudinal, behavioral, and institutional questions. It includes discussion of several individual-level and county-level studies that further suggest the importance of ethnic/racial diversity for politics.

The concluding chapter (chapter 8) summarizes the major findings, assesses those relative to the interpretation, and seeks to place the general argument in a broader perspective. It also raises certain questions about the social diversity approach.

Table 1.2 Ideas and Propositions of the Social Diversity Interpretation Concerning Aspects of State Politics and Policies

Aspect	Homogeneous	Heterogeneous	Bifurcated
General Traits			
Nature of pluralism	consensual	competitive	hierarchical
Nature of social system/ structure	simple(st) (uniform)	complex (multiple)	simple (two-segment)
Orientation to social order/ social production	community	contract/market	hierarchy
Political Institutions, Processes, and Attitudes			
Voter turnout			
absolute	high	moderate	low
relative	moderate/lower	moderate	moderate
Political parties			
Party competition			
absolute	high	moderate/high	low
relative	moderate/lower	moderate/high	low
Party organization strength	moderate	high	low
Overall level of democratization			
absolute	high	moderate	low
relative	lower	moderate	moderate/low
Issue (public opinion) polarization	high	moderate	low
Interest group strength	weak	moderate	strong
Formal Governmental Institutions			
Strength	moderate	high	low
Public Policy Outcomes			
absolute	high	moderate/high	low
relative	lower	middle	moderate/higher

The general impacts that social diversity is expected to have on state politics are outlined in table 1.2. Specific expectations, findings, and discussions about these are presented in later chapters.

Conclusion

Let me begin with the conclusion and summarize the central argument and general findings of this work at the outset. First, social diversity is a central contextual factor and should be understood as an analytical construct that is critical to understanding state politics and policy. Social diversity is conceptualized, measured, and applied to an array of central issues in state and, by implication, U.S. politics. Second, the impact of social diversity is manifested in different ways relative to different aspects and indicators and is evident in numerous dimensions of state politics and policy. These dimensions include political processes and political institutions, governmental institutions, and public policies. The evidence indicates that racial/ethnic diversity as a social and political phenomenon is very much a part of, and is imbedded in, state and national politics.

When public policies are considered in absolute terms—in aggregated ways or generally—the homogeneous states most often do "best" and the bifurcated do "worst." But that may be due largely to the substantial minority populations in the former and their relative absence in the latter. Thus, when considered in relative terms—when the evidence is "disaggregated," or assessed specifically or in terms of the differential impact on minority groups—outcomes in the homogeneous states are sometimes, indeed often "worse." These findings emerge much more frequently than commonly held views of state politics would expect. The findings in the homogeneous states are striking, particularly relative to the low racial/ethnic diversity in such states.

The social diversity perspective thus suggests that there are faces to power and inequality in state politics and policy.[87] Virtually all state-politics research has overlooked the other face; relatedly, the research has emphasized, perhaps *over*emphasized, only one dimension. Social diversity helps explain beyond that and is especially important in bringing attention to and understanding of the other face. At the same time, a central implication of the argument and findings described here is that race and ethnicity are a dilemma in all the states and thus truly are an "American dilemma." The dilemma takes different forms and is manifested differently relative to differing contexts, but is pervasive. In the process of developing this interpretation and its related arguments, this book sheds new light on many major issues and questions in state politics and policy.

2

The Social Diversity Interpretation

in Perspective

Reviewing Other Explanations

of State Politics

The social diversity interpretation is the focal point of this book. Before
further assessing it, however, a review and discussion of other approaches to state politics is useful in itself, as well as for comparative purposes. There have been so many research articles and so many explanatory
variables used in the study of state politics that any summary of approaches
is difficult and certain to be incomplete. Nonetheless, some overview is necessary and a summary can be provided.

In general, the goal of this chapter is to consider major issues and perspectives commonly found in the scholarly study of state politics; later chapters revisit these issues from the social diversity perspective. In some cases,
these perspectives are treated as variables to be explained themselves, as
"dependent variables" relative to social diversity (see, especially, chapters 3
and 4). In other cases, they are examined as alternatives or challengers to
social diversity as an interpretation of state policies (see latter parts of chapters 5 and 6). To organize and facilitate this overview of other approaches,
I draw on and parallel recent discussions by two leading scholars of state
politics.

I first, briefly return to Brace and Jewett's "state of the field" review.[1]
Then I pattern much of the chapter after Virginia Gray's discussion of the
socioeconomic and political context of states found in a leading book on
state politics.[2] However, I often depart from Gray's treatment and frequently
consider additional issues. These excursions are meant to complement Gray's
discussion and to bring closer attention to issues relevant to the social diversity thesis, thus further laying the groundwork for subsequent chapters
in this book.

Brace's Overview

Brace (and Jewett) examined six major political science journals between 1983 and 1993 to identify the number and topics of articles dealing with state politics. Brace's essay is helpful in delineating journal-based research.[3] Applying an "inclusive" definition to the articles, they found that 384 had been published during the period—an average of about 35 per year.[4] Brace groups the articles into five major categories relative to their topics, although they acknowledge that the categories frequently overlap. Those categories and their frequencies are (in descending order): elections (23 percent), governmental institutions (19 percent), policy studies (17 percent), federalism and intergovernmental relations (5 percent), and state political economy. State political economy, as defined by Brace and Jewett, includes issues such as state economies and interest groups. Brace adds that other areas of research include elite behavior and attitudes (10 percent of all the studies identified); parties and interest groups (8 percent); gender, race, and ethnicity (5 percent); public opinion, culture, and ideology (5 percent); mass behavior (3 percent); and "other" (5 percent).[5] After assessing this vast literature, Brace concludes that the research has been lacking a unifying framework, and he argues for contextual approaches (see chapter 1). Yet their own survey of existing research implies that little such analysis is to be found.

**Gray and the Socioeconomic and Political Context
of States**

In the first chapter of a major book on state politics, in its sixth edition as of 1996, Gray discusses the socioeconomic and political context of state politics.[6] The chapter sets the agenda for the remainder of the book, and subsequent chapters consider specific common concerns in state politics. Since context is the focus of Gray's concerns in this first chapter, I infer that context is, or should be, a central consideration—indeed, a starting point— in the study of state politics.[7] Gray delineates a number of variables or factors commonly viewed as important in explaining political and policy differences among the states.[8] (These are summarized in later chapters, as they appear commonly in analyses of state politics and policy.) A striking point in this chapter is that there is no specific identification or extended discussion of *theories* of state politics; indeed, it seems conspicuous by its absence. Instead, a number of variables are listed and discussed. The absence of a specific discussion of, or of a section labeled, theories does not necessarily imply any shortcomings in Gray's discussion. Rather, it is suggestive of the nature of the state-politics field at this point, and it is consistent with and implicitly supports Brace and Jewett's claims regarding the lack of a unifying theoretical framework for the study of state politics.[9]

If the amount of attention—the sheer length of discussion in the chapter—is any indicator of what variables or explanations are most important for the study of state politics, Gray's discussion implies that political culture appears to be the single most significant.[10] Other scholars seem to agree.[11] Notably, political culture is a somewhat contextual factor and is claimed to have broad significance for state politics.[12] (Political culture was discussed extensively in chapter 1 and is discussed later as well.)

Gray specifies several major types of variables or explanations of state politics, or specific dimensions thereof: political, economic (or socioeconomic), and the "broader political context."[13] Of the three, Gray discusses the first—political, as distinct from what is considered broader political— only very briefly, presumably because those factors are considered at length in subsequent chapters of her book. The political factors mentioned are party control, party competition, interest group strength, and the nature and strength of governmental institutions (for example, gubernatorial power and legislative professionalism). Considerable discussion is given to various aspects of the socioeconomic context.

Socioeconomic Factors

The People

Among the socioeconomic variables, the first Gray considers is "the people" because state populations can be thought of as "human resources." Specific population characteristics noted and discussed are size, growth, density, and composition. The great variations in size, growth, and density are discussed, particularly implications arising from those factors. For instance, Gray suggests that population size and density (itself related to population size and land area) have implications for the ease or difficulty of efficient provision of public services and economies of scale. Population size and density also may affect the style of politics, in that face-to-face campaigning and contact may be more likely in some circumstances while media campaigning is more likely in others.

Gray also notes that the most populous states tend to be among the most urbanized, although there a number of exceptions. There is also a regional pattern; states on the east and west coasts tend to be densely populated, while those in the south and the mountain west are clearly the least metropolitan. At the same time, however, the growth of metropolitan areas in the south has led to major political and social changes there. Urban versus rural splits in state politics and policies may also emerge from these patterns.[14]

Gray's discussion of population attributes and state variations brings to attention several issues that have not been fully considered in the research. These are considered later in this chapter, but it can be noted at this point that variables are often incorporated into research in several ways. Population size is commonly used to create per capita measures of public policy; urbanization is commonly accounted for in policy studies. But, as argued later, it may be that such standardization or accounting does not fully capture the importance of these variables or their complex relationships with other variables.

Under population composition, Gray considers poverty, education and skills, immigrants, and minorities. Poverty levels differ a great deal across the states, important in itself. But poverty is also associated with "a syndrome of other social problems," such as crime and the need for education.[15]

In discussing education and skills, Gray asserts that education is important for several reasons, including, its link to "income, social class, and other aspects of socioeconomic status." However, education is of further importance to a state's economic development because "businesses are reluctant to locate in states where the labor force is inadequately trained." Gray contends that education attainment also is related to a state's policy choices because "an educated citizen typically demands a higher level of public service than does an uneducated one." Furthermore, Gray adds that "without educated citizens the opportunities for democracy cannot be realized."[16] Notably, but not surprisingly, levels of education are inversely correlated with poverty levels. There is a regional pattern, with the southern states having fewer high school graduates while the western states tend to have the highest concentrations of high school graduates.[17]

Erikson, Wright, and McIver assert that education is yet more complex in its impact on state politics and policy.[18] Their study of public opinion and public policy in the states found that education has unique impacts on public opinion in terms of partisan identification and ideological identification. Specifically, education was the only variable that "pointed in different directions" on partisan versus ideological identification; that is, more education was associated with being more likely to identify as Republican *and* more likely to consider oneself liberal.[19]

In discussing immigrants, Gray begins by invoking the common idea that the United States is a "nation of immigrants." Importantly, she adds that "*much of our nation's history* can be told by reviewing the arrival of different waves of immigrants . . . [and] the process of assimilating these ethnic groups into the political system formed the *basis of many political cleavages.*" Gray also acknowledges that there have been very different patterns of immigration in the last generation compared to previous generations, with Southeast Asians and Latin Americans being the two largest waves in the 1980s and 90s.[20]

Gray's specific discussion of minorities notes that states vary as well in the "ethnic and racial composition of their populations. Ethnic and racial characteristics form the *basis of significant political conflict* in many states" (emphasis added). This has been most evident in the south, where historically "the politics of individual southern states has varied according to the *proportion of blacks.*" Gray notes that another large and rapidly growing minority group is the Hispanic or Latino population. Latinos are somewhat like blacks in that "they are a disadvantaged minority; they have low incomes and low levels of education and they suffer discrimination." Latinos differ from blacks, however, in that they, and Asians, have been the targets of measures to make English the official language in a number of states. According to Gray, "this indicates an *increase in the degree of ethnic and racial tension* and an *uneasiness* over the assimilation of *diverse groups* into American society."[21]

Gray's comments about the importance of immigrants and minorities are, clearly, consistent with the thesis developed in this book. But the social diversity perspective goes much further, treating these matters as central, and systematically and extensively assessing social diversity's manifestations and implications. In that vein, the social diversity perspective suggests that the relationships concerning immigrants and minorities are rather more complex, pervasive, and systemic than implied in Gray's overview and other analyses. The minority groups have longer and more complex histories in the United States than Gray seems to suggest. And especially in the case of Latinos and Asians, there has been and continues to be significant immigration. The experiences of more recent immigrants are somewhat distinct from those of their predecessors, but to some degree those later experiences are influenced by the earlier experiences. Recognizing and understanding this point is also important to understanding politics within the states.[22]

The Place

Another aspect of the socioeconomic environment addressed by Gray is the place—that is, land, location and climate, and natural resources. The land area and population density of states have at least several implications, including impacts on the provision of public services. Location can be an asset; being located on the ocean or other waterway, or having proximity to favorable markets or a favorable climate, may advantage states economically.

One might add that major immigration flows have been felt first and often foremost in cities located on the coasts (e.g., New York City, Boston, Miami, Los Angeles, San Francisco) or in border regions in states such as California, Texas, and Florida. Historically, this factor has been significant in influencing or significantly reshaping the politics of such states. Interior areas typically have been less dramatically affected immediately, but have had difficulties of their own in dealing with minority groups (as shown in later chapters).

Economic Context

A specific aspect of socioeconomic environment discussed by Gray is state economy. State economies vary in size, in which economic sectors are most important (e.g., manufacturing, services, mining), and in the major goods produced. As the nature of economic activity has changed owing to the globalization of capitalism and other factors, state economies have been affected. Gray and others acknowledge, indeed stress, the importance of economic change. Yet one wonders whether the state-politics research has fully appreciated the changes in type or mode of production, perceptions of economic stagnation, or other such development implications. For instance, while the decline of private-sector unionism is often noted in the research, the importance of this factor in terms of political participation and/or political influence has not been adequately considered.

State wealth, commonly measured by state personal income, is another factor on which states vary considerably.[23] In general, the southern states cluster at the bottom and the New England states, especially lower New England, and Middle Atlantic states are toward the top. According to Gray, "personal income is an important constraint upon state programs because wealth determines what a state can afford to do upon its own." There is the irony that those states that have the fewest resources, the poor states, are also the ones with the greatest *needs*. But state wealth is not directly translated or converted into expenditures for public programs. Gray argues that there are many "anomalies in state wealth and expenditure rankings" that indicate that wealth alone is not a fully convincing or complete explanation for policies. "*Politics* shape how economic resources will be translated into public policies."[24]

Along with these points raised by Gray, another can be added. A common issue in the state policy literature, albeit not always acknowledged, is the how to consider economic factors. That is, such factors may be viewed as needs or as resources; it may even be the case that what are resources can, simultaneously, generate needs. For instance, Gray suggests that a wealthier population can generate more public resources (revenues), but also have higher expectations of public services and perhaps preferences for different types of public services. The poor, while needier (by definition), also tend to be less well-organized politically, less able to articulate their concerns, and thus less able to generate responsiveness from governments. Hence, the needs and resources of states are not simple to determine, and the economic context of the states is highly complex. How to adequately account for economic complexity is another issue in studying state politics.

Peterson's Political Economy Perspective

Gray argues that politics, not just economic resources, shapes policy in the states. That view is somewhat turned on its head by political economy perspectives, such as that of Paul Peterson.[25] Peterson asserts that city and state governments are more or less willing to spend money on public programs based on the *type* of program or policy involved; they tend to embrace some policies and avoid others. This orientation results largely from two features of the U.S. political system: federalism and capitalism. Capitalism implies that private economic activity is to be relatively unregulated. But to the extent that regulation is permitted, federalism provides that the national (federal) government, not the states, has the major power to regulate interstate commerce. Thus, a state's abilities to shape private economic activity are limited and must occur through persuasion and encouragement, not command. Therefore, states tend to embrace policies that support developmental policies because they feel strong needs to protect their tax and economic base; they see other states as competitors for economic development; and they perceive economic development activities to produce net economic benefits.

In contrast to developmental policies, redistributive policies—those that take from the well-off and give to the needy, such as welfare and health care for the poor—are avoided. This avoidance stems from several related factors, including the concern that a state may become a welfare magnet; generous welfare policies may attract more poor to the state. Redistributive policies are also avoided because they are presumed to make a state less attractive for economic activity, in that they are associated with net economic cost to the state and to unproductive activities. A third type of policy, allocational, includes various activities of a maintenance, caretaker, or housekeeping variety. These are thought to be neutral in their economic consequences for states.

Peterson's argument is certainly important and has been highly influential in the study of state and local politics. It underscores the importance of a "contract" in the U.S. political system, especially if one thinks of federalism as, in part, an institution and a contract or division of authority between the states and the national government. His theory also acknowledges the importance of markets and capitalism in the U.S. political system generally and develops its implications for particular state public policy concerns.[26]

For all its insight, however, Peterson's argument has limits regarding what it tells us about state politics and policy. For instance, *why* is governmental support (expenditures) specifically committed to a particular activity or set of activities within policy domains, once the economic imperatives have set the bounds of resource commitment? Once states determine how much to spend on various policies, the specific forms and allocations that will be addressed remain important. To the extent that redistributive policy is engaged in, to whom, how, and under what conditions are resources distributed? In short, Peterson's theory tells us more about *similarities* than differences. Its ability to explain the many and extensive differences in state policies that we know exist is limited. And its utility in explaining the structure and processes of state political and policymaking institutions seems yet more limited.

The Broader Political Context of State Politics

Returning to Gray's analysis, let's review her assessment of the broader context of state politics. Gray first considers "historical differences." Almost this entire discussion is given to Elazar's political culture argument (see also the extensive discussion of Elazar's framework in chapter 1).

Political Culture Approaches

According to Gray, Elazar's political culture theory has a great deal of intuitive appeal to scholars of state politics because it is "consistent with general impressions" about state differences in "political values, style and tone." Moreover, it provides historical explanation for many differences. Indeed, its historical nature is a strength of and a distinguishing feature of Elazar's perspective, in that the state politics research has tended to be ahistorical. Another reason, I would suggest, for the influence of Elazar's cultural argument is its ostensible comprehensiveness, in that he links political culture to an array of state governmental and political phenomena. Elazar discusses and explains his view of the sources of state political cultures—religious and ethnic, especially European groups—and provides concepts and categories (moralistic/commonwealth, individualistic/marketplace, traditionalistic/status quo). But he goes well beyond that. However, some researchers question the adequacy or accuracy of Elazar's historical assumptions and arguments.[27]

Elazar hypothesizes about attitudes and outcomes regarding a number of issues in state politics, including general views of politics; what are seen as the appropriate spheres of (political) activity; new programs or policy innovation; how bureaucracy is viewed (positive, ambivalence, negative); the kind of merit system; how politics is viewed (healthy, dirty, a privilege); who should participate (everyone, professionals, the appropriate elite); the role of parties; party cohesiveness; and the kinds and nature of party competition.[28]

The intuitively appealing and broad-ranging nature of Elazar's framework has generated a great deal of research. Gray notes that many studies have subjected Elazar's ideas to empirical analysis. Lieske asserts that over 100 studies have directly used the political culture argument,[29] and Nardulli offers that "no self-respecting regression analysis concerned with state politics can ignore" the Elazar scale.[30] The array of issues that have been examined relative to political culture is likewise impressive. Also striking is how frequently research attributes significance to political-culture factors; however, sometimes no systematic analysis is provided to support the claims.[31]

With some frequency, research finds support for the Elazar framework.[32] However, other scholars claim that support for Elazar's framework is mixed. Thompson, Ellis, and Wildavsky believe that how well Elazar's theory has withstood scrutiny "is a matter of continuing debate. For every study that claims to have found Elazar's theory vindicated, there is another that claims to find it of little use."[33] Gray also notes an apparent disjunction between aggregate-and individual-level findings regarding political culture. More generally, Brace argued that existing work on state politics has not been able to reconcile differences between individual and aggregate-level findings on a number of issues—something that is often the case with political culture. I suspect this results from insufficient attention to context, as such.

Other work, which is ostensibly sympathetic to cultural approaches, has questioned Elazar's specific terminology and has also leveled major criticisms at Elazar's basic understanding of culture and history in the United States Thompson, Ellis, and Wildavsky argue that Elazar's term "moralistic" is misleading in several ways and suggest that what that culture actually entails is "egalitarian communalism."[34] They also claim that the traditionalistic category might be reconceived as "hierarchical collectivism." They suggest that hierarchical collectivism is a context where there is "a place for everyone, and [but] everyone in their place." These are important refinements and suggest at least two points. First, it indicates that Elazar's moralistic and traditionalistic cultures *both* have forms of collective or communal orientations. It also suggests is that a supposed central feature of the moralistic culture is an emphasis on equality.[35]

Lieske's Regional Subcultures

Lieske has developed an argument and provided evidence on regional subcultures in the United States. And despite its specific focus on counties, Lieske's work is relevant because it emerges from ideas closely related to Elazar's political culture framework, refining and extending that perspective. (Lieske's work is not discussed by Gray, but it deserves attention here.)

Lieske raises several criticisms of Elazar's political culture argument. Lieske notes the difficulty of measuring political cultures and suggests that Elazar's "derivation of the three political subcultures is not based on any rigorous statistical procedures. Neither are his geopolitical designations based on any empirical data, other than historical migration patterns, personal field observations, interviews, and scholarly studies of America's regions, sections, and ethnoreligious groups." Moreover, Elazar has not updated his mappings; "his state and substate classifications are the same today as they were 27 years ago."[36]

Lieske also points to the "crudeness" of Elazar's classification scheme. Political culture is defined as the persistent, generational patterns of political attitudes, values, beliefs, and behavior that characterize a group of people who live in geographical proximity. "But what constitutes distinctive subcultures is often a very subjective judgment." Lieske adds that another problem with many "cultural themes, including Elazar's, is their circularity. Thus, it is often the case that Elazar's typology relies, in part, on information about past political behavior to predict current or future political behavior." Elazar himself has acknowledged that his scheme may face the problem of circularity.[37]

To improve upon Elazar's framework, Lieske seeks "to develop and analyze . . . new measures of American subcultures that are mathematically precise and replicable, reflect current cultural conditions, and are based on nonpolitical measures of American culture" (down to the county level).[38] To accomplish this, Lieske collected data (from 1980) on 45 variables, including 5 indicators of racial origin, 11 indicators of ethnic ancestry, 14 indicators of religious affiliation, and 15 indicators of social structure (e.g., urbanization, industrialization, income inequality, family structure, cultural homogeneity). Using sophisticated statistical techniques, he produces 13 factors or clusters of regional subcultures: rurban, ethnic, border, agrarian, Nordic, Germanic, Hispanic, Mormon, Anglo-French, native, heartland, Asian, blackbelt. Lieske's mapping of U.S. counties reflects only 10 of these, however, because 3 (agrarian, native, and Asian) are too small to consider.

Note that the labels imply that 9 of the 10 cultures are primarily related to or defined in terms of ethnic/racial characteristics. This is interesting because only 16 of the variables used to created the clusters are ethnic or racial, while 14 of the variables have to do with religious affiliation and 15 are "social structure" variables, according to Lieske. This seems different from Elazar's categories, which appear as influenced by religious factors as ethnic ones; and as stressed earlier, there has been rather little attention in Elazar's analysis to racial or minority groups as such. One of the clusters, rurban, is defined mostly in nonethnic or racial terms, affected primarily by the presence of managerial/professional/college populations, high proportions of young people and low proportions of the elderly, and high urbanization.[39]

Lieske describes the subcultures in some detail. He claims that the heartland subculture, found most commonly in the lower Midwest, is "racially white and homogeneous" and has "relatively few white ethnics."[40] The Germanic culture is similar to the heartland region in being "overwhelmingly white and culturally homogeneous." The Nordic culture, closely related to the Germanic culture, is (also) "overwhelmingly white and racially homogeneous." "*Insulated* by the Germanic culture and situated off the major east-west migratory routes, the Nordic culture has enjoyed a high degree of *cultural autonomy* that is reinforced by an economic base of agriculture, natural resources, and high-tech industries." The Mormon region is described as another "relatively *insulated* subculture."[41] Note that Lieske's discussion suggests that almost half (4 of 10) of the cultures are white and racially homogeneous and/or insulated, and sometimes both.

In some contrast to these homogeneous areas, the "Anglo-French . . . represents a unique blend of the two largest ethnic groups—British and French—which are roughly the same size." Note that both groups are northern or western European (white), according to diversity interpretation, and that Lieske brings attention to the groups being of "roughly the same size"—that is, it is implied that proportionality and context are important. Also note that Elazar categorized the states where these groups are dominant as moralistic.

Yet more complex, the ethnic subculture is an "ethnic *polyglot*." Lieske's characterization suggests the presence of multiple groups, consistent with the heterogeneous, or even individualistic, context. According to Lieske, another subculture, the Hispanic, represents "the oldest . . . non-British stream." While this subculture is defined by its relatively large Latino population, Anglo groups are "*still* culturally *dominant*." "The most distinctive feature of the Blackbelt, of course, is its racial composition," and because there is so much poverty in this region, especially among blacks, this sub-culture also has the highest levels of income inequality."[42]

Lieske tests the explanatory power of his new measure, comparing it with Elazar's on a number of social, political, and policy indicators. Lieske surmises that this new typology "compares very favorably with Elazar's in accounting for differences" on a number of politics and policy indicators. And although "no more parsimonious than Elazar's typology (10 versus 9 categories), it is more precise and takes into account recent demographic changes, especially the United States greater cultural diversity." The level of explained variance of Lieske's indicators is not very high, however. Lieske adds that his "new measure may also prove useful in contextual research that conceptualizes subcultures as arenas of conflict."[43]

Lieske's article thus hints at, but does not fully develop, arguments that parallel those made here. He acknowledges increasing social diversity, but gives less attention to its historical sources and consequences than does the present argument. Nor is much attention given to political or policy consequences, particularly regarding differential impacts for specific groups.

Public Opinion

Gray discussed political culture in terms of historical differences; she also considers contemporary differences as central to state political context. Her discussion of contemporary differences emphasizes public opinion, particularly the important book *Statehouse Democracy: Public Opinion and Policy in the American States*.[44] That book argues that the key to understanding state politics and policy is to understand public opinion in the states. State public opinion is measured with survey data from CBS News/*New York Times* exit polls for 13 years (1976–1988) in terms of partisan (Democrat, Republican, Independent) and of ideological (liberal, moderate, conservative) self-identification. The authors find that many aspects of state politics, including policy liberalism and the nature of state party systems ("pragmatic" versus "responsible" parties), are best explained by public opinion.

One issue—especially relevant to the present study—is the effort to account for state differences in public opinion in the first place. Erikson, Wright, and McIver find that very little of overall public opinion is attributable to individual traits or demographic variables such as education, income, age, race, religion, gender, and size of place or residence.[45] Because so much of state public opinion is *not* explained by those micro-level factors, Erikson, Wright, and McIver go further in seeking to explain public opinion in the states by asking, "Do states matter?"[46] To assess "state effects," they undertake a series of analyses ("dummy variable" regression analyses), using two levels of regional categories and another analysis where each state is a "dummy" variable; the analyses also include the demographic variables. Their analysis can account for only 9 percent of state partisan identification and less than 4 percent of state ideological identification patterns.[47]

Erikson, Wright, and McIver find that there are, indeed, clear and strong state effects. The state of residence "appears to have a major impact on political attitudes"; "the effect of living in one state rather than another is often of about the same magnitude as the difference between one demographic category and another."[48] Thus, context—that is, states—matters. But what is it about state context that produces the state effects?

First, Erikson, Wright, and McIver examine the possibility that certain "omitted" individual-level variables, such as union membership and religious fundamentalism, may account for the state effects. The former seems of little consequence, however, the latter has some impact on ideological, but not partisan, identification. Given the limited impact of these two variables, what else might explain the state effects? Several other, broader factors are considered.

Erikson, Wright, and McIver examine the possible significance of region, Elazar's political culture, "social context" effects, and specific demographic variables (income, education, and race). None of these accounts for the state effects. After setting aside the distinctiveness of the South, the state effect does not follow a consistent geographic (regional) pattern. They also find "that state scores on Elazar's [political culture] classification are unrelated to" the state components of partisanship and ideology.[49]

Studies of contextual effects posit that "people's attitudes are influenced by the aggregated attitudes of those around them; those attitudes are "typically operationalized as the attitudes of the locally *predominant* social groups."[50] But while state residence appears to have a major impact on political attitudes, state effects "are not influenced by the attitudinal predispositions of the states' demographic groups."

After exhaustively considering the numerous broader variables, Erikson, Wright, and McIver conclude that much of the variance in state-level opinion (partisanship and ideology) "is due to state level differences . . . rather than the demographic characteristics of residents of different states" and that "the state of residence produces at least as much variation as does the typical demographic variable." However, while powerful state effects are identified, "the underlying causes of interstate differences in state effects *remain a mystery.*"[51] In short, *that* there are major state effects is clear; *what* the sources of those effects are is not known.

Erikson, Wright, and McIver provide strong evidence of the importance of public opinion in understanding various aspects of state politics and policy. However, as they acknowledge, the very sources of public opinion and other important issues elude explanation. They are not alone when, in seeking to fully explain the sources of state public opinion, they identify and assess the impacts and find linkages between aggregate (state) effects and demographic variables such as income, education, race, and religion. But in their effort to determine state effects, the specific demographic factors considered (income, education, race) may be somewhat limited and viewed only in limited, aggregated, but not fully contextual ways. For instance, they assess percent black but not percent Latino, white ethnic, and so on because (I assume) their data do not include such evidence. Similarly, other of their

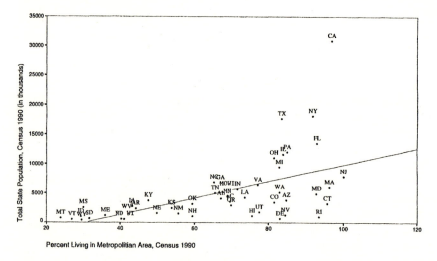

Figure 2.1 State Population with State Urbanization

sity and white ethnic diversity. Minority diversity correlates with population size ($r = .52$, $p = .00$) and with metropolitanization ($r = .51$, $p = .00$); white ethnic diversity correlates significantly with urbanization ($r = .54$, $p = .00$), but not overall population. Furthermore, homogeneous states tend to have low population density; for instance, the Dakotas, Utah, Oregon, Idaho, Minnesota, and even the geographically small states of upper New England have low population density. Finally, white ethnic diversity is strongly related to population density ($r = .88$, $p = .00$), although minority diversity is not.

2. *Poverty, income, and wealth distribution.* As might be expected, there is a rather strong relationship between state poverty level and per capita income ($r = -.69$, $p = .00$). There appear to be other general patterns, too. The homogeneous (and most moralistic) states have somewhat lower poverty rates than other states. But they also tend to have moderate to slightly below-average levels of per capita income. Bifurcated states tend to have high levels of poverty and low levels of income. The situation for heterogeneous states is less clear, but there is some tendency for them to have middle-range levels of poverty and above-average per capita income.

Percent in poverty is also related to the distribution of wealth (measured with Gini coefficients, $r = .75$, $p = .00$); poverty and income *in*equality increase together. Again, certain patterns related to diversity emerge, as suggested by the correlation between the measure of wealth inequality and minority diversity ($r = .38$, $p = .01$). Greater inequality of wealth is found in bifurcated states, but the pattern is mixed for the other types of states, except that some of those where wealth is most *equally* distributed are homogeneous states (e.g., Wisconsin, Utah, Vermont; see figure 2.2).

3. *Education and other social indicators.* Education is thought to be a

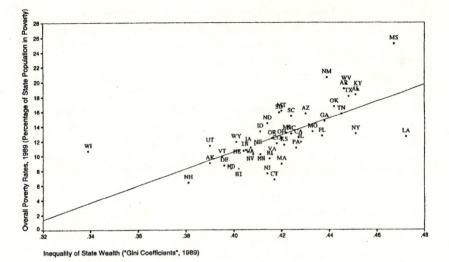

Figure 2.2 Overall Poverty Rates with Income Inequity

major variable in politics, one that affects both individual and aggregate patterns. Education—measured as the percent of a state's population (25 years of age or older) who have a high school degree or higher—shows significant relationships with other socioeconomic variables. For instance, education is positively related to per capita income ($r = .43$, $p = .002$). And it is strongly and negatively related to both income *in*equality ($r = -.72$, $p = .00$) and poverty rates ($r = -.67$, $p = .00$). But levels of education are not strongly related to urbanization ($r = .02$).

Figure 2.3 indicates what might be hypothesized as broad tendencies of state overall socio-economic patterns related to social diversity. The bifurcated environment would be hypothesized to appear most like a pyramid, with whites on top, blacks and minorities at the bottom, and poor whites

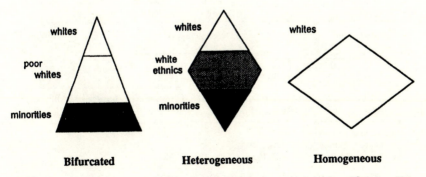

Figure 2.3 Hypothesized Social Diversity and Socioeconomic Stratification Patterns

in between. The heterogeneous pattern would be hypothesized as somewhat less pyramid shaped than the bifurcated; it indicates a reasonably large middle class that includes white ethnics, but minorities still tend to be disproportionately present toward the bottom. The homogeneous has the largest middle class, with relatively smaller upper and relatively smaller lower classes.[53]

Clearly the impact of the numerous socioeconomic variables, and the relationships among the variables, may be quite complex. But the situation may be even more complex than has been suggested here. As Brace indicates, sometimes the impact of variables appears inconsistent when assessed at macro versus micro levels. Erikson, Wright, and McIver underscore the point well:

> Consider state income: Wealthy states are often suspected of being more liberal even though individual wealth breeds Republicanism and conservatism. Consider education. It might be that a more educated populace affects the political climate perhaps encouraging liberalism, but possibly Republicanism as well. Consider race. The size of the local black population sometimes makes whites more racially reactive.[54]

Thus, particular variables may be interrelated, but they may simultaneously have impacts that seem inconsistent with one another. That appears to happen a great deal, as will be evident in subsequent chapters of this book. I suggest later that some of those inconsistencies might be explicable in terms of context, the social diversity context in particular.

The broader frameworks discussed in this chapter may also have parallel yet distinctive implications. Likewise, social diversity may have some common, but also some distinct, assumptions, insights, and implications compared to other perspectives. For instance, the social diversity argument shares some outlooks with Elazar's political culture argument, as well as Lieske's extension of political culture, as may be apparent (and as is further indicated in figure 2.4). The social diversity view is also fundamentally different from the political culture view, however. Social diversity emphasizes diversity, of course, hence it conceptualizes and views the essential factors of state politics

1. Homogeneous		Heterogeneous		Bifurcated	
2. ⌐M MI	⌐IM⌐ I	IT	⌐TI⌐ T	TM⌐	
3. Anglo/French Mormon	Nordic Germanic Rurban	Ethnic Heartland	Border	Black Hispanic	

1. Social diversity (Hero 1996)
2. Political Culture (Elazar 1966, 1984)
3. Regional Subcultures (Lieske 1993)

Figure 2.4 Social Diversity and Elazar's Political Culture/Lieske's Regional Subcultures

differently from other frameworks. Moreover, social diversity brings attention to faces or aspects of state politics and policy typically overlooked in other approaches (see chapter 1).

State contexts are important yet complex phenomena. A central concern of this book is to consider the nature of and extent to which the social diversity context helps explain variations in aspects or levels of state politics and policy.

A Note on the Presentation of Evidence

In the chapters that follow, the social diversity interpretation is examined relative to a large number of questions, issues, or variables (i.e., dependent variables). Scatterplots are often used to illustrate general patterns and, in most instances, statistical evidence is examined and is noted in the body of the discussion; unstandardized regression coefficients, b's, and statistical significance, p, are typically noted. The direction and statistical significance are also summarized in tables, but much other detail is not. That is, summaries of the direction and statistical significance of the social diversity indicators, and other variables, are often presented, but much other statistical data or output (e.g., the specific unstandardized regression coefficients, standardized regression coefficients, standard errors, and so on) are not detailed in the tables.

I present the evidence in this fashion because I wish to maintain a focus on the big picture—the theoretical issues and arguments that lie at the heart of the social diversity interpretation. An overly detailed data presentation may detract from that goal, and may bring a "tedium of typical scholarly work"[55] that I wish to avoid. The nature of the data presentation does not, it seems to me, compromise the rigor or systematic nature of the broader endeavor. However, I expect—indeed, I anticipate—that some researchers will find the data presentation too limited and/or otherwise unsatisfactory. So be it. The goal of this study is to present and consider a new perspective; I wish to ensure that the tail (data and statistical analysis) does not wag the dog (theory). This also seems consistent with Brace's view, with which I agree, that state politics research has been weak on theory despite ostensibly impressive quantitative analysis.[56]

The next chapter thus continues to address these goals by examining political processes, attitudes, and political institutions.

3

Social Diversity and Political Institutions, Political Processes, and Attitudes

Political processes and political institutions in the states encompass a number of activities. Most commonly these include processes associated with voting, levels of voter participation, the nature and impact of political parties and party systems, and interest groups. This chapter considers an array of such issues from the standpoint of the social diversity interpretation. Matters such as political participation and parties are often considered part of state processes.[1] But they can also be thought of more specifically as political institutions or organizations because each of these processes has a set or rules, structures, and mechanisms that are important rules of the game in state politics. Their significance as such is commonly understood at a general level, but it is not always incorporated into thinking about and studies of state politics. Yet theoretical leverage may be gained by thinking about such processes as institutions or organizations because the processes may reflect and/or institutionalize certain factors or social forces, including social diversity.

Scholars commonly speak of party systems or interest group systems, and they often view both parties and interest groups as "mobilizing institutions." The works of Key and of Schattschneider, for example, emphasized that parties as organizations are critical to democracy because they provide some continuity and coherence in the political process. Key emphasized that *organized* political party competition was critical if the "have-nots" were to be effectively heard in state politics.[2] Schattschneider stressed that all organizational processes have biases toward certain outcomes and groups, resulting from their particular processes and structures.[3]

Another reason to consider organizations, especially political parties, as institutions is because of their treatment and their place in U.S. politics. Bibby and Holbrook stress that political parties in the United States are highly regulated by state government, and that political parties are virtually quasi-governmental entities.[4] While in other western democracies political parties are viewed as private associations, in the United States parties function in a manner not unlike public utilities.[5] Among the most significant state regulation has been the requirement that parties nominate their candidates via the direct primary. This requirement emerged in the Progressive era, when a vast array of institutional reforms were adopted in state and local government. But Bibby and Holbrook add that state regulation extends well beyond specifying nominating procedures to include issues of party membership, organizational structure, access to the ballot, and campaign finance. All but five states specify in statutes some aspect of the party's internal organization structure, the composition of its most important units, and its internal operating procedures and rules.

Viewing political processes as institutions has also been practiced and understood historically. We commonly speak of the institution of slavery as a political, economic, and social phenomenon, and we readily acknowledge its legacy in our social and political systems. With the abolition of this "peculiar institution," the South enacted a number of practices—a legal system—designed to maintain the political segregation and inequality that we think of as institutions: the "Jim Crow system" with its poll taxes, literacy tests for voting, white primaries, and the like. Also, political machines, or political party organizations with specific institutional features, existed in the South as well as in the Northeast and Midwest, and they created various linkages among governmental officials, party structures, and various groups.[6]

Finally, in assessing the power of interest-group systems within states, scholars typically note factors that can be viewed as institutional or structural.[7] They discuss the state policy domain, the level or institutionalization of state government, the extensiveness and enforcement of state lobbying laws, and so on. Also, almost half the states have the institution of the initiative, though their rules, regulations, and procedures vary considerably. Political and policy implications are associated with those rules and procedures.[8] Thus, these political institutions (or processes) are integral to state government and politics.

This chapter examines various political processes and institutions in state politics, and considers the issues relative to social diversity in the states. The analysis draws on both findings of previous research and original research; the evidence is presented so as to highlight the issues relative to social diversity.

Voting Rights, Voter Turnout, Parties, and Democracy in the States

Hill delineates, explains, and assesses the policy impact of "democracy in the states."[9] He measures the level of democracy in states according to three factors—the right to vote, voter turnout, party competition—and according to its overall democratization, providing specific scores on these dimensions for the 50 states, comparing the 1980s and the 1940s.

Parts of Hill's analysis are revisited here, and some of his findings are considered in assessing levels of democracy relative to social diversity. Along with specific parts of Hill's analysis, I give attention to some of his general discussion.

The Right to Vote

Hill notes that throughout most of the 20th century, until the mid-to late-1960s, the right to vote was constrained to some degree by malapportionment in *all* 50 states. That is, the basic standard of "one person, one vote" was established only rather recently. Beyond that, Hill indicates that voting rights during the 1940s were constrained in a number of states by institutional rules such as extensive restrictions based on ethnicity, restrictions based on literacy or ethnicity, and constraints emanating from the activities of political machines.

Hill presents evidence indicating that all the states of the old Confederacy practiced the first—that is, restrictions based on ethnicity, although Hill also clearly includes or means to emphasize race. Two additional states, Arizona and New Mexico, are classified as having had restrictions based on literacy and ethnicity. Given the population composition of those states, we can assume that the main groups affected were Latinos and Native Americans. Moreover, for two states in the 1940s—Texas and New Mexico—"there is substantial evidence that political machines operated to manipulate the votes of ethnic minorities in a clearly undemocratic fashion."[10] These states had, and have, relatively large Mexican-American (Latino) populations.

Hill places New Mexico in the category of "highly undemocratic" on voting rights for the 1940s, saying that "while some might question" whether New Mexico belongs in that category, "the obstacles to Native American and Mexican American voting rights . . . [were] sufficiently high" that it be labeled as such.[11] Arizona is rated as "undemocratic" on voting rights in the 1940s; given Arizona's population composition, it would appear that its low rating is due to reasons similar to those for New Mexico.

With the implementation of the federal Voting Rights Act of 1965 (VRA) and its later amendments, variations in voting rights among the states have narrowed considerably. As with malapportionment, the importance of federalism and "liberal" values in reshaping the institutional practices of the states is evident in the VRA legislation. In fact, federal policies have led to such minimal variation in formal voting rights, at least as measured by Hill, that statistical analysis of data on voting rights for the 1980s is not feasible (although that measure is incorporated into the overall democratization indicator examined later). Still, the evidence warrants discussion.

For the 1980s, Hill's scale of the right to vote indicates that the seven states in the lowest category are all Old South or bifurcated states (Alabama,

Georgia, Louisiana, Minnesota, North Carolina, South Carolina, Texas). The vast majority of states ($n = 42$) are in the middle category, and only one, North Dakota, is in the highest category. Thus, the remaining variation in the right to vote is still associated with high racial/ethnic diversity (in the case of the Old South states), and low social diversity (in the case of North Dakota); refer to figure 1.1. These patterns are hardly surprising, but they remind us of the legacy of institutions and traditions typically associated with social diversity.

Voter Turnout

Hill measures voter turnout based on average state turnout in gubernatorial elections from 1980 to 1986.[12] That turnout indicator is analyzed here relative to social diversity (minority and white ethnic) as well as other variables—urbanization, education, per capita income, and party competition.[13] Greater minority diversity is significantly related to lower voter turnout ($b = -17.2, p = .03$); education is also significant ($b = .63, p = .03$), but the other variables are not. The scatterplot in figure 3.1 shows the patterns. In addition to the general patterns, note that three states classified most differently by the social diversity and the political culture frameworks—California, Colorado, and Michigan—do not have an especially high turnout; their turnout seems lower than political culture would lead us to expect.

In another study, Hill and Leighley examined mobilizing institutions and voter turnout, and found that racial diversity provided a powerful explanation of turnout (their measure of racial diversity is somewhat similar, but not exactly like, the social diversity indicator used here).[14] Their measure of racial diversity is consistently related to the strength of mobilizing institu-

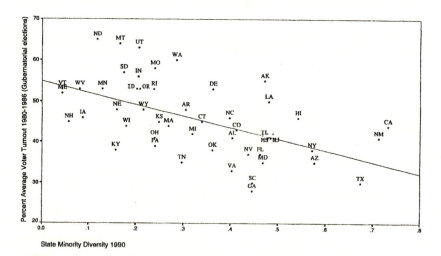

Figure 3.1 Voter Turnout with State Minority Diversity

tions—party competition, liberalism of party elites, and the difficulty of voter registration. Social diversity has a greater impact than various socioeconomic factors, and is significant even in the face of controls for those factors. Moreover, Hill and Leighley's findings hold in both southern and nonsouthern states. Thus, the impact of racial diversity is not merely important in one region.[15]

That study also found that racial diversity and education levels were the strongest predictors of voter turnout in 1982, in both the south and the nonsouth, controlling for other variables such as income, income inequality, and urbanization. Also, racial diversity was more strongly related to voter turnout in 1980 and 1982, in both the south and nonsouth than other mobilizing factors such as party competition, the relative liberalism of Democratic and Republican elites, and the difficulty of voter registration. While Hill and Leighley's analysis focused on the 1980s, they indicated that patterns in the 1950s and 1990s were similar.[16] Clearly, Hill and Leighley's findings are quite supportive of the social diversity argument as it pertains to several political processes.

Party Competition and Related Issues

Another element of democracy in the states considered by Hill is party competition. Party competition (as measured by the "folded Ranney index"[17]) was examined here relative to social diversity and to education, urbanization, and income. Only education is significantly related to party competition; that none of the other variables is significant is surprising and the reasons for this are unclear.[18] However, Bibby and Holbrook, among others, have noted several problems with the Ranney index of party competition.[19] When an alternative measure of party competition was used, that of Holbrook and Van Dunk,[20] minority diversity has a significant negative relationship to that indicator ($b = -19.5$, $p = .06$). Education also has a significant, positive impact ($b = .936$, $p = .01$).

There is more to political party systems than just their levels of competition. The strength of the party organization is also important. Dwyre et al.'s study of decision-making processes and the distribution of tax burdens in New York and California found that institutional patterns—party organizational structure—affected policy outcomes.[21] In New York, the reform of the state's tax system was decided by cohesive, constituency-based legislative parties. This led to a more equitably distributed tax burden than in California, where policies were decided mainly through a "series of disconnected public referenda." That is, Dwyre et al. found that the nature or strength of party organization is important for policy outcomes.[22] Party organization was found to play a more important role in heterogeneous New York than in more bifurcated California; the absence versus the presence of another political institution—the initiative—also appears important. Whether social diversity is related to party organizational strength deserves further exploration.

Social diversity was examined here relative to the strength of state party organizations,[23] and appears to have some impact. Social diversity (for 1980) was examined relative to the strength of state Democratic Party and state Republican Party organizations (for 1975–1980), controlling for several variables. Greater minority diversity is related to weaker Democratic Party organizational strength ($b = -.715$, $p = .02$; urbanization is also significantly related, positively $p = .01$). This likely reflects the weakness of Democratic Party organizations in the South. At the same time, white ethnic diversity has a significant, negative relationship to Republican Party organizational strength ($b = -1.15$, $p = .02$). Because party organizational strength appears to be an important factor in understanding state politics and policy outcomes,[24] and social diversity has an impact on party organizational strength, social diversity is important. (Later discussion in this chapter concerning the Erikson, Wright, and McIver research extends and expands on this evidence.)

Overall Democratization

Hill also assesses levels of overall democratization in the states in both the 1940s and 1980s; the indicator for this is an index that combines data on the right to vote, turnout, and party competition.[25] For the 1940s, Hill categorizes all the Old South states in the lowest category, and New Mexico and Arizona are just above those states on this score.[26] Thus, historically the presence of other minorities—Latinos and Native Americans, not only blacks—appears related to less democracy.[27]

In analyzing the factors associated with overall democratization for the 1980s, Hill finds that racial heterogeneity and political culture both are strongly related to the overall democratization scores; recall that in chapter 1 political culture was shown to be closely related to social diversity. Two other variables considered—economic development (per capita income) and income inequality—are also associated with democratization. (Recall that evidence in chapter 2, showed significant relationships between diversity and income inequality).

Does social diversity help explain the overall democratization scores? As might be expected from the foregoing discussion, it does. When the social diversity indicators and other variables (urbanization, income, and education) are considered relative to the overall democracy measure, both minority and white ethnic diversity are found to be significantly related, the former negatively and the latter positively ($b = -1.43$, $p = .06$, and $b = 3.23$, $p = .10$). Education has a significant positive effect ($b = .11$, $p = .001$), but urbanization and income have no significant independent effect. Social diversity, as defined here (and as defined by others as well),[28] helps explain several aspects of democracy in the states beyond what socioeconomic factors explain. But social diversity's significance for state political institutions seems yet greater.

Social Diversity and Party Composition

There is more to state political parties than just the level of interparty competition, or even which party is in control of government. Brown argues that the basic nature of political parties is critical to understand, and he views "social composition"—essentially social diversity—as a central feature of parties and party systems in the states.[29] His study focuses on the social group bias of the party coalitions; parties can be thought of as aggregates of social interests that link the mass public to government. Brown delineates the social group basis of party coalitions in the states relative to several demographic group traits: race (black and white), religion (Protestant, Catholic, Jewish), education (college degree versus not), income (high and low), gender, and union membership. To appropriately understand party coalitions, Brown emphasizes, "we need to know how group characteristics incline an individual toward a particular partisanship *and* we need to know the relative *size* of each group in the state populations."[30]

Using data from 1976 to 1988, Brown determines the state party cleavages and categorizes states relative to three major types of cleavages: southern, New Deal, and post–New Deal. In the southern partisan cleavage, "race plays the fundamental role in differentiating the support coalitions of the two parties."[31] As implied by its name, this cleavage includes the Old South states; Oklahoma is also included, but Arkansas and Kentucky are not (and these two states do not conform to any of the three party cleavages identified by Brown). Notably, but not surprisingly, this cleavage is also very similar to the bifurcated states.

The New Deal cleavage contains the largest number of states—19. Brown describes this cleavage in terms of economic class—that is, high versus low income, and religion, but not race or ethnicity. The social diversity perspective would bring attention to other factors, however, and may help clarify why Brown finds race/ethnicity less salient in this cleavage.

Fifteen of the 19 states (79 percent) that Brown includes in the New Deal cleavage were below the national average in terms of minority diversity, and most of them were well below that average (based on the 1980 data on diversity). And 16 of the 19 had rather low levels of white ethnic diversity. In fact, 13 of the 19 are among the more homogeneous states—Vermont, Maine, New Hampshire, Montanna, Minnesota, Utah, Iowa, South Dakota, North Dakota, Indianna, Nebraska, Washington, Oregon. Three states (Massachusetts, Rhode Island, and Connecticut) are among the states that social diversity classifies as simple heterogeneity, having high white ethnic, but somewhat low minority diversity. It is highly improbable that racial/ethnic factors would be important to state party composition patterns where there is so little minority presence in the first place. The three remaining New Deal cleavage states are above the average for minority populations, but all are notable for their large Latino populations—New Mexico, Arizona, and Colorado—and have small black populations. Hence, social diversity, or particular configurations thereof, may also be relevant to this cleavage, although it is not fully acknowledged in the Brown framework.

Several issues regarding Brown's data and arguments should be noted. The data Brown uses to derive the cleavage categories do not include Latinos or other minority groups, or white ethnics. Thus, assigning certain states to the New Deal cleavage may partly be due to data availability[32] and may not fully capture the social group elements of those states' party systems. Some of the racial/ethnic diversity may be subsumed in the religion variable, but that is not apparent in Brown's analysis. Considering a broader array of racial and ethnic characteristics might lead to a modification of the assignment of states to cleavage categories.

The post–New Deal cleavage, Brown argues, in many ways combines "the characteristics of the first two cleavages, most notably with regard to race and class as dominant characteristics" of party bias. In states categorized in this cleavage, "class-related characteristics are important" but "race is also a dominant characteristic."[33] Again, the diversity perspective suggests several points.

Seven of the 14 states in this category are above average in terms of both minority and white ethnic diversity (New York, New Jersey, Delaware, Illinois, Michigan, Nevada, Maryland in the 1980s). These tend to be heterogeneous states according to the diversity interpretation. Another state listed under this cleavage is California, where the Latino population is not only very large (over 25 percent) but also substantially larger than the black population numerically. Yet owing to several factors, the Latino population's electoral impact is much less than the numbers suggest. Also, recall that earlier discussion indicated that the political culture framework misclassifies California because aspects of its diversity context are overlooked (see chapter 1 regarding Elazar's cultural classification). One scholar argues that California has a two-tiered political and social system, with whites in one tier and minorities, with Latinos numerically dominant, in the other.[34] And, as discussed earlier, Dwyre et al. argue that weak party structure and heavy use of initiatives are important features of California's politics.[35] Thus, the post–New Deal cleavage may be yet more affected by social diversity than Brown's analysis acknowledges.

Another important impact of racial context on party patterns is identified by Giles and Hertz.[36] Their study of Louisiana parishes ("counties") indicates that as the size of parishes' black population increased there was a significantly stronger tendency of whites to join the Republican party.[37] Race may "structure" parties. Glaser also found that racial context—the size of black populations within counties, both within and outside the south—has major impacts on various racial attitudes.[38] These two studies thus point to the significance of the social diversity context for political parties.

Brown's analysis is insightful, but it may actually understate and/or partly misperceive the importance of social diversity, or absence thereof, on the party cleavages he identifies. Overall, the evidence indicates that social diversity has a substantial impact on political parties as institutions and as aggregates of social groups and interests. Social diversity has implications for political attitudes within states as well, as the following evidence underscores.

Social Diversity and Public Opinion

Along with enhancing the understanding of parties as products of social group cleavages, social diversity may help understand public opinion in the states and associated workings of state party systems. Erikson, Wright, and McIver assessed partisan identification and ideological identification as aspects of public opinion in the states. However, as they acknowledge, their data are actually most reflective of "active electorates."[39] (Certain groups, especially racial/ethnic minorities, tend to be substantially underrepresented in the active electorate.) Regarding partisan identification, Erikson, Wright, and McIver determined the relative size of Democratic versus Republican identifiers in each state; they also specified, but focused less attention on, percent of independents. As discussed earlier (chapter 2), they identified important state effects on public opinion among the electorate, but they were largely unable to determine the source of state effects. It may be that social diversity helps explain partisan and ideological identification;[40] this is explored below.

Social Diversity and Partisan/Independent Identification

Social diversity is first examined, through regression analysis, relative to the indicator of mean party identification—that is, percent of Democrat versus Republican identifiers; education, income, and urbanization are also included. Neither of the diversity indicators is significantly related to average partisan identification, but education (percent who are high school graduates or more) is significant. Like Erikson, Wright, and McIver,[41] it is hard to pinpoint the direct impact of a contextual factor—here, social diversity—on partisan identification in the states. Brown's analysis, however, emphasizes social diversity's impact on party composition and, in turn, on state public policy.[42]

Little research attention has been given to independent identification among state voters; as noted, Erikson, Wright, and McIver's measure focused on Democratic and Republican identification. Diversity may, however, have an impact on the percent identifying as independent; thus, it and the several other variables noted above were examined relative to "percent independent." White ethnic diversity is strongly and positively related to the percent independent; more white ethnics are related to more independents in the electorate ($b = 56.5$, $p = .002$), although minority diversity is not. Education is also positively related ($b = .49$, $p = .02$), but the other variables are not. It thus appears that at least some of the contextual or state effects on independent/partisan identification that Erikson, Wright, and McIver were unable to account for are related to social diversity.[45]

Social Diversity and Ideological Identification

Is social diversity associated with the *ideological* identification patterns among state voters, as measured by "percent liberal minus percent conservative?"[44] It appears so, at least to some degree. White ethnic diversity is positively and significantly related to average (mean) self-identification across the states ($b = 33.7$, $p = .03$, even with controls for urbanization, education, and income); minority diversity has no significant independent impact. However, social diversity appears to have other impacts on ideological patterns within states.

When social diversity is considered relative to "percent moderate" in the states (a dimension of state ideology not examined directly by Erikson, Wright, and McIver), minority diversity is found to have a significant negative relationship. More minority diversity is related to fewer moderates ($b = -5.8$, $p = .01$); more white ethnic diversity is also significantly, negatively related to persons identifying themselves as moderates ($b = -9.6$, $p = .08$). Income and education are also significantly related to "percent moderate," but the direction of the impact differs: the former is positive and the latter is negative. Social diversity's impact on ideology seems to follow a broad pattern. The evidence of liberal/conservative patterns along with these of moderate identification suggests that white ethnic diversity is associated with aggregate liberal leanings and minority diversity with overall conservative leanings in the active electorate as a whole. Put another way, homogeneity—fewer minorities and fewer white ethnics—appears linked to higher proportions of moderates. Higher levels of self-identification as moderate and, perhaps, moderation, and maybe even moralistic orientations, seem affected by social context—specifically social diversity.

The evidence suggests that social diversity seems to account for some of the ideological patterns in the states, as measured in the Erikson, Wright, and McIver study. If so, this is an important contribution to understanding state public opinion, and it underscores the importance of social diversity as an analytic construct.

Social Diversity and Ideology of Party Elite

Party Elite Ideology—Polarization

Erikson, Wright, and McIver examined the ideology and attitudes of party elites. They found that party elites in some states—moralistic ones—tend to be not only the most ideological but also the most ideologically polarized. They examined patterns relative to Elazar's three-category framework of political culture,[45] and their findings seem to provide substantial support for that framework. That is, the assumption is that party elites in moralistic cultures are the most ideological because issues drive politics in this environment. Party elite ideology is less polarized in the individualistic and traditionalistic cultures.[46]

What might explain the patterns of party elite polarization? As noted, Erikson, Wright, and McIver cast the issue in terms of Elazar's political culture, but social diversity offers a different perspective. It might be that the social diversity context of states, in conjunction with states' general or mass ideological orientations, helps account for patterns of party elite ideology. The social diversity view suggests the following interpretation.

In more heterogeneous contexts, an ideological profile (liberal, moderate, conservative) among the masses approximating a normal curve would be anticipated. Erikson, Wright, and McIver's data actually suggest such a pattern, except that the curve is a bit skewed to the conservative end. Important from the social diversity standpoint is the assumption that this aggregate ideological pattern is underlain by a somewhat diverse configuration of the electorate resulting from heterogeneity. That is, in this context, consensus does not run especially deep; legitimacy is fragile because group differences, linked to heterogeneity, are constraining (see the discussion of competitive pluralism in chapter 1 and figure 1.4.) Social diversity suggests that this helps explain the pragmatic/responsive versus responsible party systems often found in the heterogeneous context; group competition, linked to heterogeneity, encourages compromise toward the middle (see figure 3.2A). Thus, the social diversity view may agree with other views that come to similar conclusions,[47] but attributes those outcomes to different forces and dynamics.

In homogeneous environments, the distribution of party elite ideology relative to mass ideology is the most difficult to assess and describe. The states classified as the most homogeneous (see figure 1.2) vary considerably in their mass ideological patterns. Some are rather liberal (e.g., Minnesota, Wisconsin, Vermont), according to the Erikson, Wright, McIver data. Others are among the most conservative states (e.g., Utah, Idaho, and the Dakotas); in fact, these states are about as conservative as Old South states. But party elites in homogeneous (moralistic) states tend to be the among the most ideologically polarized.[48] How can this be? What might explain this ostensibly contradictory pattern?

The social diversity perspective suggests that what may allow this polarization of ideology among party elite opinion is the *little social diversity* among the mass population—and among the party elite—in socially homogeneous settings. That is, elites and the mass population may be relatively "freer to disagree"; there is less need to close ranks, owing to a relative absence of redistributive issues directly tied to matters that have often been divisive in U.S. politics—that is, race and ethnicity. Perhaps, paradoxically, greater freedom for issue politics may exist where there is less diversity because the political stakes are not starkly defined in racial or ethnic terms—

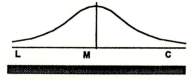

A. Heterogeneous

L   M   C

(underlying heterogeneity)

B. Homogeneous

L   M   C

(underlying homogeneity)

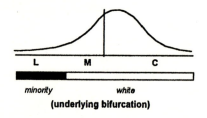

C. Bifurcated

L   M   C

minority   *white*

(underlying bifurcation)

Figure 3.2 Hypothesized Ideological Patterns and Underlying Social Diversity

that is, in terms of a major "American dilemma." This, social diversity suggests, is a major reason that the responsible party model appears more common in homogeneous states.[49] This was also implied in the characterization of homogeneous states as having a consensual pluralism (see chapter 1) and earlier in this chapter with regard to Brown's analysis of party cleavage structures.[50]

What, then, might be the configuration of opinion in homogeneous settings? It is unclear in the aggregate because the ideological variation across the homogeneous states is quite high, but collectively, it may take on the appearance of a flattened normal curve (see figure 3.2B). Guessing at the specifics is much less important, however; whatever the ideological configuration is, it is, in fact, undergirded by homogeneity. The nature of the ideological profile and the extent of ideological polarization among elites and/or the electorate play different roles, and may be less critical, because they are muted by the relative absence of racial/ethnic division.

In the bifurcated context, social diversity would expect a distribution with a very strong tilt, or skew, toward the conservative end (see figure 3.2C). This relatively high cohesion of conservatism is underlain by a consensus among dominant groups to essentially maintain stratification, itself related to bifurcation. Minorities would be expected to be somewhat more liberal, at least on issues of economic and social equality. However, the existing research on state public opinion drawn on here does not permit the analysis of dimensions of ideology—for example, social versus economic liberalism.

Apart from this speculation, is there any evidence that social diversity has an impact on party elites' ideological polarization? There is. I derived a simple measure of the distance between, or the polarization of, Democratic versus Republican Party elites,[51] and analyzed it relative to the social diversity measures, the three socio-economic measures, and mass polarization (through regression analysis).

White ethnic diversity is negatively and significantly related to the distance between party elites ($b = -11.7, p = .01$); more white ethnic diversity among a state's population is related to less distance between party elites. Minority diversity is related to more distance between party elites, but is not significant statistically. Greater education is related to greater ideological distance between party elites, but is not significant. Notably, white ethnic diversity is significant and ideological polarization in the general, or mass, population is also significant in explaining party elite polarization.

These findings may help explain why the heterogeneous (or individualistic) states appear to have a pragmatic party model: heterogeneity may necessitate compromise or movement toward the middle among political elites.[52] While the impact of white ethnic diversity on mass ideological identification is to make it slightly more liberal, among elites it seems associated with more ideological convergence.

These arguments may also help reconcile what appears to be a contradiction, although one that is usually overlooked, in Elazar's work. Elazar claims that the moralistic culture is cooperative and has a commonwealth orientation. At the same time, he argues that issue politics are central in this culture and that issues are intensely debated, often generating high levels of party competition. But the cooperation/commonwealth orientation and the simultaneous issue intensity seem incompatible, prima facie.

What, if anything, might reconcile this issue intensity and competitiveness with a commonwealth outlook that is also said to exist? Elazar seems unclear about this. But the social diversity view would suggest that the underlying homogeneity may well be the missing link in reconciling the ostensibly contradictory claims. That is, issue intensity and commonwealth may both occur because a context of homogeneity limits or manages the situation. (This was suggested earlier and is further developed later in this chapter.)

Another implication of these claims about ideology and social diversity context is that most of the ideological debate in homogeneous settings is likely to be issue-based—that is, it is about the application or interpretation of values, the means rather than the basic values themselves, on which the social diversity view assumes there is considerable agreement.[53] This may also help explain why homogenous states vary considerably in mass ideology—with some quite liberal and others quite conservative, compared to heterogeneous and bifurcated states—but are similar in having more polarization among party elites.[54] Furthermore, this line of argument implies that ideological differences in heterogeneous contexts results from both issue and basic values dimensions. In bifurcated contexts, especially of the Old South variety, there is rather less ideological division regarding either issues or basic values, especially within the historically dominant—that is, the white groups or population.[55]

While these latter speculations appear plausible, they are difficult to assess because existing data on ideological identification in the states do not distinguish between issue and basic values as aspects of, or contributors to, ideology.[56] Indeed, this is a limitation of the public opinion research on state politics. Similarly, the state public opinion research does not adequately consider whether identifying oneself as a liberal (or moderate or conservative) means the same thing in different social contexts. For example, calling oneself a liberal in New York versus Mississippi, or Minnesota versus New Mexico, probably has somewhat different meanings and implication in each context. What one is liberal or conservative *about* may differ considerably according to context. There are difficulties in assessing the propositions about party or ideological patterns and social diversity, and there are limitations in the public opinion data. These matters notwithstanding, there is another important question that deserves attention: social diversity's relation to the party elite's overall ideology.

Party Elite Ideology—Overall Patterns and Their Significance

Certain findings of the Erikson, Wright, and McIver study make the impact of social diversity on the overall ideological leanings of state party elites—as distinct from the ideological distance, or polarization, just discussed—especially important to consider. Challenging much theory and numerous empirical claims, Erikson, Wright, and McIver argue that the *overall*, or average, ideological leaning (or liberalness) of state party elites—not ideological polarization of party elites per se—is the critical factor in determining the substantive implications, the policy impacts, of state party systems.[57] That is, they conclude that the policy relevance of state parties is determined by the party elite's aggregate ideology, not elite polarization. Given that claim, a critical question is: What accounts for party elite ideology in the first place?

Democratic Party elite ideology and Republican Party elite ideology were examined relative to the social diversity measures, and several other variables were controlled (average mass ideology in the electorate, along with the three socioeconomic variables). White ethnic diversity is negatively and significantly related to Democratic Party elite ideology ($b = -8.45$, $p = .03$); minority diversity is also negatively related, but not significantly so. Overall (mean) mass ideology has the strongest impact and education is also significant. But that white ethnic diversity has this level of impact, in the face of numerous other variables and controls, is notable.

Turning to the ideological patterns of Republican Party elites, we find that their ideology is negatively and strongly significantly related to minority diversity ($b = -3.2$, $p = .01$, again with controls for the several other variables), but white ethnic diversity is not. More minority diversity is related to more conservative Republican Party elites. Average (mean) state ideology of the electorate is also strongly significant. Thus, overall ideology has a major impact on the party elite's ideology for both parties; the earlier finding that social diversity has some impact on mass ideology takes on yet more importance.

Generally, it seems that social diversity has an impact on the party elite's overall ideology. This is especially critical because party elite ideology seems to be the driving force in state party systems as they affect public policy, according to Erikson, Wright, and McIver.[58] Social diversity's impact on party elite polarization is clearer and stronger. The finding that social diversity shapes party elite ideology advances the understanding of state political and policy processes. This, along with other findings reported above, suggests the importance of social diversity for various dimensions and dynamics of state parties in the electorate as well as party organization elites.

Further Comments on Social Diversity, Party Systems, and Public Opinion

While social diversity has been shown to be relevant to state political processes, it may also have broader significance with regard to party systems and their role as institutions that aggregate and organize political activity. Party systems seem related to broader issues of political and social order. The heterogeneous environment is in several respect the most complex. Politics in such environments is often seen as "dirty."[59] However, from the social diversity standpoint, it may be more appropriate to call it "messiest" because the level and nature of ethnic/racial compositions are vast and quite differentiated, especially in complex heterogeneous states—New York, for example. Party organization and the two-party systems common in these settings seem to serve as institutions central to simplifying, organizing, and bringing some order to that complexity. Whether parties have adequately, efficiently or equitably done so in this setting is another matter.

The bifurcated setting, with two major racial groups (whites and minorities), tends to be a simpler social context, with the legal, political, and social lines more clearly drawn. Historically, bifurcation has been further simplified by closing ranks around one-party systems and promoting a relatively cohesive antiegalitarian ideology. While there is now more party competition in the bifurcated states, it continues to occur within relatively narrow ideological parameters.[60] Both the heterogeneous and the bifurcated states, therefore, have significant levels of social diversity, albeit differing in the nature and extent of that diversity. In both cases, party systems seem to simplify, narrow, manage, or control that diversity in rather different ways, for different reasons, and with different effects.

In homogeneous states, political parties do not need to play the same managing or controlling role because the setting is already or naturally simplified, since there is very little racial or ethnic diversity in the first place. Thus, it is appears less surprising that this simpler social order is often the setting for ideological, issue polarization, and that "third parties are popular."[61] Political energy need not be expended on directly confronting social diversity or complexity in this context, and may thus be directed elsewhere. Again, there is little need to close ranks and individuals may be freer to disagree.

Many scholars have noted that states vary in terms of two-party competitiveness, one-party dominance, and cohesiveness of party systems.[62] However, these patterns have not always been linked specifically to social diversity patterns (heterogeneity, bifurcation, and homogeneity). But social diversity seems to be an important dimension of those patterns, one often imbedded in one state's social composition and political systems.[63]

Interest Groups

Interest groups are generally perceived to exert a major influence in state politics. Supported by the earliest systematic studies, various scholars have found that interest groups play a substantial role in state political systems. This section briefly summarizes some recent research on interest groups; it also explores whether social diversity affects interest group systems in the states.

Recently, several systematic efforts have been undertaken to assess the impact of interest group systems. Probably the leading example is a series of articles and a subsequent book by Gray and Lowery.[64] Among their contributions, Lowery and Gray present an intriguing theoretical approach to studying interest groups grounded in population ecology concepts. They argue that interest group systems in the states can be explained by environmental factors, particularly (1) the potential gains from interest group activity, or "energy"; (2) the stability of the governmental system, or "stability"; and (3) the number of potential constituents, which is affected by "area." They apply this ESA model of population ecology to help explain state interest group systems. In the process of testing their ideas, they develop measures of the density (number of groups) and diversity (the extent of economic and/or social sector differentiation) of interest group systems.

Gray and Lowery's theory and analysis provide several important and sometimes counterintuitive findings. One finding contrary to prevailing theory is that growth in the number of interest groups is not necessarily linear. Beyond a certain point, the number of groups is checked by the competition for scarce resources and thus leads to a natural equilibrium. Another is that interest group density is bounded in certain ways at the lower end, in that all states have some minimum numbers and types of interest groups because there is a basic similarity in the presence of certain groups across states.

Thomas and Hrebenar,[65] and scholars who analyzed interest groups earlier, have identified a host of factors associated with the "systemic" or collective influence of interest groups relative to other components of state governmental and political systems. Four factors are listed under the socioeconomic and political environment: the level of socioeconomic development; political attitudes, especially political culture and ideology; the strength or weakness of political parties; and the level of campaign costs and sources of support. Other variables discussed by Thomas and Hrebenar are structural or federal in nature, such as the policy domains or authority of state governments and policy priorities in a given period.

Incorporating these variables, and drawing on a team of research experts in each of the states, Thomas and Hrebenar provide a ranking of interest group system influence for the states. In 7 states the impact of interest groups is rated as "dominant." In 21 states, the interest group system is rated as "dominant/complementary." Seventeen states are rated as having "complementary" interest group systems, and 5 as "complementary/ subordinate;" in no state are interest groups categorized as "subordinate."

What explains the specific patterns—that is, why do states have more or less powerful interest group systems? Thomas and Hrebenar carefully discuss this relative to the variables they identify. They claim that "there is likely a connection between the political culture of a state and the extent of group system power. States that have moralistic political cultures . . . are likely to have less powerful group systems than states that have more individualistic cultures. Socioeconomic development also has its effects, usually by increasing the number of groups and reducing the likelihood that the state will be dominated by one or a few interests."[66]

Certain points are not clear in the Thomas and Hrebenar discussion, however. For example, as factors explaining interest group system influence, socioeconomic development and political culture may point in different directions. That is, less socioeconomic development is assumed to strengthen interest group influence, while a moralistic culture is presumably related to weaker interest group influence; but most of the moralistic states are somewhat less developed socioeconomically (as is suggested in chapter 2). Additionally, it appears that Thomas and Hrebenar, as well as Gray and Lowery, emphasize *economic* development when they discuss socioeconomic development or complexity in the states. Ethnic/racial diversity, as a social factor, is not specifically raised.

Thomas and Hrebenar do not systematically assess the extent or the details of whether and why states do or do not fit with the expectations posed. Moreover, it is difficult to determine what factors should be included in a systematic analysis, given that the ratings or rankings of interest group systems reported for states appear to *already* incorporate the important variables. But it does not appear that ethnic/racial diversity is directly incorporated into their ratings of state interest group systems. Therefore, several questions about interest groups are considered here.

For instance, are the density and diversity of interest group systems delineated by Gray and Lowery related to social diversity? Are density and diversity, as measured by Gray and Lowery, related to interest group system power, as delineated by Thomas and Hrebenar? What would be the expected relationship between social diversity and interest group system, and why? Is social diversity related to interest group system power in state politics? I begin with, and emphasize, the latter two questions.

The social diversity view suggests that in homogeneous contexts the power of interest groups as a system is expected to be relatively weak or low because groups do not appear to represent dramatically divergent interests, at least not very divergent in racial or ethnic terms. At the same, this racial or ethnic homogeneity may mute certain economic differences to some degree. The number of groups will be moderate to fairly high, probably slightly above average, because of the ostensible issue politics possible in these environments, owing to the underlying social similarity and related political consensus. These expectations are consistent with—indeed, are a part of—the consensual pluralism discussed earlier (see chapter 1).

In the heterogeneous context, interest group power is anticipated to be middle range or moderate. This is because heterogeneity, racial/ethnic and otherwise, likely leads to the existence of many competing groups. Thus the expectation is of large numbers of groups that compete significantly with each other and moderate the overall impact of groups. The level of group competition has a moderating effect on the power of any one or any one set or type of groups. Again, this is consistent with the competitive pluralism discussed in chapter 1 and consistent with much theorizing.

In more bifurcated environments, the overall interest group system will be quite powerful, the highest of the three types of states. A rather "undiverse" set of interest groups would be expected because group activities have been limited historically by social, political, and institutional constraints. Many of the constraints were directed at minority groups. That there is a somewhat limited number, and relatively powerful groups, is central to hierarchical or limited pluralism (see chapter 1).

What patterns exist? Do these expectations hold up? To assess this, Thomas and Hrebenar's interest groups system reputation measures—interest group dominance scores—are considered relative to social diversity and other variables.[67] Gray and Lowery's interest group density and diversity scores are also examined. Thomas and Hrebenar developed interest group system ratings for two recent periods; scores for both periods were considered relative to the social diversity indicators (for the appropriate period);

the three socioeconomic factors considered earlier are also included. The analysis indicates some support for the social diversity perspective relative to Thomas and Hrebenar's interest group system scores.

When the two social diversity indicators were examined relative to the Thomas and Hrebenar interest groups scores, minority diversity was found to be positively and significantly related for *both* periods ($b = 3.13$, $p = .002$ for the 1980s measure, and $b = 2.13$, $p = .01$ for the 1994 measure). As the social diversity view anticipated, more minority diversity is related to more powerful interest group systems. Very important, however, groups directly representing minority interests are not among the powerful interest groups; indeed, such groups are seldom seen as very influential at all.[68]

In both periods the relationship with white ethnic diversity is negative—again, as expected. For the 1980s, the relationship is significant (at.10, $b = -3.89$); for 1990, white ethnic diversity is not significantly associated with interest group system strength. The significant relationship holds when the socioeconomic variables are also included, but the socioeconomic variables themselves are not significant. That ethnic/racial diversity shows a significant relationship with interest group system strength, but that socioeconomic variables may not, is striking. Most research has focused on economic variables. Yet this finding suggests that they are of little importance—at least the specific variables used and the way they are measured here. The interest group diversity (numbers) and density indicators of Gray and Lowery, themselves presumably related to socioeconomic factors, seem not to be related to either of the two interest group system measures (nor for either period) of Thomas and Hrebenar's data, and are only weakly related to social diversity. In short, social diversity may be an important aspect in understanding state interest group system. This has not been stressed in previous studies.

Direct Democracy

Practices referred to as "direct democracy"—particularly the initiative and referendum—might also be viewed as institutions in that they have particular rules and procedures and, perhaps most important, can produce important procedural and/or substantive policies in the states (see chapter 7). The initiative is particularly important in this regard because it is something like governing or policymaking institutions, such as legislatures and governors. Notably, however, little systematic attention has been given to direct democracy in much of the state-politics literature, including major overview books.[69] But scholars who have examined the impact of initiatives have raised serious questions about its democratic nature in general and its impact on minorities, especially ethnic and racial groups.[70]

The substantive use of initiatives and their significance for minority groups are considered in later chapters. For the moment, however, several points can be noted. First, some evidence suggests that ethnic or racial minorities are less likely to vote in initiative elections than are nonminorities,

In the bifurcated environment, the clientele that has benefited historically has been the white population, while the social, economic, and political costs are borne by blacks and poor whites. Here, there also appear to be winners, the "haves," historically almost exclusively whites, and losers, the "have-nots," minorities and poor whites. Poor whites have benefited to the extent that they have received higher legal and social status than blacks. But many critical observers would suggest that, in fact, there have been no real winners. Evidence suggesting that no one really wins is the political and economic inequality, high poverty, and generally lower socioeconomic development common in bifurcated environments (see chapter 2).

Homogeneity implies that the costs and benefits of public policies are less likely to fall disproportionately or visibly on any identifiable racial or ethnic group because there just are few such group members in these states. However, for groups that are distinctive, this may not necessarily hold, as is shown in later chapters. Overall, majoritarian politics, a kind of win-win situation, is more common and more readily achieved politics in homogeneous environments (see figure 3.3). In short, there may be broad but systematic political and policy patterns and outcomes associated with the several diversity contexts.

Conclusion

This chapter strongly suggests that social diversity is related to and, indeed, seems presently and historically imbedded in major political processes and institutions in the states. An array of processes and activities typically seen as the core of state politics are importantly affected by social diversity. And particular impacts of different types of diversity are evident. The importance of social diversity is supported by previous research as well as present analysis.

Hill, and Hill and Leighley demonstrate racial diversity's impact on a

		Benefits	
		Concentrated	Diffuse
	Concentrated	Heterogeneity (Group Competition)	(Entrepreneurial)
Costs			
	Diffuse	Bifurcated (Clientele)	Homogeneity (Majoritarian)

Note: Wilson's policy types relative to the concentration/diffusion of benefits and costs are noted in parentheses.

Figure 3.3 Social Diversity and Wilson's Framework

Table 3.1 State Political Processes and Institutions
on Which Social Diversity Has an Impact

Right to vote
Voter turnout
Party competition
Overall democratization
Party composition
Percent independent
Overall (mean) ideology
Percent moderate
(Relation of Mass Ideology to Party Elites' Ideology)
Party elite ideology
   Polarization
   Overall
General nature of party system
   Pragmatic vs responsible party systems
   Parties as simplifying institutions
Interest group system Strength

Note: The arguments and evidence regarding these issues are developed in the body of this chapter. In most instances, the social diversity measures are directly examined relative to these issues. In others, I make linkages to and draw inferences from other research. And in one or two instances the claims are somewhat speculative, but are linked to theory and other evidence. Finally, a number of the above relationships were also considered with Elazar's political culture scale included in the regression analysis; the political culture scale had no independent impact when included with the social diversity and other variables.

number of aspects of state political processes, institutions, and on overall democratization.[75,76] Brown essentially defines political parties as social group organizations.[77] Research findings of Giles and Hertz and Glaser similarly are supportive of the diversity argument.[78,79]

The original research presented in this chapter extends and adds to the evidence in behalf of social diversity. Social diversity provides new insights and evidence as well as helps reinterpret and reaffirm previous research. For example, social diversity helps explain moderate ideological identification and independent (versus Democratic or Republican) identification of the electorate across the states. It also helps explain, and offers various propositions concerning, the interaction of mass ideological patterns and party elite ideologies. For instance, both party elite polarization and overall party elite ideology appear affected by state social diversity. The ostensible impact of social diversity on overall party elite ideology is especially important because that ideology has been identified as the critical factor affecting the policy relevance of party systems. Social Diversity is significantly related to state interest group systems. Finally, I suggest that social diversity patterns have implications for broad political patterns and relations—patterns that parallel the Wilson framework.

Overall, this chapter provides compelling evidence that social diversity is directly and extensively implicated regarding major aspects of political institutions, processes, and public opinion in the states. (A summary list is provided in table 3.1.) I next consider social diversity's relationship to formal institutions.

4

Social Diversity and the Formal Institutions of State Government

State governmental institutions—state legislatures, governors or executives, the bureaucracy, the courts, and, in some states, "direct democracy" structures—are the formal policymaking bodies in the states. While these institutions are studied frequently, the studies tend to be rather compartmentalized.[1] The tendency is to examine particular aspects of one institution or another, but few studies consider institutions as a whole or the interrelationships of institutions.[2] And the issues have not been considered from the standpoint of social diversity.

Studies that focus on institutions as a whole often consider only one or a few states, perhaps because of the sheer complexity encountered when assessing these intricate entities. Studies that examine all the states are also limited by the variations, complexity, and the numerous incommensurabilities of state institutions; thus, research tends to focus on a few of the more apparent and measurable dimensions of state institutions. But it is not altogether clear that the most apparent and/or measurable traits are necessarily the most important or interesting. This is not to criticize the previous research; indeed, studying institutions as a topic (and as an approach to studying state politics) is highly desirable. However, the difficulties and limitations of studying state governmental institutions evident in previous research also have consequences for analyzing social diversity relative to those institutions.

This chapter examines the formal institutions of state government, focusing primarily on two major issues in relation to social diversity: formal institutional structure or characteristics, and descriptive representation or institutional composition. Both of these are important, commonly addressed issues in the literature, although the former, in particular, is seldom considered from the standpoint of a social diversity interpretation. First, the formal powers, the strength, and the institutional capability of individual institutions are considered to the extent that such analysis is feasible, as are the interrelationships of institutions. The central issue is whether there is evidence that social diversity shapes the general structure or strength of institutions. Second, the degree of descriptive representation—the extent to which the racial/ethnic (social) diversity of states is reflected in the membership or composition within the institutions—is examined.

The Nature and Strength of State Government Institutions

Previous research and theorizing imply some general, although not always detailed, expectations about state institutional traits or structures. Those expectations tend to be derived from the socioeconomic perspective on state politics, although they are not necessarily incompatible with the social diversity outlook. For instance, scholarship implies that more professional legislatures are more likely to be found in states with greater social and economic complexity. Similarly, the formal powers of governors might be expected to be greater in larger, more economically and socially complex states. And professionalism and merit in bureaucracies also appear related to socioeconomic development.

Elazar argued that political culture influences the nature of and attitudes toward bureaucracies in states.[3] He claimed that merit systems and bureaucratic professionalism are more common and viewed more positively in the moralistic culture, reasoning that once governmental action is deemed necessary, bureaucratic neutrality and potential efficiency are seen as desirable in that context. Bureaucracies are least favored in the traditionalistic environment, with the individualistic in between. Some evidence supports Elazar's claims, finding that the strength of merit systems is consistent with his predictions.[4] However, Elazar did not discuss political culture relative to the other institutions of state government, such as governors, legislatures, and courts, and their strength individually or relative to each other.

Overall, then, the mainstream state politics research provides somewhat limited guidance into the historical or institutional nature of formal state policymaking entities, although there are some general expectations about state institutions taken individually. This is partly because governmental institutions are often studied as independent rather than dependent variables, as that which explains politics and outcomes rather than that which is to be explained. Beyond the broad expectations in the existing literature, what might the diversity perspective suggest?

Social Diversity's Expectations Regarding State Institutions

If states have general orientations to politics and social order, as argued earlier (see chapter 1), institutional strength and structures might reflect that. Formal governmental institutions might be more or less powerful in themselves, and also vary in their relationships to one another, in part because of social diversity environments. Moreover, social diversity suggests that institutions should be thought of collectively, not just individually.

Institutionalist or new institutionalist approaches to studying politics might well claim, however, that institutions are much more than simple reflections of society. Institutions are viewed as relatively autonomous entities that independently shape politics, policy, and society. Institutions, some suggest, do not necessarily respond to, and may in fact impede, be contrary to, or channel social forces. However, I am simply suggesting that there would presumably be some broad consistency between institutions and social factors because, without that, some crisis might result. Perhaps recent enactments of term limits, restrictions on a government's tax-raising capacity, and the like can be understood as efforts to rein-in institutions.

The simple suggestion here is that governmental institutional structures may differ relative to social diversity, in part because institutions grapple with that diversity at the same time as they shape that diversity through decision-making structures and processes. Indeed, Cain has argued that the use of the initiative, itself an institution, has been critical in reconfiguring the California legislature through term limits and other devices; that reconfiguration and other uses of the initiative have, in part, been due to concerns about state government's responsiveness, or what some see as over-responsiveness, to social diversity concerns.[5] How strong or professional is the state legislature, the governor, and the two considered together? What is the general character of the state courts and of the bureaucracy? The social diversity perspective puts forth certain expectations about these questions.

Formal institutions, especially the elected or political ones (i.e., legislature and governor), would be expected to be strongest overall in the heterogeneous states because that heterogeneity suggests the need for a government that is sufficiently strong to establish and maintain a modicum of social order in a diverse social and economic setting. (In some states, judges are also elected; see below.) More complex social patterns may be associated with more complex formal structures. However, complexity might work against the establishment of strong governmental institutions, in that diversity and complexity may make agreement on creating strong institutions difficult. Recall that heterogeneity is expected to be related to moderate levels of issue consensus and basic value consensus (see figure 1.4) and, thus, may also limit the strength of formal institutions. Nonetheless, the major expectation of relatively strong institutions remains, with the recognition that while institutions may be strongest in this context, they may be somewhat less powerful than expected because social diversity may both increase and decrease the authority different (ethnic/racial) groups are willing to grant to government. Population size and other socioeconomic factors might also modify this.

The weakest formal institutions are expected in the bifurcated environment. In this context, strong government is perceived as neither necessary nor particularly desirable because the essence of power is lies in society—

that is, outside government—and in social stratification (bifurcation) or hierarchy. Government need only be strong enough to help maintain that stratification.[6]

Formal institutions in homogeneous contexts are expected to be moderately strong or in between the heterogeneous and bifurcated patterns. In this setting there may not be a need for especially strong government because homogeneity underlies the political system, helping produce the consensual pluralism suggested earlier. But policy debates may need to be moderated through or mediated by reasonably strong institutions because issue politics (as distinct from debate over basic values or redistributive policies) seems to be common here (see chapters 1 and 3). Also, because the underlying social consensus may, in fact, produce considerable policy agreement and policy activity, there is a need for somewhat strong, if not large, government to implement those policies.

Evidence on Social Diversity and State Institutions

State Legislatures

State legislatures are recognized as the formal lawmaking bodies of state government. For many years, including through much of the 20th century, state legislatures were viewed as backward and ineffective institutions, overly dominated by interest groups and plagued by inappropriate operating procedures, inadequate information sources, low pay for members, and a host of other problems. During the 1960s and 70s, a movement arose to improve the structures and processes of state legislatures, to make them more professional. Some reformers argued that legislatures needed to be made more "FAIIR"—that is, Functional, Accountable, Independent, Informed, and Representative.[7] "More representative" referred, in part, to descriptive representation, an issue considered later in this chapter. Toward these ends, a number of reforms were proposed, including (1) allowing state legislatures to meet longer, so that they could have adequate time to address and consider legislation; (2) higher salaries to attract a broader array of and higher quality individuals to seek legislative office; (3) better staff support and research capability to provide more and better independent sources of information; (4) making the legislatures smaller so that they could function more efficiently and citizens would be in a better position to ascertain accountability; (5) having clearer, more easily understood legislative procedures so that legislators and citizens alike could have a better sense of the openness and fairness of the legislative process. Reform groups rated the state legislatures relative to their adoption of various measures relevant to the reform agenda.

Some research—for example, that of Carmines,[8] found that legislative professionalism was a significant variable in effecting policies in the states. Professionalism was identified as an important factor in facilitating the translation of party competition into policy outputs, specifically welfare policy. Thus, it appeared that legislative professionalism was an important intervening variable shaping redistributive outcomes in state politics. Later research, however, has not always shown professionalism to be as important as Carmines found.

Various scholars have created measures of legislative professionalism. Recently, Squire developed an index of state legislative professionalization based on three indicators: legislators' salaries, levels of staff support, and time spent in session.[9] This index is helpful, and is used below, but it has limitations. Among those limitations is that it taps only those three dimensions of legislative professionalism and does not address others, such as the size of legislative bodies, general legislative rules and processes, committee rules, processes and power, and party cohesion and organizational strength within the legislature. These untapped dimensions are quite difficult to ascertain and very difficult to measure. Moreover, there are numerous informal aspects of state legislative politics that comparative statistical research has difficulty addressing. The limitations in the index of formal professionalism aside, the measure was examined relative to the social diversity indicators.

Neither of the social diversity indicators (minority and white ethnic) is significantly related to the legislative professionalism index.[10] Minority diversity approaches but does not achieve statistical significance ($p = .14$); contrary to expectation, the relationship of minority diversity to legislative professionalism is positive. California, the very highest on minority diversity in 1990, is among the most professionalized; New York is also somewhat high on minority diversity (see figure 4.1). Thus, two states that are high on professionalism and moderate to quite high on diversity seem to produce that finding. White ethnic diversity is positively but not significantly related.

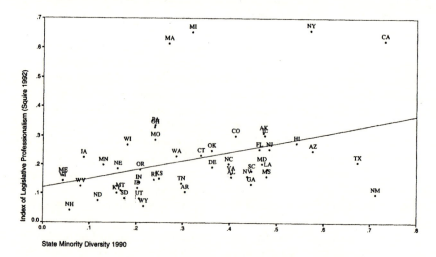

Figure 4.1 Legislative Professionalism with State Minority Diversity

At the same time, none of the socioeconomic variables (urbanization, education, and income) has a significant relationship.

That California, a bifurcated state according to the social diversity index, places where it does on the legislative professionalism index may seem to contradict the hypothesis offered earlier. To some degree it does; however, two important points might be noted. California was among the first states to adopt a term limits measure; that measure also reduced staff support for the legislature. And the measure that limited terms and reduced staff in California was adopted through an alternative institution, the initiative. Additionally, other research finds that greater increases in minority diversity over time, between 1980 and 1990, are positively related to state adoption of term limits.[11] The other three states with the highest levels of professionalism tend to be heterogeneous states, consistent with expectations. Also, none of the homogeneous or bifurcated states (other than California) is particularly high on the legislative professionalism index. Thus, there is some evidence consistent with the expectations, although the expectations are not strongly evident in the aggregate patterns when all the states are examined.

Governor's Formal Powers

Studies of gubernatorial power most often consider governors formal, legal, or institutional authority. Those powers include authority regarding vetoes, appointments to the executive branch, control over the budget process relative to state legislatures, tenure potential (length of terms and ability to succeed oneself), the number and the significance of separately elected executive officials in the state (e.g., attorney general, secretary of state), and party control in the state legislature.[12] At the same time, scholars acknowledge and have sought to measure numerous informal or personal dimensions of a governor's influence, such as popularity, style, electoral mandate, and stage in the term.[13] As with the legislatures, the powers and roles of governors have evolved over time. Since the 1950s, there has been some tendency toward having stronger governors than in previous eras, with various forms of authority to act as the states' executive leaders, although governors' powers may have weakened on some dimensions.

Scholars have rated or summarized a governor's powers with various indices.[14] Again, the indicators of gubernatorial power have limitations.[15] For instance, the indices typically weigh each dimension equally, but it is not clear that this is the best approach generally nor that it is most appropriate in particular types of states or over the period of a governor's term. And it is doubtful that the indicators can effectively measure such a complex and ambiguous phenomenon as gubernatorial power and/or leadership. Nonetheless, an index is examined relative to social diversity and other variables.[16]

Social diversity does not have a statistically significant relationship with formal gubernatorial powers. Of the variables assessed along with social diversity, only state per capita income has a significant relationship (at

p =.08); wealthier states have more powerful governors, presumably consistent with expectations of the socioeconomic school of thought.

A Collective Look at State Legislatures and Governors

Social diversity shows no clear or strong relationship to the index of legislative professionalism nor to the index of formal gubernatorial powers taken alone. The suggestion earlier, however, was that governmental institutions should be considered collectively. Figure 4.2 indicates the state positions on two indicators of state institutions—legislative professionalism and formal gubernatorial power.

The expectation was that states might fall into patterns such as "strong overall" (i.e., strong both in terms of gubernatorial power and legislative professionalism, with heterogeneous states anticipated to be most numerous in that quadrant), "weak overall" (i.e., weak on both dimensions, with bifurcated states likely to fall here), "legislative-centered" (with relatively strong legislatures and formally weak governors), or "governor-" or "executive-centered" (strong governor and weak legislature). Homogeneous states were expected to be distributed between these latter two. Note that while four states (Massachusetts, New York, California, Michigan) stand out, there is less variation on legislative professionalism among the remaining states.

To further assess whether social diversity is related to legislative professionalism and gubernatorial power, the two were combined through multi-dimensional scaling techniques, and that indicator was examined relative to social diversity. There is no relationship between this indicator and social diversity—not surprising, given the findings just presented.

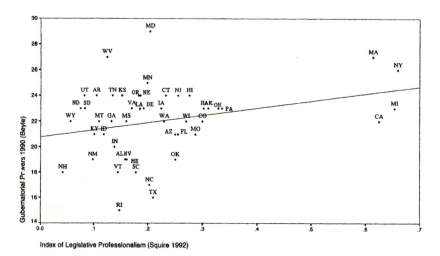

Figure 4.2 Gubernatorial Powers with Legislative Professionalism

The broader implications of these nonfindings are unclear. Most simply, they may mean that diversity just does not have an impact, at least not a direct one, on the strength of the governorship and legislative institutions. On the other hand, it may mean that any social diversity influences that may exist are not evident in the measures of governmental institutions—or aspects of institutions commonly studied. Or social diversity may have an impact on institutions in other informal, not readily measurable ways. Also, because the institutions most often were established in earlier periods, they may not have been (or are not) directly affected by contemporary societal diversity. Yet state constitutions and formal governmental institutions have been frequently changed, which might lead us to expect that social change would have some impact on this constitutional or institutional change.

The institutional patterns that do exist would be expected to have consequences for how (contemporary) social diversity and other influences are responded to.[17] Those issues are examined in later chapters.

Courts

The courts and the bureaucracy both differ somewhat from the legislatures and governors in that they are less visible governmental institutions, are sometimes thought of as nonpolitical, and appear to derive much of their power or legitimacy from their presumed expertise and neutrality. These two institutions are difficult to analyze in relation to social diversity (or other analytical approaches, for that matter), for several reasons.

In seeking to study the state Courts as institutions in relation to social diversity, determining the appropriate indicators is not simple or clear. And the issues are further complicated by the nature and roles of state court systems. Jacob argues that different levels of state courts are distinct in important ways. Trial courts, on one hand, have certain traits and procedures not unlike those of administrative agencies, in that they have a high volume of activity; often follow routines or standard operating procedures; and have limited discretion.[18] Trial courts are involved in the administration of justice, just or simply implementing the law. Yet the simple administration of justice has important implications (see chapter 6). Appellate courts, on the other hand, wield more and broader power in the legal and political arenas, and function more as policymakers.

Despite the limitations and difficulties in assessing state courts relative to social diversity, the issue is worth exploring. In this exploratory effort, I draw upon several indicators noted by leading scholars of state courts. Jacob provides evidence on several aspects of state courts, including reputational indicators for state supreme courts and the methods of selecting judges.[19] Such indicators provide some, albeit far from perfect, analytical basis to examine state courts.

1. *Social diversity and state supreme courts reputation.* Three reputational indicators are drawn from other research and include (a) the number of states citing the particular state's supreme court decisions; (b) a general

prestige score, and (c) tort law innovation adoption patterns.[20] Minority diversity has a negative and significant relationship, with the number of states citing its supreme court (b = 11.9, p = .08); the higher a state's minority diversity the less its decisions are cited by other states. White ethnic diversity is also negative but is not significant. Higher urbanization has a strong positive impact on citations.

Neither the social diversity nor the socioeconomic variables have a significant relation with the general reputational score for state courts. However, regarding the states' tort innovation score, white ethnic diversity is negatively and significantly related (b = −.52, p = .10); minority diversity is also negatively, but not significantly, related. Education and urbanization are significantly related to tort innovation, but the former is negative while the latter is positive.

Social diversity, thus, has some relationship to two of the three court reputation indicators. This suggests some importance for social diversity in how a state's courts are perceived by other states, but the full meaning and implications remain to be explored and are beyond the scope of the present study. Socioeconomic variables also show some relationship, but the directions are somewhat erratic. Social diversity may also have some indirect impact, in that both minority and white ethnic diversity are at least moderately related to urbanization, which itself shows an impact on the court's reputation (simple correlations of the social diversity measures with urbanization are .51 and .54, respectively; see chapter 2).

2. Social diversity and state court selection methods. States use several methods to select judges, and different methods may be used for different levels of courts. For example, trial court and state supreme court judges may be selected differently, although there is some tendency to use the same method for various courts. The major selection methods include partisan elections, nonpartisan elections, appointment (by the governor or legislature, most often the former) and the merit (or Missouri) system, which involves gubernatorial appointment and subsequent, periodic judicial retention elections.[21]

Assessing judicial selection practices relative to social diversity, or other factors for that matter, poses several problems. First, as noted, judicial positions within a state may be selected differently, thus, the analysis is separated accordingly. Also, not all states have intermediate appellate courts, and the analysis is thus limited to the states that have such courts (n = 38).

Second, it is unclear how to measure or rate the selection processes in relation to one another. That is, there is no clear and simple (numerical) ordering of selection methods upon which all scholars would likely agree. One might distinguish between elective versus nonelective (appointed), and/or make various other distinctions. However, it is not obvious how to compare the merit system, with its retention elections, to nonpartisan elections, and so on. Therefore, the selection methods were examined through a series of "0, 1" analyses (i.e., the state does not have = 0; does have = 1) relative to social diversity and other variables.

The evidence indicates that social diversity has some relationship to selection methods. The four selection methods for each of the several types of courts—highest, intermediate appellate, and trial courts—are discussed in turn.

Selection Methods for Highest Courts

- Partisan election. Both social diversity indicators are positively related to partisan election, but neither is strong. However, higher levels of education are negatively and significantly related to partisan elections for the highest courts ($p = .02$).
- Nonpartisan election. Minority diversity has a moderately strong, and negative, relationship to nonpartisan election to the highest courts ($b = -5.6$, $p = .07$). White ethnic diversity is also negatively, but rather weakly, related to this selection method. The socioeconomic indicators show no significant relation.
- Appointment. There is a positive, but nonsignificant relationship between this selection method for the highest court and the white ethnic indicator. Minority diversity shows no relationship. Of the socioeconomic variables, both income and urbanization are significant ($p = .06$ and $p = .10$, respectively); the former is positive while the latter is negative, however.
- Merit system. While neither social diversity measure is significant, white ethnic diversity is negatively related to merit selection while minority diversity is positively related. Education is positively and significantly related to merit selection ($p = .01$).

Selection Methods for Intermediate Appellate Courts

- Partisan election. As with selection to the highest courts, both minority and white ethnic diversity are positively related to partisan elections, although the relationships are not significant. Only education has a significant impact, and it is negative.
- Nonpartisan election. Minority diversity is negatively and strongly related to nonpartisan election of intermediate appellate court judges ($b = -11.2$, $p = .03$); white ethnic diversity shows no relationship. Urbanization has a modest positive relationship ($p = .09$) and per capita income has about an equally strong negative relationship; again, the socioeconomic indicators point in different directions.
- Appointment. Neither of the social diversity indicators shows much relationship to this selection method for intermediate appellate courts. The several socioeconomic indicators, likewise, appear not to have much impact.
- Merit system. None of the variables—neither social diversity nor socioeconomic—have a significant impact on merit system selection for intermediate appellate courts.

Selection Methods for Trial Courts

Neither social diversity measure shows a relationship to partisan elections for trial courts; only education has a significant ($p = .01$) impact and that is negative. Both social diversity measures have a negative relationship with nonpartisan elections, but both are not significant. Greater urbanization shows a positive relationship, however. The social diversity indicators seem to have no impact relative to the appointment method for trial court selection. Per capita income has a significant positive impact, however.

Social diversity does appear to have some impact relative to merit selection for trial court judges. Minority diversity is positively and significantly related ($b = 15.1, p = .06$). This is something of a surprising finding. White ethnic diversity, on the other hand, is negatively related and approaches, but does not reach, statistical significance ($p = .12$). Education is positively and significantly related ($p = .03$).

A Summary of Social Diversity and Court Selection Methods

Only a few of the relationships between judicial selection methods and social diversity seem strong. But there is some tendency for the diversity indicators to have specific directional patterns relative to methods of selection. For example, minority diversity is negatively related to the nonpartisan election and the appointment selection methods for all three levels of court. White ethnic diversity is negatively related to nonpartisan elections and to merit selection for all three levels. Social diversity seems broadly, if somewhat weakly, related to judicial selection methods, and that seems grounded in historical institutional patterns.

Bureaucracy

The courts and other institutions of state government are quite difficult to measure or summarize for aggregate analytical purposes. Much the same can be said of the bureaucracy. Earlier research had, in fact, presented different indicators of bureaucratic quality or capability,[22] but a more recent study by Barrilleaux et al. claimed that measuring state bureaucracy is, essentially, futile.[23] Hence, I do not venture into that thicket directly. Instead, a simple, and admittedly limited, indicator is used.

A sometimes-used, but clearly rough indicator of bureaucratic quality is the average salary of state employees. When this indicator is examined, social diversity has no apparent impact;[24] only per capita income shows a significant (positive) relationship.

The Initiative

As suggested earlier (see chapter 3), the initiative and the referendum may be seen as institutions, in that authoritative decisions—constitutional and/or statutory laws—can be enacted through these mechanisms in the states that provide for them. The particular structures of initiatives vary in states concerning whether they apply to state statutes, the constitution, or both, the number of signatures necessary to get on the ballot; the percentage of votes necessary for adoption; and other dimensions. Issues briefly considered here, however, concern the historical reasons why states do or do not adopt the initiative. Social diversity appears central to that story. (The frequency and the particular ends to which the initiative has been used, especially in recent years, are addressed in later chapters.)

The adoption of the initiative is often viewed in regional terms, in that states in the western United States were the most likely to adopt the initiative. This, according to scholars, is traceable to several reasons. One is that the Progressive movement swept the western states only a few decades after most had attained statehood and, thus, "political institutions . . . were not as firmly rooted in traditions as they were [in other states]."[25] Thus, newer states were more likely to adopt the initiative. Racial/ethnic factors also appear central.

Schmidt argues that a major "factor that hindered the establishment of I&R [i.e., the initiative and referendum] in the Northeast was the *high proportion of immigrants* in the cities." Most of the immigrants—from southern and eastern Europe—were poorer and less educated than their northern European predecessors and the "political differences between the two groups were immense." "*White Anglo-Saxon Protestants feared the immigrants'* potential voting power and doubted their ability to read, much less comprehend, ballot questions."[26]

Also, Schmidt suggests that racism and related factors influenced the adoption of the initiative. Schmidt speaks of the "tendency of rural white politicians in the East and South [in the early 1900s] to oppose I&R, fearing that the urban masses, once empowered by I&R, would overrule the decisions of malapportioned legislatures dominated by rural interests." Thus, a frequent pattern was that legislatures allowed the initiative in cities, but not statewide. Part of the reason that western states adopted the initiative statewide was that "the majority of residents in the boom towns of the West were white *native U.S.* citizens who had moved in from other states, *not other countries*, and therefore *did not represent the same kind of threat*."[27]

Schmidt also argues that differences in social diversity in the West and the South are central to understanding why the initiative was commonly adopted in the former but not in the latter states during the Progressive era: "In contrast with the self-reliant egalitarianism of the West, *southern politics was still steeped in aristocratic—and racist—traditions. Not that westerners were not racist*—it was simply that *the victims of western racism were not numerous enough to outvote the native U.S. citizens*."[28]

In short, what Limerick has referred to as the "conquest" of minority groups in the western United States helps explain institutional patterns—the presence of the initiative—in that region.[29] Furthermore, Schmidt shows that resistance to the initiative in the South was related to fears of Negro influence. Memories of Reconstruction were such that concerns over the possibility that blacks might regain political influence stifled support for the initiative.

Overall, then, the historical record strongly suggests that social diversity concerns have affected the (non)adoption of the initiative, a component of direct democracy. The present study shows how the western United States has changed substantially in its ethnic/racial composition and how politics has been affected accordingly.

Descriptive Representation Within State Governmental Institutions

Descriptive representation within institutions is another important, and complicated, matter. "Parity" in descriptive representation means that various groups hold approximately the same proportion of positions within governmental institutions (legislatures, executive branch officials, bureaucracies, court judges) as they constitute in a political jurisdiction, in this case the states. The focus here is on racial/ethnic minorities, especially blacks and Latinos, for these have been the major focus of previous research and for which data are available. To a considerable degree, federal government actions have had an impact in this regard. As discussed earlier, a number of reapportionment cases, along with the federal voting rights legislation, have targeted state legislative electoral processes. And federal equal employment opportunity legislation, beginning in the early 1970s, sought to make employment in state and local government more open to minorities and provided the federal government authority to monitor patterns.

Descriptive Representation in State Legislatures

In a number of states, especially those with little social diversity, one would expect to find little if any presence of minority group members. And that turns out to be the case. However, the question for the moment is not so much the number but the proportion in the institution relative to the proportion in the population. Evidence of descriptive representational parity in state legislatures for minorities overall is presented in figure 4.3.[30]

The evidence suggests several points. First, the overall extent of descriptive representation of minorities is quite low; no state achieves parity and most fall well short of it. This is important, but is only one aspect of the issue. A second issue is whether social diversity helps explain the patterns. The analysis shows that it does.

There is a strong relationship between minority diversity and minority underrepresentation in state legislatures; the larger the minority population,

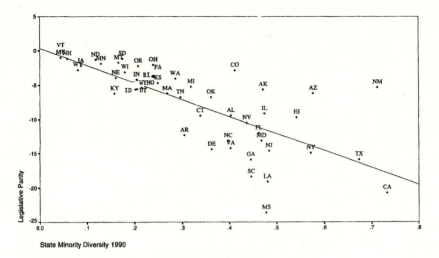

State Minority Diversity 1990

Figure 4.3 Legislative Parity with State Minority Diversity

the greater the degree of underrepresentation ($b = -20.4; p = .00$). This is most evident for Old South states such as Mississippi, Louisiana, and South Carolina.[31] White ethnic diversity is positively related to minority representational parity, but not significantly so. Both education and income are significantly related, but the former is positive while the latter is negative in the multivariate case.

Descriptive Representation in State Bureaucracies

Evaluating descriptive representation in bureaucracies is difficult because of the manner in which the Equal Employment Opportunity Commission presents data.[32] But the issue is addressed with the available evidence. Both minority and white ethnic diversity are negatively related to the indicator of bureaucratic parity—more diversity, less parity. But the latter is significant ($b = -1.25, p = .10$) while the former is not. This may suggest competition for state jobs between the old (white ethnics) and new ethnics (i.e., minorities). Furthermore, both education and urbanization are significantly related to bureaucratic parity, but education has a negative and urbanization a positive relationship.

Evidence on overall descriptive representation in the bureaucracy is presented in figure 4.4. A number of states ($n = 17$) have parity ratios of 1 or greater,[33] meaning the achievement of parity. Of many issues addressed in this book, this is one of but a very few where parity occurs in more than a few states. These tend to be states with large minority populations. On the other hand, a number of the most homogeneous states (e.g., Vermont, Maine, New Hampshire, the Dakotas, Montana, and Idaho) have among

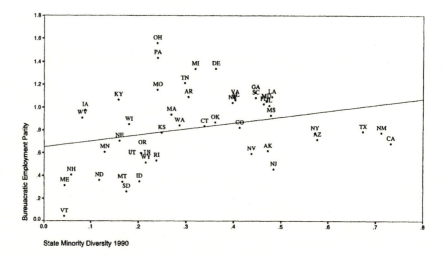

Figure 4.4 Bureaucratic Employment Parity with State Minority Diversity

the lowest parity ratios. What might explain this? This question is not easily answered, but some possible explanations can be offered.

It may be that a group must attain a certain population size and/or proportion within a state before it can effectively mobilize to achieve equal access to public employment.[34] This seems quite plausible. However, some scholars take the opposite position, arguing that when a group is small it is less threatening and thus can, perhaps should, more easily achieve access or inclusion, even assimilation into a social and political system.[35] Another possibility is that in some states the private sector offers ample economic opportunities, thus making the public sector bureaucracy a less necessary or attractive avenue of employment. But it is not immediately clear why this would differ so much in some states than in others.[36]

A caveat should be added to these findings. The data just noted on minority presence in state bureaucracies do not consider issues of job stratification or segmented inequality—that is, "disparities in the *type* and *quality* of jobs that are held by groups,"[37] in a given jurisdiction or state. For instance, it is not uncommon to find that the proportion of ethnic or racial minorities among public employees is similar to that for a city as a whole.[38] But minorities are typically disproportionately holders of the lowest level jobs. Thus, while there may be overall, or "block," equality, there may simultaneously be considerable segmented inequality.[39] The data examined here address only the former dimension and thus understate the extent of inequality, perhaps substantially so. That makes the findings of a high degree of block inequality in a number of states especially striking.

Overall, the relationships between social diversity and bureaucratic parity are not very strong, but low minority diversity appears to have an especially strong association with low bureaucratic representation in homogeneous settings. The impact of white ethnic minority diversity on bureaucratic parity is slightly negative, while minority diversity's impact on legislative parity is strongly negative (as seen earlier). Thus, the extent of social diversity's impact varies relative to different formal institutions.

The matter of descriptive representation might be considered further—to examine patterns among state executive officials and/or among state court judges, for instance. But the general evidence indicates that the numbers (and percentages) of minorities among those positions are so small as to make systematic analysis infeasible. That is, itself, suggestive.

Conclusion

Social diversity's relationship to the strength and nature of the two major political institutions of state government—the legislature and governorship—is not as strong or as consistent as expected. While several heterogeneous states have the relatively strong legislatures and/or governors anticipated, most other states have somewhat less strong institutions, and the overall relationships are weak. This may simply suggest that social diversity provides little insight on the structure of these two political institutions. Or it may be that diversity is not related to the aspects of those institutions tapped by the commonly used measures. Another distinct possibility is that new institutionalist views are correct in claiming that institutions are, indeed, relatively autonomous entities in political systems. The analysis also indicates that socioeconomic variables have some, but not especially strong or consistent, relationships with legislative professionalism or governors' formal powers. Despite these weaker than expected findings, I would suggest that the issues and hypotheses offered here are the kind that need to be explored in future research.

On the other hand, evidence suggests that social diversity clearly has had an impact on several other state government institutions. Social diversity shows some relationship to state court reputation and also seems to have some relationship with methods for judicial selection in states, albeit limited. Moreover, some historical accounts claim that the presence or absence of the institution of the initiative is/was strongly shaped by social diversity.

Social diversity, specifically minority diversity, shows a clear relationship to descriptive representation—that is, the social composition—of a central state institution, state legislatures. Higher minority diversity is related to high underrepresentation in legislatures. Legislatures in homogeneous states have few minorities, but that is consistent with their homogeneity (and leads to minimal departures from parity.) Homogeneity is often associated with a *high* degree of minority underrepresentation in state bureaucracies, a striking finding. And white ethnic diversity is negatively related to bureaucratic parity. The indicator of bureaucratic descriptive representation focused on block, not segmented, inequality. Hence, the degree of equality indicated by the data is probably better than evidence on segmented inequality would suggest. Again, there are different faces or patterns associated with descriptive underrepresentation in different state institutions.

Overall, there are some limited links between institutional structures and social diversity suggested in the analysis. On the other hand, relationships between social diversity and descriptive representation within two major state governmental institutions are apparent. Formal institutions may be important not only in their structure and composition but also in their impacts on public policies. The next two chapters examine policies directly and extensively.

5

Social Diversity and
State Public Policies
Education, Health,

and Welfare

Thus far, social diversity has been shown to influence an array of state political phenomena. Especially apparent is the relationship with various political processes (chapter 3), and descriptive representation in governmental institutions (chapter 4). The focus now turns to public policies, an area where diversity is expected and, indeed, has been previously shown to have important and intriguing implications.[1] A number of policies and/or dimensions of policies are examined in this and the next chapter. The policies considered include those commonly viewed as central in state politics, such as education, health, welfare, and criminal justice.[2] Related issues having to do with particular or differential dimensions of the policies are also considered because social diversity's impact may also be manifested there.

The goal, then, is to examine policies that are clearly central to states and, at the same time, to consider a variety of policies and/or subpolicies. In short, social diversity is examined comprehensively relative to policies. In some instances, the present analysis extends in time and/or in other ways extends previous research on diversity and state public policy;[3] in other instances, initial examination of diversity relative to policies is undertaken and presented.

Public policy is important in itself and for a host of reasons. As two leading scholars of public policy contend, "public policy is an especially important phenomenon to study because it reflects human agency. . . . Through public policy collective choices are made with significant consequences as to how and whether problems are resolved, how benefits and costs are distributed, how target groups are viewed by themselves and others, and how such groups regard—and participate in—politics." But, they also note, "public policy is a complex combination of elements, including goals and objectives, agents and implementation structures, targets, tools, rules, and rationales."[4] Thus, policies and dimensions of policies are examined here because of their inherent importance and are considered relative to social diversity as that is essential to the larger arguments developed in this book.

While the policies are sometimes examined with expenditure indicators, the emphasis tends to be on nonexpenditure measures; considering nonexpenditure indicators should lessen the impact of wealth as a factor that influences policy patterns. The policies are selected based on their general importance in state politics, and the disaggregated indicators focus on the differential policy impact on minority groups, and with attention to a variety of types of policies.[5] The differential policy indicators also tend to focus on issues of equality of racial/ethnic minorities relative to the general populations of states.

There are numerous policies and subpolicies that might be considered under the broad rubric of any one "policy area." Deciding which ones are most appropriate to examine is itself difficult, and there appears to be little consensus in the literature. Moreover, deciding how to measure the policies and subpolicies is difficult. For example, one recent book on state public opinion and public policy examined education policy with per pupil expenditures.[6] But others might suggest that per capita expenditures[7] or education spending as percent of the state budget are equally good if not better indicators. Yet another project measured education with indicators such as graduation rates, the extent of and pattern of tracking (of blacks and Latinos) students into classes for the gifted and remedial classes, and a host of similar measures.[8] This latter study thus focused more directly on issues of educational equality.

To take another example, some have studied welfare policy with various indicators of state financial effort, such as state welfare expenditure per $1000 personal income, welfare as percentage of total state general expenditure, and number of AFDC recipients per 1000 population.[9] Others have examined the scope of welfare, or states' extension of eligibility for AFDC (the major welfare program) beyond the minimal levels required by federal regulations.[10] The findings and the conclusions that may be drawn by using alternative policy indicators may differ substantially. What these welfare measures do have in common, however, is that they stress aggregate or general rather than disaggregated or differential aspects of state policies.

Thus, selection of indicators appears somewhat subjective, and there has been little consistency in the measures selected and examined in research, except that there has been a strong tendency to examine aggregate or general patterns. That tendency may explain much of the empirical support for the political culture view and several other interpretations.

In the analysis that follows, both aggregated and differentiated indicators are considered. The attention to the latter leads to a different outlook, a significant reconceptualization of state politics and policy, and further underscores the importance of social diversity. But social diversity's impact is also evident concerning general policies.

tion of black populations; 37 states were included in the analysis (refer to endnote 1).

Blacks had substantially lower graduation and significantly higher suspension ratios across the states,[17] consistent with the diversity interpretation and with the arguments that "two-tiered pluralism"[18] and "second generation discrimination"[19] occur within state policy systems. But an especially distinct and notable finding of the social diversity interpretation was that minority diversity was actually positively related to graduation ratios—that is, as states had more minority diversity, blacks had higher graduation ratios. Homogeneous states—those with small minority populations—generally had *lower* black/white graduation ratios than did states with large minority populations.

Several homogeneous states—Wisconsin, Minnesota, Washington, and Utah—were found to have substantially lower black graduation ratios than bifurcated states such as South Carolina, Alabama, Mississippi, and Texas. Racial/ethnic diversity explained a considerable portion of the variation in black graduation ratios in those states from which data could be drawn. This implies that minority diversity is considerably more problematic in the homogeneous environment than is generally expected, recognized, or understood in other analyses.[20]

A similar pattern was found regarding suspension ratios for blacks. Minority diversity and white ethnic diversity were found to be inversely related to suspension ratios—the states with the smallest minority and ethnic populations had the highest suspension ratios for blacks. That is, the disparity in the outcomes for blacks tended to be most pronounced in the most homogeneous states. But aggregate policy indicators mask these findings and studies that focus only or primarily on general patterns overlook this.[21]

In short, the previous analysis of differential state educational outcomes did not seem to support claims about the commonwealth outlook of the moralistic culture, at least with respect to minority groups.[22] But if egalitarianism is taken to be a central trait of the moralistic culture,[23] that is quite telling. Hence, the better aggregate or overall policy outcomes in homogeneous states appeared to result from a more homogeneous racial/ethnic context than moralism per se. The little racial/ethnic diversity that exists in homogenous environments was found to be associated with relatively worse policy outcomes for minorities.

Evidence on education outcomes for the mid-1980s seems understandable from a social diversity perspective, but other interpretations seem less able to explain them. In any case, additional evidence deserves attention; thus, the issues just summarized are assessed further. Education policies are further examined in several ways and for a different time frame, the early 1990s.

Education Policies in the 1990s

Caveats

Assessing education policies, especially with aggregate or general measures, requires caution. Some states do not spend especially large amounts of money relative to other states, yet they have relatively high levels of education as measured by graduation rates and percent of the population with a high school degree or more. They may spend less because the need is not as great; states such as Iowa and Minnesota appear to be in this category. Other states spend more, but have lesser outcomes. These points should be kept in mind as a preface to the following analysis.

Other caveats should also be noted. Examining differential educational outcomes in the states poses some difficulties. Central among these is that statistical analysis may have difficulty in coping with the some of the major indicators (or dependent variables). Specifically, for several of the indicators of differential outcomes—minority suspension ratios, for example—states with very low numbers or proportions of minorities may be somewhat different relative to each other and relative to states with larger minority populations.

To examine the diversity thesis without being stymied by this problem, the analysis that follows uses several approaches, as necessary. First, scatterplots indicating patterns relative to social (minority) diversity for all states are presented relative to a number of issues. This allows us to see and visibly identify the patterns and all of the states relative to the particular issues (dependent variables). The scatterplots focus on minority diversity because the indicators of differential outcome provide data relative to minority, but not white ethnic, populations. Further analysis (regression analysis) is then undertaken in two ways: (1) analyses of all the states is conducted ($n = 50$, in most instances) and, (2) analysis that considers only those states with a minimum threshold of minority populations ($n = 41$, in most instances).[24] Findings are often discussed with respect to both sets of cases (as appropriate; i.e., when both sets need to be considered and/or when the findings regarding the two sets are substantially different).

Common statistical techniques, such as regression analysis, may have difficulty fully grappling with the phenomenon of interest. But that should not preclude the pursuit of important theoretical issues. The use of more advanced statistical techniques in the future may help refine the findings, but at this juncture, it may only impede posing and considering the central theoretical concerns of the diversity interpretation. And developing the theoretical arguments are the major concern of this project. The methods and analysis are more than adequate for present purposes.

Education Expenditures and Effort

First considered are education expenditures and effort (using data from 1990 from the Statistical Abstract); the former is defined as per capita spending on education (including both elementary/secondary and higher education), the latter as state per capita expenditure on education divided by state per capita income. The findings for both measures are rather similar. Both diversity indicators are significantly related to effort, but not necessarily in the ways that might be expected. Minority diversity is related to more education effort ($b = .03$, $p = .02$) while white ethnic diversity is related to somewhat lower effort ($b = -.04$, $p = .11$). Greater urbanization tends to have a negative significant impact on education spending and effort, while existing levels of education in a state have a positive impact.

Perhaps surprisingly, then, bifurcation is related to greater effort regarding education. This may partly reflect the greater need associated with larger minority populations. But several homogeneous (moralistic) states are notable for low education spending. For example, New Hampshire was ranked 43rd in per capita elementary/secondary spending and 50th in higher education spending in the late 1980s. On the other hand, New Mexico, one of the financially poorest states, ranked 6th and 9th in per capita spending for pre-college and higher education, respectively.[25] Despite greater effort, the policy outcomes in high minority diversity (bifurcated) contexts, tend not to be higher in absolute/general terms, as indicated in such measures as overall graduation rates.

Education Outputs and Outcomes

It is important to examine education outputs and outcomes other than or beyond those associated with expenditures and effort.[26] Here the question is, once a state has made a particular level of financial commitment (i.e., expenditures and/or effort), what is the outcome? Those issues are examined in general and in differential terms regarding several indicators. The policy indicators are calculated with data from the U.S. Department of Education, Office of Civil Rights.

1. *Total or overall graduation rates.* One indicator of education policy is overall graduation rates in a state. Does social diversity have an impact on this? Yes. Analysis indicates that more minority diversity is significantly related to *lower* overall graduation rates ($p = .05/.06$ for 50/41 state analysis, respectively; see table 5.1). More minorities are related to lower overall graduation rates. White ethnic diversity is positively related, but does not quite achieve statistical significance ($p =$ about .15 for both the *n* of 41 and 50). Of the three socioeconomic variables, only urbanization has a significant impact, and it is negative. Thus, minority diversity has a negative impact, or racial homogeneity has a positive impact, on overall graduation rates, as might be expected from conventional wisdom and other perspectives. This impact holds when the socioeconomic variables are considered.

Table 5.1 Social Diversity and Overall Graduation Rates

Independent Variables	Overall Graduation Rates ($n = 50$)		Overall Graduation Rates ($n = 41$)	
	a	b	a	b
Social Diversity				
Minority diversity	—**	—**	—**	—*
White ethnic diversity	+	+	+	+
Controls				
Education	+	+	+	+
Urban	—**	—**	—**	—**
Income	+	+	+	+

Source: *Statistical Abstract*, 1995, and Department of Education, Office of Civil Rights.

* $p < .10$
** $p < .05$

a = Reduced model (the social diversity, and the control variables examined separately)
b = Expanded model (all variables examined together)

2. *Minority versus overall graduation rates.* What is the pattern when a differential measure—the graduation rates for minorities compared to overall graduation rates—is examined? Evidence is presented in the scatterplot (figure 5.1), which reveals several points. First, in all but one or two states, minority graduation ratios are below parity (1.0) relative to overall rates, clearly indicating a pattern of negatively differential outcomes; in many instances, they are well below parity. Second, larger minority population is actually associated with higher graduation ratios for minorities.

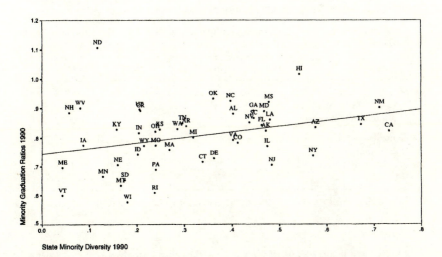

Figure 5.1 Minority Graduation Ratios with State Minority Diversity

Note that a number of homogeneous (moralistic) states—Wisconsin, Minnesota, Montana, Vermont, and South Dakota, for example—are some of the states with the worst minority versus overall graduation ratios. But this is consistent with the previous research findings from the 1980s.[27] Several homogeneous states do relatively well, however—for example, North Dakota, New Hampshire, Utah, and Oregon. But as or more often than not, homogeneity is associated with lesser outcomes for minorities. White ethnic population is associated with lower minority graduation rates. When the two diversity measures are considered alone, both have a significant effect.

When considered along with the socioeconomic factors, the impact of white ethnic diversity remains; it continues to have a negative impact.[28] (See table 5.2). Perhaps this suggests tension between the old—that is, white ethnics—and the new ethnics—blacks and Latinos—in education politics. Minority diversity retains some significance when the socioeconomic variables are examined ($b = .17, p = .08$, for $n = 41$), and its positive relationship with differential graduation rates remains. Notably, the socioeconomic indicators themselves have little or no significant impact, either. The patterns suggest that minority diversity interacts with the socioeconomic factors in complicated ways, but that social diversity retains important influence. And given that it is more likely that race or ethnicity explains the socioeconomic variables, rather than vice versa, the findings are especially noteworthy.

3. *Minority versus overall suspension ratios.* Another differential dimension to consider is a regulatory policy within school politics—suspension ratios. Here again, the scatterplot is revealing (see figure 5.2). The highest minority suspension ratios are in six rather homogeneous states—the two Dakotas, Nebraska, Iowa, Minnesota, Nebraska, and Idaho. All these states

Table 5.2 Social Diversity and Minority Graduation Ratios

Independent Variables	Minority Graduation Ratios ($n = 50$)		Minority Graduation Ratios ($n = 41$)	
	a	b	a	b
Social Diversity				
Minority diversity	+*	+	+*	+*
White ethnic diversity	−**	−**	−*	−*
Controls				
Education	+	−	+	−
Urbanization	+	+	+*	+*
Income	−	+	−	−

Source: *Statistical Abstract*, 1995, and Department of Education, Office of Civil Rights.

* $p < .10$
** $p < .05$

a = Reduced model (the social diversity, and the control variables examined separately)
b = Expanded model (all variables examined together)

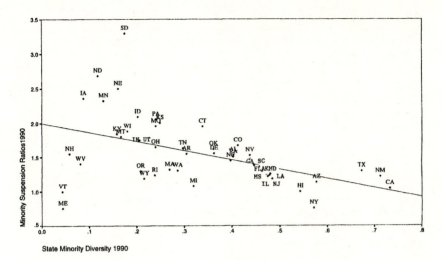

Figure 5.2 Minority Suspension Ratios with State Minority Diversity

have suspension ratios for minorities twice as high as the overall state average. Five of these are moralistic in Elazar's political culture categorization, and several of these states also stood out regarding minority versus overall graduation ratios (see above).

The regression analyses further support the implications of the scatterplot (See table 5.3). Minority diversity is negatively and significantly related to minority suspension ratios ($b = -1.6$, $p = .001$ for $n = 50$; $b = -1.9$, $p = .001$ for $n = 41$). White ethnic diversity is also negatively related to minority versus overall suspension ratios ($b = -2.5$, $p = .06$ for $n = 50$; $b = -1.6$, not significant for $n = 41$). And the socioeconomic indicators have no significant impact. In short, the importance of social diversity, especially minority diversity, for suspension ratios is strong and consistent. Equally important, the patterns suggest that states with low minority diversity are often among the relatively most punitive toward minorities. Both of these are notable findings in themselves; moreover, they are consistent with past research findings.[29]

Social Diversity and Education—Further Comments

Social diversity is frequently significantly related to education policies, with respect to both aggregate/general and disaggregated/differential indicators. But the directions of those relationships are also important to note. For instance, minority diversity is negatively related to total graduation rates and positively related to minority graduation ratios. Thus, while social diversity commonly has an impact, the specific direction varies somewhat relative to specific policy indicators; it appears that policy influences the particular politics associated with social diversity.[30] There is a need to better understand

Table 5.3 Social Diversity and Minority Suspension Ratios

Independent Variables	Minority Suspension Ratios ($n = 50$)		Minority Suspension Ratios ($n = 41$)	
	a	b	a	b
Social Diversity				
Minority diversity	$-$***	$-$***	$-$***	$-$**
White ethnic diversity	$-$*	$-$*	$-$	$-$
Controls				
Education	$+$*	$-$	$+$	$-$
Urban	$-$	$+$	$-$	$-$
Income	$-$	$+$	$-$	$+$

Source: Department of Education, Office of Civil Rights.

* $p < .10$
** $p < .05$
***$p < .01$

a = Reduced model (the social diversity, and the control variables examined separately)
b = Expanded model (all variables examined together)

the specific politics of the various dimensions of educational policy. However, one pattern seems consistent: minority diversity is consistently related to lower or worse outcomes, in either absolute terms or relative terms. Thus, when this other face of state politics is considered, different conclusions may be drawn. These findings on education policies also indicate that racial and ethnic factors are a dilemma across the states, although the specific direction or forms differ in different contexts.

Welfare and Health

The states have had an important but shared responsibility with the federal government in the areas of welfare and health policy.[31] The state role expanded with the 1996 welfare reform legislation, but the federal government historically has played a major role in defining eligibility and providing financial assistance in these areas. The federal government plays a important role in these areas, more so than in other policy areas, such as education. Because the federal government has, in fact, had an important presence in these areas, especially during the period examined here, it would be anticipated that state-level traits, such as social diversity, might have somewhat less impact in explaining state policy activity.

Welfare Policy

Within welfare policy, Aid to Families with Dependent Children (AFDC) is the major federal-state shared program. It is the focus here and various indicators of welfare spending are examined. In examining state welfare policies, others have focused on the scope of welfare policies[32]—that is, the measure stresses state provision of services beyond those required by federal regulations. However, this may be an indicator of potential provision of welfare programs rather than an indicator of actual provision or use. While expenditure measures are not without their own shortcomings, they suffice for present purposes and are supplemented with other types of indicators.

Previous Research Findings on Welfare Policy

Several studies found that higher racial diversity is related to less support for welfare policy. Brown found a negative relationship between percent of blacks and state welfare efforts, controlling for a number of other factors (the overall size of the welfare recipient population, state wealth, party elite liberalism, and the nature of party cleavages).[33] Similarly, Radcliff and Saiz found strong negative relationships between black political participation and several policy measures, including welfare spending.[34] Thus, substantial previous research indicates an impact of minority diversity on welfare policy.

Various indicators of welfare spending are examined here. Those include AFDC benefits per recipient,[35] per capita welfare spending, and welfare effort (state per capita spending divided by per capita income). Other nonexpenditure indicators might be preferable. Because of reservations about expenditure indicators, the analysis considers and presents both the bivariate and multivariate evidence. The indicators are first examined relative to social diversity and to the socioeconomic variables separately; then the two sets of variables are examined together for the several policy indicators.

Welfare Spending

1. *Welfare payments per recipient.* When examined alone, white ethnic diversity has a positive and significant relationship to per recipient payments ($p = .005$); minority diversity is negatively but not significantly related. Both per capita income and education show strong positive relationships ($p = .0002$);[36] urbanization is negatively but not significantly related ($p = .12$).

When all the variables are examined, neither of the diversity indicators is significant, although white ethnic diversity approaches significance. The socioeconomic variables are significant and show a pattern very similar to the bivariate patterns.[37]

2. *Welfare spending per capita.* When examined alone, white ethnic diversity has a positive and significant relationship to per capita welfare spending per capita ($p = .002$). In contrast to the per recipient indicator, minority diversity is positively, but not significantly, related to per capita spending. Of the several socioeconomic variables, only income shows a significant relationship, and it is positive.

Neither the diversity nor the socioeconomic variables shows a significant independent impact to welfare spending per capita when considered simultaneously. This is somewhat like the pattern found for Medicaid spending (see below) and suggests complex interactive effects between the two sets of variables and, perhaps, other variables also interact with these.

3. *Welfare effort*. Minority diversity is significantly and negatively related to welfare effort ($p = .08$) while white ethnic diversity is positively, but not significantly related when examined alone. Education is the only one of the socioeconomic variables to be significantly related in the bivariate analysis.

White ethnic diversity indicator has a weak significant impact on AFDC effort when all the variables are examined ($b = .06$, $p = .09$), but minority diversity is not significant. Education also has a significant impact, and it is positive.

4. *Proportion of minority recipients*. A final way of examining welfare spending patterns is considering the proportion of welfare recipients who are of minority background. As noted earlier, several previous studies have found a negative relationship between the proportion of minorities as program recipients and policy outputs.[38]

To pursue such an analysis, the minority diversity indicator was removed and another indicator, minorities as a percent of welfare recipients, replaced it. Analyses of this and the other variables relative to welfare payments per recipient, welfare spending per capita, and welfare effort was then undertaken. Minorities as a percent of welfare recipients has a negative relationship with each of the three indicators. More minorities as welfare recipients leads to lower welfare effort, beyond the impact of other factors. But it is significantly related only to AFDC effort ($p = .08$) when the several other variables are accounted for.

Health Policy

Medicaid is a major health policy program in which states share financial and administrative authority with the federal government, and is thus examined here. Infant mortality rates, another important indicator of health policy where state-level factors would be expected to be important, is also considered.

Previous Research Findings on Social Diversity and Health Policy

The pattern found in previous research concerning a number of indicators of social well-being—infant mortality rates and Medicaid expenditures—broadly parallels those for education policy. Previous studies indicated a negative relationship between higher minority diversity and state spending on Medicaid; greater minority diversity is related to lower Medicaid expenditures,[39] which is consistent with other research findings. For example, Plotnick and Winters found a negative relationship between a state's nonwhite population and financial support for Medicaid in their political and economic analysis of state income redistribution.[40] Similarly, Grogan notes that studies suggest that "racial prejudice" influences state's social welfare policies, and her own study found that the race of Medicaid recipients is related to at least two dimensions of state Medicaid policies—financial eligibility and benefit coverage.[41]

Other earlier research also found that higher minority diversity was related to higher overall infant mortality rates.[42] At the general level, infant mortality rates were highest in bifurcated (traditionalistic) states and lowest in homogeneous (moralistic) states. On the other hand, black infant mortality ratios were relatively higher in homogeneous states. State minority diversity was inversely related to black infant mortality ratios—the ratio of black infant mortality rates to total state infant mortality rates. Infant mortality rates for blacks in such homogeneous states as Minnesota and Iowa, for instance, were found to be over twice the overall state average.[43] Yet in a number of southern, bifurcated states (Arkansas, Alabama, North Carolina, Georgia, Louisiana, South Carolina, and Mississippi), black infant mortality rates were higher than the overall rates, but to a much lesser degree—that is, those states had better ratios.[44] Hence, the finding of relatively worse policy outcomes for blacks in homogeneous (moralistic) environments was not confined to education policies.

The previous findings regarding homogeneity and infant mortality patterns are neither anticipated nor explained by theories of race/ethnicity and state policy studies.[45] Whether such patterns continue to appear in data from the early 1990s is examined below.

Medicaid Spending

There are a number of dimensions one might consider to assess state Medicaid policy.[46] Spending is one. Several indicators of Medicaid spending are considered relative to the social diversity argument.

1. *Medicaid payments per recipient.* When the diversity indicators are examined alone (in the bivariate case) relative to Medicaid payments per recipient, both are significantly related, white ethnic diversity positively ($p = .00$) and minority diversity negatively ($p = .06$ for $n = 50$). Per capita income is significantly related positively ($p = .00$) and urbanization is negatively related ($p = .08$) when examined without the diversity measures.

White ethnic diversity maintains its significant positive relationship with Medicaid spending per recipient when the other variables are also considered ($p = .04$). Minority diversity continues to be negatively related and approaches, but does not quite achieve, statistical significance ($p = .11$). Per capita income retains a significant positive relationship ($p = .02$). These findings, particularly that minority diversity is related to lower and income is related to higher Medicaid payments, are consistent with conventional wisdom. But the impact of white ethnic diversity has not been directly identified in most of the previous research (see chapter 3).

2. *Medicaid spending per capita.* White ethnic diversity is positively and significantly related to per capita Medicaid spending ($p = .00$); minority diversity is negatively but not significantly related. Of the socioeconomic variables, per capita income has a significant positive relationship ($p = .01$) and education is significantly negatively related ($p = .01$).

In the multivariate case, only white ethnic diversity has a significant relationship ($p = .01$), and it is positive. Minority diversity is negative, but not significant. At the same time, it is notable that none of the several socioeconomic variables is significant, either.[47]

3. *Medicaid effort.* Medicaid effort is calculated as state per capita spending on Medicaid divided by per capita income. When the diversity indicators alone are examined relative to this measure of Medicaid policy, both are positive but neither is significant. Education is negatively and strongly related, and urbanization shows no relationship (per capita income is not considered as it is incorporated into the dependent variable).

When all the variables are examined, patterns somewhat distinct from those of the bivariate analysis (just presented) are found. White ethnic diversity retains a positive relationship, but now is significant; thus, only when the impact of other variables is accounted for does the importance of white ethnic diversity emerge. Minority diversity now has a positive relationship, but remains nonsignificant.

Education continues to have a strong negative relationship. While urbanization continues not to be significant its negative impact approaches statistical significance in the multivariate case ($p = .13$) while it did not in the bivariate case. Thus, there appear interactive effects of white ethnic diversity and urbanization regarding Medicaid effort.[48]

4. *Proportion of minority recipients.* A final way of examining Medicaid spending patterns is considering the proportion of Medicaid recipients who are of minority background. As noted earlier, several previous studies have found a negative relationship between the proportion of minorities as program recipients and policy outputs.[49] To pursue such an analysis, the minority diversity indicator was removed and another indicator, minorities as percent of Medicaid recipients, replaced it. Analyses of this and the other variables relative to Medicaid payments per recipient, Medicaid spending per capita, and Medicaid effort was then undertaken.

Minorities as percent of Medicaid recipients has a negative but not significant relation to Medicaid payments per recipient. It also has a negative nonsignificant relationship to per capita Medicaid spending and a positive but nonsignificant relationship with Medicaid effort. Thus, the pattern is for larger percentages of minorities as Medicaid recipients to lower Medicaid spending, which is in line previous findings.[50] But the relationships found here tend not to be statistically significant, particularly in the multivariate analyses. Thus, previous studies actually provide stronger support for the social diversity perspective than do the present findings.

Infant Mortality Rates

Another often-used indicator of state policies in the health arena is infant mortality rates.[51] General/aggregate and specific/differential indicators of infant mortality rates are examined.

1. *Overall infant mortality rates.* As with the earlier research findings,[52] greater minority diversity is associated with significantly higher infant mortality rates, or smaller minority population is related to lower infant mortality rates ($b = 2.29$, $p = .07$). White ethnic diversity is negatively but not significantly related. Generally, homogeneity (moralism) is associated with better infant mortality conditions, the typical expectation. Also, higher levels of education in a state are related to lower rates ($p = .002$).

2. *Minority versus overall infant mortality rates.* The patterns for the differential pattern of infant mortality are in stark contrast to the aggregate patterns just noted. Figure 5.3 suggests that minority diversity is negatively related to minority versus overall infant mortality rates. As there are more minorities and white ethnics, there are better ratios. Infant mortality rates for minorities are, on the whole, worse in *homogeneous* (moralistic) states. Similar to the 1980s data, the evidence for 1990 indicates that Minnesota and Iowa have minority infant mortality ratios twice that of their overall pattern, and have minority ratios worse than a number of southern states, although several homogeneous states do relatively well. White ethnic diversity also has a strong negative relationship.

The visual patterns of figure 5.3 are affirmed in the regression analyses (see table 5.4). Both diversity indicators have negative and significant relationships, whether all 50 or just 41 states are examined ($p = .003$, at minimum, for the *n* of 41 or of 50). These relations occur even in the face of

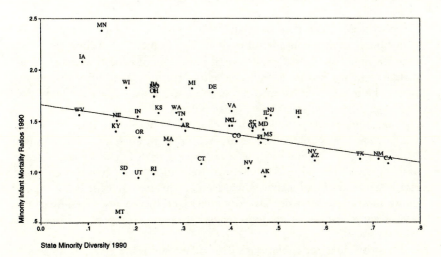

Figure 5.3 Minority Infant Mortality with State Minority Diversity

Table 5.4   Social Diversity and Infant Mortality Rates

Independent Variables	Overall Infant Mortality Rates		Minority/Overall Infant Mortality Ratios	
	a	b	a	b
Social Diversity				
Minority diversity	+**	+*	−**	−***
White ethnic diversity	−	−	−	−***
Controls				
Education	−***	−**	−	−**
Urban	+	−	+	+**
Income	−	+	+	+**

Sources: *Statistical Abstract of the United States*, 1993 (data are for 1990).

Note: $N = 50$ for overall infant mortality rates and $N = 42$ for minority versus overall infant mortality ratios; minority infant mortality data are unavailable for several states.

* $p < .10$
** $p < .05$
***$p < .01$

a = Reduced model (the social diversity, and the control variables examined separately)
b = Expanded model (all variables examined together)

controls for socioeconomic factors, which themselves also tend to have significant impacts. These findings reaffirm that homogeneity is clearly and strongly related to negatively disparate infant mortality ratios for minorities. Again, other interpretations do not identify nor account for such findings.

Summarizing and Interpreting the Findings

The evidence suggests that the relationship between social diversity and three major public policy issues is substantial. Significant relationships are found between minority diversity and several indicators of education policy: education spending efforts, overall graduation rates, and minority suspension rates. The relationships tend to be strong and consistent. The findings also challenge other interpretations of state politics.

Concerning welfare policy, significant relationships are found between white ethnic diversity and welfare expenditure indicators; minority diversity, or more specifically, minorities as a proportion of recipients, is significantly and negatively related to AFDC effort. Regarding health policy, significant relationships are found between white ethnic diversity and Medicaid expenditure indicators. Minority diversity consistently has a negative impact on expenditures, but not as strong as might be expected from previous research findings.[53]

Minority diversity's relationship to infant mortality rates, both aggregated (general) and disaggregated (differential), is especially striking. Higher minority diversity is related to better ratios. Conversely, homogeneity is related to significantly worse minority vs. overall infant mortality rates.

Some might question, or dismiss, the findings of differential outcomes for minorities in homogeneous settings. It might be argued that minority political weakness, owing to lack of population size and/or critical mass, is what explains these findings. That may be so, at least in part. But that is not the argument of such interpretations as political culture and the "minority threat hypothesis," or other common interpretations of state politics, to the extent that those other interpretations address these issues at all. Political culture's claims about a commonwealth orientation, an "undivided interest," and egalitarian concerns seem quite inconsistent with much of the present set of findings. Moreover, the political culture argument implies that moralistic states will "do the right thing," even in the absence of pressures or demands for certain policies.[54]

The minority threat hypothesis specifies a marked increase in threat concerns as minority population sizes increase, resulting in worse outcomes for minorities. But the evidence here indicates that where small minority populations are present, minorities often have highly disparate outcomes, and those disparate outcomes may actually be relatively higher in more homogeneous settings. Thus, at least two common interpretations seem not to explain some of the findings.

The situation for minority groups regarding the several policies examined in this chapter is frequently one where they either have *relatively high* (but still lower) outcomes in states that have *low overall outcomes*, or *relatively low* outcomes in states with *high overall outcomes*. Thus, black students in Minnesota may have higher graduation rates than do black students in Alabama, for example. However, *relative* black educational outcomes are such that blacks do substantially worse than their white counterparts in Minnesota than do blacks compared to their white counterparts in Alabama. Yet the quality of education in the latter may not be especially high.

These patterns underscore the various faces, the complexity, and the pervasiveness of the "American dilemma" as played out in several state policy arenas. It also suggests that the minority threat hypothesis is only partially correct. Policies such as highly disproportionate minority versus overall suspension and infant mortality ratios that occur in homogeneous settings are found when differential or relative policies are considered. Thus, other theories overlook major dimensions of important state policies. And other perspectives do not explain much of the differential policies either, as developed later in this and the next chapter.

Another point should be added here. Some observers might suggest that the differential outcomes are attributable to other factors, such as relative poverty rates for whites versus minorities. This possibility was examined; a ratio of minority versus overall poverty rates was added to the analysis. When this was done, the basic findings (developed above) remain. Accounting for minority versus overall poverty rates does not affect the findings on minority versus overall graduation or minority versus overall suspension ratios, and the relative poverty rate is not itself significant. On the other hand, relative poverty rates do have an independent impact on minority versus overall infant mortality rates. However, minority diversity itself remains significant. Thus, the several significant differential patterns found earlier (graduation, suspension, infant mortality) are related to minority diversity, and cannot be explained away by minority poverty rates. In any case, to challenge the differential findings by raising the issue of differential poverty rates in homogeneous settings begs the question, it seems to me. Why the poverty rates are as high as they are to begin with in those settings is something not adequately addressed by the political culture argument or others.

Considering Alternative Interpretations

Social diversity has important impacts on several major state policy areas and dimensions thereof, especially education and infant mortality. And socioeconomic variables are important in various ways and to various degrees, although the strength and direction of impact of these variables is not always high or consistent.

While the evidence in support of the social diversity thesis is considerable, do other theories or perspectives help explain the same policies? A number of alternative interpretations, common in the literature, were considered relative to the various policies examined earlier in this chapter. On the whole, they do not do as well as social diversity in explaining policies.

The other alternative interpretations, beyond the socioeconomic (already considered), that were examined are political culture,[55] ideology,[56] party competition,[57] legislative professionalism,[58] and gubernatorial power.[59] Variables reflective of each of these interpretations (alone) were analyzed (through regression equations) that also included the two diversity measures and the socioeconomic variables. And the analyses were undertaken both for all the states and for only the states that meet the minority diversity threshold ($n = 41$, see endnotes 15 and 24), much as the issues were assessed above.

In comparing the alternatives with the diversity interpretation, I considered whether the alternative interpretations had significant independent explanatory power themselves and whether the explanatory power was more than that of social diversity. In general, seldom do the alternative interpretations explain the policy indicators better than social diversity and also achieve statistical significance. In most of the relatively few instances where they do, it is with respect to aggregate/general rather than differential/disaggregated policy indicators. The important substantive findings regarding the alternative interpretations are summarized below for the policies; the policies are discussed in the same order as above.

Political culture is significantly related to and has a stronger statistical relationship with total graduation rates than does social diversity. But for other indicators of education, political culture has little significance while social diversity does. Importantly, political culture shows no relationship to differential policies such as minority versus overall suspension rates. Political culture and social diversity indicators have about equally strong relationships to Medicaid effort, but political culture shows no impact on minority versus total infant mortality rates. Of the several welfare (AFDC) indicators, political culture does slightly better than social diversity on some but not necessarily other measures. Regarding the differential or ethnic/racial equality aspects of the several public policies, political culture clearly provides little insight.

Of the several policy education indicators assessed earlier, *ideology* has a significant impact on only one—minority suspension ratios. More liberal ideology is related to lower minority versus overall suspension rates. But minority diversity has a stronger impact for both sets of states (i.e., $n = 50$ or $n = 41$, as indicated by regression coefficients).[60] While average ideology has a significant impact on Medicaid payments per recipient ($n = 50$), white ethnic diversity has a stronger impact (see chapter 3). Ideology has no impact on differential infant mortality rates. Its impact on several welfare expenditure and/or effort indicators is somewhat stronger in some instances than that of diversity, however. While more liberal ideology might be assumed to be related to greater concern for equality, or more similar outcomes across racial groups, the evidence examined for several differential policy measures suggests no such relationship. On the other hand, ethnic/racial diversity clearly does show a relationship.

Party Competition has a significant impact on per capita education spending and on effort when all states are considered, but not for the subset of states (i.e., $n = 41$). However, minority diversity is more strongly related and has significant impacts for both sets on this (i.e., all states and $n = 41$). Party competition has no significant impact on the other general education measures or on the differential education indicators; diversity does, especially on the latter. Party competition does have a significant positive relationship to welfare expenditure indicators, as well as a significant positive impact on Medicaid effort ($p = .10$, for $n = 50$, but not for $n = 41$). White ethnic diversity has a stronger impact on these policy indicators, and does so for both sets of states. Party competition has no impact on either of the infant mortality rate indicators.

The indicators of the strength of formal government institutions—*legislative professionalism* and *gubernatorial powers*—do not have significant relationships with education policies (in either set of cases), including the differential indicators. On the other hand, both more professional legislatures and stronger governorships are related to somewhat greater Medicaid spending and/or effort. But neither has an impact on other differential health indicators such as minority infant mortality rates. Legislative professionalism shows consistent and strong impacts on welfare spending indicators—clearly stronger than social diversity—but the governor's power does not appear important.

Conclusion

This chapter has shown that social diversity has clear and strong implications for several major state public policies and/or dimensions thereof. Notably, homogeneous settings are often associated with *relatively* worse policy outcomes concerning minorities despite better absolute patterns. Policies for minorities in homogeneous environments may be less visible because the size of the minority population is by definition smaller in such contexts. But when the disaggregated or differential patterns are examined, the patterns are rather clear; there are larger relative gaps. These findings, for evidence from the early 1990s, corroborate and significantly extend findings from the mid-1980s.[61] They also hold even when several socioeconomic variables are considered or controlled.

Equally striking, additional analysis showed that social diversity commonly provides as good, and often a better, explanation of various education, health, and welfare policies than do other interpretations (political culture, ideology, etc.). This is especially so for differential or disaggregated policies.

In short, ethnic/racial diversity is clearly an important factor in understanding several major state public policies. But these findings also show that the importance of ethnic/racial factors in state politics and policy is greater, more widespread, and more complex than any other interpretations have previously suggested, much less understood. The next chapter continues this exploration, focusing on other state public policies.

6

Social Diversity and
State Public Policies

Other Issues

The previous chapter considered several policies often viewed as social and/or redistributive in nature, such as welfare and certain health policies. Social diversity was found to have substantial and consistent relationships to several of the policies, especially their differential dimensions. This chapter examines various other policies, some of which appear directly relevant for minority groups and, thus, perhaps particularly understandable in social diversity terms. Yet other of the policies considered, such as family policy, might not be viewed as ones where social diversity is germane because the link between social diversity and policy is likely more indirect than for others. However, because states play major roles in these policies, they deserve consideration.

Criminal Justice

Criminal justice is a major policy, a form of regulatory policy concerning individual behavior over which states have primary authority and responsibility. It is also an issue where social diversity might be expected to have an impact, based on numerous questions about the fairness of the justice system in the United States. In fact, Skogan has claimed that the racial disparities in the imposition of prison sentences and the death penalty are "the most serious—and potentially the most explosive—issue facing the American system of justice."[1] Hence, its importance as a policy and the states' central role suggest that it be examined.

Incarceration Rates and Drug Arrest Rates

1. *Aggregate or overall incarceration rates.* Scholars view incarceration rates as a useful indicator of criminal justice policy. Thus, diversity is first ex-

amined relative to state overall incarceration rates. Minority diversity has a significant positive relationship with overall incarceration rates; there are higher incarceration rates overall where there are more minorities, a finding that is not especially surprising. Also, white ethnic diversity has a positive and significant relationship. Two socioeconomic variables also have significant impacts but in different directions: higher levels of education are related to higher incarceration rates while higher per capita income is related to lower rates.

2. *Black versus overall incarceration rates.* Another dimension of state criminal justice policy, one focused on differential outcomes, concerns the situation for minorities in that system. According to a leading scholar of criminal justice policy in the states, "one of the greatest challenges to the system of justice in the American states remains the apparent racial disparities in how it operates. African Americans are disproportionately represented at every step in the criminal justice process from arrest to imprisonment." Skogan explains some of the reasons for this, including that "blacks commit (relatively) more crimes" and that "black offenders are even more likely to be arrested."[2]

Skogan notes that the patterns "vary from state to state, one obvious reason being the differences in the racial composition of the states." But Skogan also claims that patterns may vary considerably between states similar in their racial/ethnic composition. What does the present evidence indicate concerning minority/overall patterns? Because data on Latinos are not provided in the data used,[3] only data on blacks are examined.

First, the evidence (see figure 6.1) indicates that black/white incarceration ratios clearly diverge from—that is, are much higher than, parity across

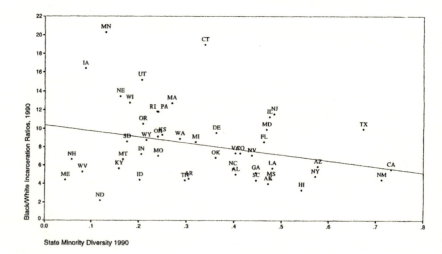

Figure 6.1 Black/White Incarceration with State Minority Diversity

the states. Second, the ratios are actually more similar—are less disparate—where there are larger minority populations. As the scatterplot shows, the greatest disparity in incarceration ratios is in Minnesota, followed by Iowa, Connecticut, and Utah. While several racially homogeneous (and moralistic) states have lower differential ratios, so do bifurcated states such as South Carolina and Mississippi. Thus, homogeneity is more often than not related to less equitable patterns overall. On the other hand, more white ethnic diversity is related to higher minority versus overall incarceration rates, another notable finding and dimension of ethnic/racial patterns.

The patterns just described are supported by the formal (regression) analyses. Minority diversity has a significant, negative relationship to differential incarceration rates (for both the n of 50 and n of 41, $p = .01$). White ethnic diversity has a significant positive relationship (for the n of 41, $p = .02$; the relationship is positive but not significant for $n = 50$). Urbanization and education both are positively and significantly related—that is, both are associated with more disparate or differential incarceration rates for blacks compared to overall rates (for both sets of states).

That greater minority diversity is related to less disparity in incarceration rates is noteworthy. And this is yet another finding not easily accommodated by dominant interpretations of state politics, such as political culture. White ethnic diversity's positive impact is also notable. That is, larger white populations, whether white or white ethnic, are related to greater disparity of minority incarceration. How and why education is positively and significantly related to more disparate outcomes is not readily obvious. Furthermore, these findings hold even when an additional variable, minority versus overall poverty rates, is accounted for. While that additional variable is itself significant, the impact of the two diversity indicators remains when relative poverty rates and the several socioeconomic variables are considered. Thus, the findings cannot be attributed to other factors.

3. *Drug-related arrests: black versus overall patterns.* Some observers have suggested that part of the disproportionate incarceration rates of blacks and other minorities (noted above) are the result of blacks being jailed for possession and use of illegal drugs. Thus, evidence on drug arrests also was examined. A pattern of relationships similar to that for differential incarceration emerges.

Minority diversity is negatively and significantly related to drug arrests for blacks for both sets of states. States with fewer minorities have *higher* black versus overall drug arrest ratios ($b = -7.4$, $p = .01$). White ethnic diversity is positively related, but not significantly so. Urbanization is the only other indicator to have a significant impact, and it is positive. The relationships between black versus overall drug arrest ratios are quite similar to those for minority versus overall incarceration rates. More minorities are related to less disparity in drug arrest ratios. Social diversity's impact on certain aspects of criminal justice policy seems clear. Whether it is apparent in other areas is explored next.

Official English

In the mid-to late-1980s, "Official English" measures were widely adopted by state legislatures and through citizen initiatives. Latinos as well as Asians were generally opposed to such measures, perceiving them as exclusionary, not "assimilationist," in intent.[4]

A U.S. Senator from California, S. I. Hayakawa (Republican), first proposed an amendment to the U.S. Constitution in 1981 to declare English the nation's official language. This English Language amendment was reintroduced in 1983 and 1985, but did not win congressional approval. In 1983, Hayakawa founded the advocacy group U.S. English, which sponsored ballot initiatives to declare English the official language across the states.

Proponents of Official English claim that their goal was to speed assimilation and end bilingual education that keeps children speaking in their native tongues. They contend that historical experience teaches that linguistic diversity threatens political cohesion and stability. Previous generations of immigrants understood, proponents contend, that English proficiency was necessary for economic mobility and social integration, creating the great "melting pot" that defined American society. Recently, some proponents of Official English support it because they claim it will discourage immigration itself.[5] Opponents argue that Official English targets linguistic minorities (primarily Latino and Asians). Such measures are seen as mechanisms of exclusion rather than assimilation, and such policies condemn the multicultural traditions of minority populations. Official English laws also imply future discrimination against language minorities and threaten the continuation of services that are necessary for participation in the political process. Critics contend that the campaign for Official English is "at best unnecessary and at worst a thinly veiled form of racism and xenophobia."[6]

Citrin et al. suggest that patriotism and "Americanism," rather than an antiminority sentiment per se, are the key symbols raised by language policy.[7] Feelings of nationalism were identified as the principal source for mass support for Official English among California's 1986 electorate. Citrin et al. claim that a general belief that speaking and writing English is very important in making one a "true" American is related to support for Official English measures. The "positive attachment to the symbol of nationhood, whether self-conscious or just reflexive contributed significantly to the pervasive approval for 'Official English.' "[8]

Without denying the role played by sentiments of nationalism, the social diversity perspective suggests that Official English is one of a series of policies that are more likely to be adopted in states with high ethnic or racial diversity, in bifurcated, than in more heterogeneous states. But it also appears that homogeneous settings adopt such measures. This pattern—where diversity has an impact across various settings, but manifests itself differently—is not unlike that found for other policies such as education outcomes, especially student suspension patterns, infant mortality, and incarceration rates.

Analyses of racial/ethnic diversity and state adoption of Official English measures have been undertaken. According to Citrin et al., there are "two distinct contexts" where Official English was adopted.[9] The states that enacted Official English measures through their legislatures during the 1980s were "mainly . . . Southern states with largely Anglo-Saxon populations and tiny proportions of foreign-born, Hispanic or Asian residents."[10] In four states—Arizona, California, Colorado, and Florida—Official English laws were enacted through voter initiative after having been defeated in the legislature. "These states . . . experienced the highest rate of growth in their Hispanic and foreign-born populations between 1970 and 1980."[11]

Also, virtually all states that enacted Official English measures through their legislatures had above-average minority populations; the minority population in these states was primarily black (Arkansas, Georgia, Indiana, Kentucky, Mississippi, North Carolina, North Dakota, South Carolina, Tennessee, and Virginia). Most of these states are classified as bifurcated in social diversity analysis. The social diversity approach suggests that these states have an antiminority outlook, even when the particular minority group (Latinos or Asians) that may be targeted by the policy is not present in large numbers. But North Dakota, a homogeneous state, also adopted a measure during the 1980s, and several other relatively homogeneous states—New Hampshire, Montana, and South Dakota—did likewise in the mid-1990s.

Other analysis supports the finding that bifurcated states were more likely to adopt Official English measures. A significant positive relationship was found between minority diversity and adoption of Official English ($p = .01$); white ethnic diversity was negatively, but not significantly related. The statistical model correctly predicted 72 percent of the "cases," or states.[12] In short, social diversity appears to have had a major impact on Official English (non)adoption. Other common interpretations of state policies seem not to explain Official English very well (if at all), compared to social diversity. The Citrin et al. study, for example, found the relationship between political culture and Official English to be "unclear."[13]

Family Policy

States are major policymakers regarding family policy. While "family policy" may be defined in various ways, Welch, Thomas, and Ambrosius[14] define it as "policy specifically directed toward family well-being." Welch et al. undertook an analysis that focused on several aspects of family policy, including abortion and helping parents balance work and child care through parental leave policies. They also identified indicators of family policy.[15] Several of those are examined here relative to social diversity.

1. *Family leave.* "Family leave policies are those guaranteeing employees a minimum benefit that would entitle them to keep their jobs even if they had to take a few days, weeks, or possibly months off to care for a new child, disabled parent, or other family member." Welch et al. also suggest that there are some implicit social class biases in family leave policy. Many employees are not able to take advantage of these leaves because the policy only guarantees leave; "employers are not obligated to provide any pay, and most do not. Thus, family leave policy will likely affect middle-and upper-income workers much more than lower-income ones, and two-earner families more than single parent households."[16]

Welch et al.'s study specifies whether states have such a policy at all, and of those that do, whether it applies to public employers only, or to both public and private employers; they use these as an indicator of state family leave policy. Therefore, this focuses on the scope of state family leave policy; the indicator does not consider actual use of the policy in general, nor does it assess the policy differentially—that is, by different income and/or ethnic/racial groups within or across states. Welch et al. examined their indicator relative to two variables—state political culture and financial resources. They found that "family leave laws are significantly more likely to be found in states with moralistic cultures and those of higher incomes."[17]

Here, the same indicator—scope of family leave policy—was reexamined relative to the social diversity indicators and the several socioeconomic variables. The findings parallel those of Welch et al. Both social diversity indicators are negatively, but neither is significantly, related. More minority diversity (less homogeneity and/or less moralism) is related negatively to the policy ($b = -1.2$, $p = .17$). Only state per capita income has a significant relationship ($p = .04$), and it is positive.

It may be that political culture better explains this indicator of family policy, but recall that the policy indicator is a scope measure and does not address actual use or implementation of the policy, nor does it consider differential patterns. Based on the findings concerning other policies discussed earlier in this chapter, one might expect that analysis of indicators that better or more directly tap differential patterns would support the diversity interpretation.

2. *Abortion policy.* Welch et al. extensively discuss and undertake analysis of state abortion policies. They claim that "political culture is . . . modestly related to the presence of restrictive abortion" and that the moralistic states . . . have the fewest restrictions on abortion.[18]

Welch et al. also provide evidence that classifies states in terms of their "post-*Roe*" policies; that is, how a state's policies on abortion developed in the aftermath (1973 to 1989) of the U.S. Supreme Court decision in *Roe v. Wade* (1973).[19] The policies of 15 states were classified as "challenging" the *Roe* decision. Twelve states, labeled "codifiers," passed restrictions that were upheld as constitutional while "acquiescers" have "ignored the issue for the most part or passed limited restrictions" ($n = 14$). Nine states have been "supporters" of *Roe* in their policies.

Here, the 1 to 4 scale classifying states concerning post-*Roe* policies was examined in relation to social diversity. Minority diversity has a significant relationship ($p = .10$) and it is positive; that is, more minority diversity is related to greater agreement with the Court's decision. Perhaps this is surprising. But several homogeneous states are classified as "challengers" (Idaho, Minnesota, North Dakota, and Utah, coded 1) and several others are "codifiers" (Maine, Montana, and South Dakota, coded 2). On the other hand, several states with substantial minority populations (Alabama, Mississippi, North Carolina, South Carolina, New Mexico, and Texas, along with New York and New Jersey) are "acquiescers" (coded 3). White ethnic diversity is not related. Per capita income is significantly, positively related; urbanization is, perhaps surprisingly, negatively and significantly related.

Thus, minority diversity appears to have some impact on state abortion policies, but its direction may be other than and more complicated than what might be expected.[20] However, if the ethnic/racial, social class, and other patterns were more specifically examined within or across states, as well as the differential access and funding, different conclusions might be drawn. In any case, it appears that other interpretations may not explain state abortion policies as well as first appears.

Tax Progressivity

Tax progressivity has to do with how equitable a state's tax system is in terms of distributing the burden of taxes in accordance with ability to pay. A "regressive" tax system places a greater burden on low-income than on high-income citizens, while under a "progressive" system, taxes increase as a percentage of a person's income as that income rises. I draw on an indicator of state tax system regressivity provided by Winters to examine the question:[21] Does social diversity have an impact on state tax structures?

Figure 6.2 indicates the pattern regarding minority diversity in scatterplot form. The regression analysis indicates that neither diversity indicator shows much of a statistical relationship to the tax progressivity measure. However, the location of several states is interesting. Two rather homogeneous (and relatively moralistic) states, Washington and South Dakota, have among the most regressive tax systems and New Hampshire (also moralistic) also has a rather regressive tax system. On the other hand, several more bifurcated states, such as Alabama, Louisiana, the Carolinas, Georgia, and Mississippi, have less regressive systems than the several states just noted. Thus, while social diversity may not have a consistent impact, claims about the egalitarian orientation of certain political cultures are not supported, either.[22] At the same time, the several socioeconomic variables also show no relationship to tax regressivity.

There are no direct indicators of differential tax progressivity (i.e., relative to ethnic/racial diversity groupings) readily available. However, minorities are almost certainly disproportionately affected by whatever level of regres-

2. *Entrepreneurial policies.* Entrepreneurial development policies "shift the aims of economic development incentives from affecting locational decisions to fostering indigenous capacities to serve new or expanding demands by providing resources that permit direct penetration or capture of a particular market or that permit a risky but potentially productive undertaking that would not have gone forward without government support."[27]

Minority diversity has a negative and significant impact on entrepreneurial policy (for 1991; $b = -1.13$, $p = .09$); states with larger minority population tend to be less entrepreneurial. None of the other variables considered has a significant relationship (although for income $p = .11$ and is positive). The reasons for and the implications of the significant impact of minority diversity is not clear, but that the relationship is significant with this (ostensibly) nonredistributive and nonsocial policy is notable in itself.

Composite Policy Liberalism

In their large study of public opinion and public policy in the states, Erikson, Wright, and McIver developed a "composite policy liberalism" score for each state.[28] The scores were a summary measure of state policies concerning: per pupil education expenditures, the scope of AFDC and the scope of Medicaid coverage, consumer protection legislation, criminal justice, and legalized gambling, equal rights policy, and tax progressivity.[29] They found that, "opinion liberalism"—that is, overall state ideology—was strongly related to this summary indicator of state policy liberalism.[30]

Does social diversity help explain composite policy liberalism as defined and measured by Erikson, Wright, and McIver?[31] White ethnic diversity is positively and significantly related ($b = 3.69$, $p = .07$); recall that white ethnic diversity was earlier found to be significantly related to a state's overall opinion liberalism (see chapter 3). Minority diversity is negatively, but not significantly, related to the overall liberalism indicator. Education has a positive and significant impact ($p = .05$).

While diversity does have some impact then, it may not be as strong as expected. This is probably due to the definitions and/or indicators used in the other study versus the present study (see endnote). That is, the Erikson, Wright, and McIver study focuses on aggregate policies, and in some instances what appear to be potential policies. In contrast, the present study brings closer attention to differential policies.

Governance Policies

During the late 1980s, and especially during the 1990s, states adopted a number of "governance" policies.[32] Governance policies constrain the processes of and/or the resources available to state government institutions; they are procedural policies that change the internal rules of the game that public officials must follow in such areas as elections, levying taxes, or allocating governmental resources. While these may not on the surface appear affected by racial or ethnic factors, some have speculated that these policies have emerged because of concerns about state government policies that have been "overly responsive" to various groups, including or especially minority groups.[33] Governance policies may be seen as a backlash and a way of constraining the perceived "excessive" responsiveness. Several of the policies are examined below.

State Legislative Term Limits

Term limitations on legislative tenure directly control legislative eligibility and incumbency. Since 1990, when legislative term limits were first adopted in California, Colorado, and Oklahoma, term limits have been adopted in 22 states. Each state varies in the length of terms and/or years and whether the measure sought to restrict both state legislative and congressional officeholders (although the latter restraints were found unconstitutional by the U.S. Supreme Court). Although there is some variation in the length of terms for state officeholders, strict limits permit only 6 years in office while more lenient allow 12 years.

An analysis of state adoption of legislative term limits found that a substantial increase in state minority population during the 1980s was positively related to the adoption of term limits; states with the largest increase in minority population were the most likely to adopt term limits. While other variables, such as level of usage of the initiative process and support for independent candidates, were also found to be important, the impact of increased minority population remained after accounting for these and other factors, such as legislative professionalism and legislative turnover.[34]

State Tax and Expenditure Limitations (TELS)

State tax and expenditure limits bring fiscal controls on state legislatures that limit their taxing and spending authority. Beginning with the late 1970s tax revolt, state tax and expenditure limitations have been enacted in 21 states (as of 1994); 11 were adopted since 1980. These measures weaken the ability of legislative institutions to collect revenues and provide public services.

Increases in state minority population (from 1980 to 1990) were found to be significantly related to the adoption of tax and expenditure limitations, even after accounting for the impact of other variables, such as frequency of usage of the initiative, wealth distribution, and state/local tax burdens.

Legislative Supermajority for Tax Increases

Eleven states have adopted constitutional provisions requiring a "supermajority" vote in the legislature to pass some or all tax increases. In 1992, four states (Arizona, Colorado, Oklahoma, and Washington) enacted amendments requiring that tax increases be approved by a margin larger than a simple majority of both houses of the state legislature. Supermajority requirements, along with voter approval requirements to enact all tax increases, have been called "second-generation" tax and expenditure limitations. In contrast to the 1970s tax revolt that specifically targeted the property tax with tax rated limits, revenue limits and caps on the increase in assessment ratios, the 1990s tax reforms limit the long-term growth in government and all tax types through procedural constraints on legislatures.

Research that assessed the impact of minority diversity on the adoption of legislative supermajority rules found that "an increase in state minority populations . . . has a positive impact;" that is "states with the largest increase in minority populations in the 1980s [were] the most likely to adopt" such measures.

Other Issues

Racial/ethnic diversity appears to be important for other levels of U.S. politics as well. Some of the citizen anger and antigovernment sentiment evident in the early 1990s may be related to ethnic/racial change. For instance, one study suggests that a vote for Perot in the 1992 presidential election was related to voter anger.[35] Minority diversity was significantly related to the state vote for Perot; as minority diversity in a state increased between 1980 and 1990, so did the percent vote for Perot. But blacks and Latinos voted for Perot much less frequently than did the rest of the population. Thus, racial/ethnic diversity seems related to broad political and electoral patterns across the states (including at the substate level; also see chapter 7).

Considering Alternative Interpretations

This chapter indicates that social diversity is significantly related to several policy areas, especially the criminal justice issue of differential incarceration rates for blacks. Social diversity's impact was examined and found to hold, even when considered along with several socioeconomic variables (income, education, and urbanization). Do other variables or interpretations provide as good or better explanations than does social diversity?

As in the previous chapter, in comparing the alternatives with the social diversity interpretation, I considered whether alternative indicators had statistically significant independent explanatory power themselves and whether the explanatory power was clearly more than that of social diversity. Seldom do the alternative interpretations explain the policy indicators better than social diversity and also achieve statistical significance. In most of the few instances where they do, it is with respect to aggregate/general, rather than differential/disaggregated, policy indicators. The major findings regarding the alternative interpretations are summarized below.

Political culture[36] does not explain—that is, does not show significant relationships with—either incarceration rates or drug arrest rates for either the general or differential indicators when social diversity is accounted for (and this is so whether all states or just the 41 states are examined). Political culture has a statistically significant impact on state family leave policies and on locational economic development policy (in both instances, for $n = 50$, but not for $n = 41$). But for none of the other policies considered in this chapter does political culture show much of a relationship. Thus, social diversity emerges as a stronger explanation of the several policies than does political culture.

State ideology[37] does not have a significant impact on any of the differential policy indicators considered in this chapter. Indeed, of the numerous policies examined, when diversity and socioeconomic factors are accounted for, ideology has a significant relationship only with composite policy liberalism, tax progressivity, and family leave policies ($p = .07$ for the latter). Similarly, *party competition*[38] also shows little or no relationship to the numerous policies and policy indicators considered in this chapter (when diversity and socioeconomic factors are also considered). Only for composite policy liberalism does party competition have a significant relationship. Thus, the importance of party competition is limited regarding certain aspects of distributional equality.

When considered along with social diversity and the socioeconomic variables, *legislative professionalism*[39] has a clear and consistent impact only on locational and entrepreneurial economic development policies, as well as on overall policy liberalism. For entrepreneurial economic policy and composite policy liberalism, minority diversity is also significant when legislative professionalism is included in the analysis.

Only for the two economic development policies (locational and entrepreneurial) do formal *governors powers*[40] have greater importance (a stronger statistical relationship) than does social diversity, when considered together, along with socioeconomic variables. Noting this importance of a governor's powers is useful for general purposes. However, social diversity has more consistent and typically stronger relationships on a host of policies.

Social Diversity and Public Policies: Further Consideration

The evidence and discussion in this and in the previous chapter suggest some general patterns regarding state policies. Frequently states that have high or good aggregate outcomes have rather low or bad outcomes relative to differential indicators. It may be useful to illustrate this; thus, figures are presented to indicate these patterns for several policies addressed in the present and previous chapters. Again, social diversity seems able to account for both sets of patterns while other perspectives barely acknowledge, much less explain, the latter.

Overall state education and differential graduation rates are compared in figure 6.3. While the patterns and relationships are not necessarily simple or straightforward, note that several of the states with the *lowest minority graduation ratios* have *above-average percentages of high school graduates*; these tend to be relatively homogeneous states (Wisconsin, Vermont, Minnesota, Maine). On the other hand, a number of Old South or border states have below-average high school graduates and have above-average minority graduation ratios (Mississippi, Alabama, South Carolina, Louisiana, Georgia, and North Carolina, for example).

There tends to be a pattern regarding suspension ratios. Figure 6.4 shows that five of the six states with the highest minority suspension ratios have average or below-average total suspension ratios. These states (the Dakotas, Nebraska, Iowa, Minnesota, and Idaho) are relatively homogeneous. They also tend to have moralism as their predominant political culture,[41] but their differential patterns do not appear consistent with what might be expected from that interpretation.

The patterns for aggregate and differential infant mortality ratios is shown in figure 6.5. While there is not a clear pattern, the location of some states is notable. Of the states in the bottom-right quadrant (better than average on total rates, worse or above average on minority ratios), six are among the more homogenous, and five of the six have moralism as their predominant political culture. A number of the states that are somewhat above average on both dimensions (upper-right quadrant) tend to be in the middle range of minority diversity. The states with low overall and low minority infant mortality ratios include quite a mix; several are fairly ho-

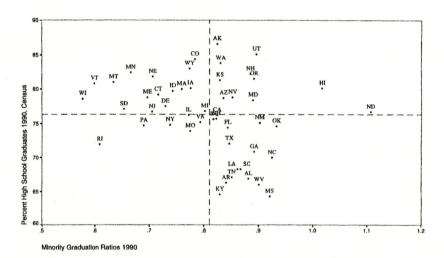

Figure 6.3 Percent High School Grads with Minority Graduation Ratios

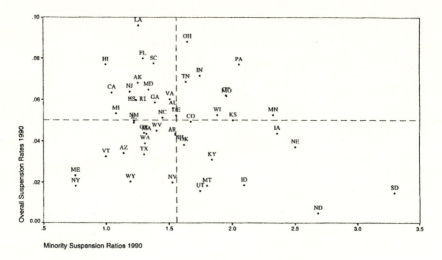

Figure 6.4 Overall Suspension Rates with Minority Suspension Ratios

mogeneous states (e.g., Utah, Montana), others are bifurcated (California and Texas), and others are mixed.

Regarding incarceration rates, there are again high overall disparities, and a number of relatively bifurcated states are found in the upper-left quadrant (see figure 6.6), having high (above-average) overall incarceration rates and relatively low black to white incarceration ratios (e.g., California, Arizona, South Carolina, Louisiana). Relatively homogeneous states are often among those with below-average overall rates but above-average black to white ratios (lower-right quadrant, e.g., Minnesota, Iowa, Utah, and Wisconsin,

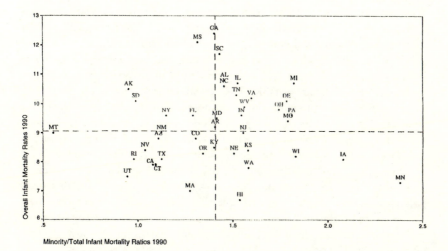

Figure 6.5 Overall Infant Mortality Rates with Minority/Total Infant Mort Ratios

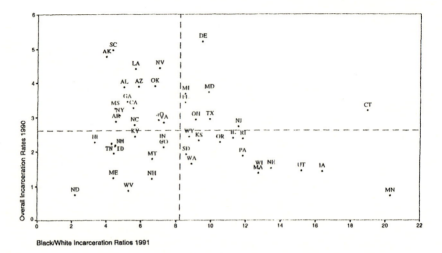

Figure 6.6 Overall Incarceration Rates with Black / White Incarceration Ratio

among others). This is a most surprising finding given the arguments of other research.[42] Several other rather homogeneous states have both low overall and low relative rates (lower-left quadrant; e.g., North Dakota, Maine, Idaho, New Hampshire), but several states that are more bifurcated are also in this quadrant (Hawaii, New Mexico, Colorado).

Conclusion

Overall, social diversity—minority and/or white ethnic diversity—appears to have significance for several policies considered in this chapter including criminal justice, particularly incarceration ratios, Official English, several governance policies, and composite policy liberalism. Its impact on several other policies is less clear or strong. Nonetheless, because several of these policies might not be expected to be influenced by diversity at all, any significant relationships are notable. Also, social diversity's impact is commonly as or more important than that of the socioeconomic or other interpretations such as political culture, ideology, party competition, legislative professionalism, or gubernatorial powers. This is especially so for differential policy indicators, where the alternative interpretations provide little insight.

This chapter further illustrates points suggested in chapter 5. Overall, racial disparities are quite common across the states. Significantly disparate policy outcomes, related to social diversity, are often found, but they may be manifested differently. On the one hand, it is not unusual for homogeneous states to have high absolute or general outcomes and low relative outcomes. On the other hand, high minority diversity is commonly associated with low aggregate and higher relative policy outcomes. Again, it appears that social diversity is important for many policies, but its faces or forms differ. The "American dilemma" is commonly evident across the states and in states' public policies. That dilemma may appear as often in homogeneous settings as in others; it may just be less visible because aggregate data obscure the evidence and previous analyses have not really looked for such evidence.

Social Diversity at

the Substate Level

Chapters 3–6 examined the relationship of social diversity to a variety of state political phenomena, including political processes, institutions, and public policies. This chapter extends the argument to another level, examining social diversity at the substate level and addressing several sets of issues. If there is further evidence to support the diversity interpretation below the state level, the interpretation gains greater credibility and potential significance.

First, I draw evidence from and summarize several studies that indicate the impact of the social diversity context on individual-level attitudes. The studies suggest considerable support for the importance of social diversity. Second, social diversity within several states, at the county level, is used to examine extensively adoption of public policies through the initiative process. Third, the formal structures of urban governmental institutions are discussed. Historical and contemporary commentary again suggests links to ethnicity and race. Collectively, the evidence from these several levels and types of analyses significantly supports the social diversity perspective.

Social Diversity and Threat and/or Isolation

Evidence from Other Studies

A great deal of research, based in individual-level data, has examined and often supported a "racial threat hypothesis." Specifically, much evidence indicates that large black populations have often been seen as a threat to and lead to distinct political attitudes and behaviors among whites. Key's analysis of southern politics, especially his arguments about the politics of "black-belt" counties, is the classic statement in this regard.[1] Key found that whites living in areas with large black populations were commonly the most likely to support segregationist candidates and policies. Recently, a number of other studies have come to similar conclusions. The findings of these studies are consistent with the argument and evidence on social diversity presented in chapters 1 and 3–6.

In a series of articles, Giles has shown that racial threat, or large black populations, affected such behaviors as voting in the 1990 U.S. Senate race involving David Duke, and the likelihood that whites changed partisan identification (from Democrat to Republican) in Louisiana parishes (counties)[2] Similarly, Glaser found that "racial environment has a strong and consistent effect on racial-political attitudes"[3] and that his data support "the contention that threat, in the form of group conflict, influences political positions on racial issues."[4]

In a study of white attitudes about several matters—minority groups (generally), equal opportunity, and multiculturalism—Link and Oldendick found that "negative constructions of racial groups [blacks, Asians, and Hispanics] lower one's support for policies aimed at these groups."[5] Regional differences in whites' general racial attitudes also were evident. Living in the South had an impact on whites' views of blacks, but not concerning Asians and Hispanics. Note that there are rather few Asians and, with the exception of Florida, there are also very few Hispanics in the South. Furthermore, "differences in the construction of blacks, Asians, and Hispanics were smaller among those in living in the West, while white Midwesterners exhibited a larger differential in their construction of Asians."[6] Regarding equal opportunity, individuals who perceived greater differences between whites and blacks tended to be less supportive, but perceived differences between whites and both Asian and Hispanic Americans had little impact on attitudes toward equal opportunity.

In examining attitudes toward multiculturalism, Link and Oldendick also investigated the perceived implications of increasingly large Asian and Hispanic populations on U.S. "ideas and customs," levels of taxes, and "jobs for people already here." They found that views toward multiculturalism "are significantly different across different regions of the country." Those in the "South, Midwest, and West were significantly less positive in their views of the effects of growing racial diversity . . . than were individuals living in the Northeast."[7] Readers should recognize that these patterns are broadly consistent with the findings presented in earlier chapters: homogeneous and bifurcated contexts are often associated with worse policies (absolutely or relatively) while heterogeneous contexts, often found in the Northeast, are more often associated with in-between patterns. Overall, the study found that the social construction of groups, itself influenced by social context, has a strong effect on white perceptions of multiculturalism. In short, extensive evidence from studies focusing at the individual level indicate that large and/ or growing minority populations may lead to negative attitudes among whites—and that there are contextual, regional differences.

Another important finding of earlier chapters of this book is that homogeneity is often associated with relatively poorer differential policy outcomes for minorities. Is there any evidence, from individual-level studies, that living among fewer minorities—that is, a context of more homogeneity—might lead to attitudes that, in turn, lead to the policy outcomes found earlier? There is.

Kinder and Mendelberg found that "racial *isolation* generally *increases* the importance of prejudice to white public opinion."[8] This result "holds up across a *variety of policies* and is *often sizable*."[9] They also conclude that the impact of racial prejudice is evident in white attitudes toward a number of "racial policies," and that when indirect effects are considered, it is quite significant even for policies that are only implicitly racial, such as the death penalty, welfare, and policies for cities. Hence, isolation, or homogeneity, not just the presence of large minority populations (bifurcation), has been found in previous individual-level research to be related to negative racial attitudes. Therefore, findings from earlier chapters on social diversity's relationship to political processes and public policies are broadly congruent with these just-noted research findings, findings focused at a different level of analysis, the individual level, giving added plausibility to the earlier findings.

Evidence of Initiative Voting

Beyond the attitudinal and related evidence just summarized, considerable voting data are consistent with the social diversity argument. State-level patterns on Official English were examined in chapter 6; here, substate—specifically, county level—voting on Official English measures within several states is considered to further assess the social diversity thesis. County-level voting on California's illegal-immigration initiative is also studied.

Official English

During the 1980s and 1990s, a number of states enacted Official English laws, several through ballot initiative. California voters adopted an English Language Amendment (Proposition 63) to the state's constitution in 1986; it aimed to enforce the status and primacy of English as the state's official language and to "preserve, protect and strengthen the English language, the common language of the people of the United States." That measure was the model for initiatives adopted two years later in Colorado, Florida, and other states. The sentiments expressed in the Official English measures continue to resonate. In 1994, California voters adopted an initiative to deny social services to illegal immigrants (discussed below). That same year witnessed dramatic changes in the partisan control of state governments and the U.S. Congress. An antiaffirmative action initiative was enacted in California in 1996 by a 54–46 percent margin overall, although about two-thirds or more of Latinos and blacks voted against the measure. And there has been increasing discussion of an Official English amendment to the U.S.

Constitution, as well as stricter immigration policies, denying welfare benefits to legal and illegal immigrants, and reforming national affirmative action laws.[10]

Here, the enactment of Official English in three states that adopted it through ballot initiative—California (1986), Colorado, (1988) and Florida (1988)—is considered extensively. States with the initiative process provide a mechanism for public policies, rather than just candidates, to be directly considered by voters. (Also, see the discussion in chapter 3 concerning adoption of the initiative itself). Moreover, initiatives can be thought of as a form of "at large" versus district elections.[11] With Anglos and other whites the majority of the electorate in all three states, the initiative process provides a mechanism for the numerically and politically dominant white population to adopt policies they prefer, over the opposition of minority groups. All three Official English initiatives were adopted by wide margins; the popular vote was 64 percent in Colorado, 73 percent in California, and 84 percent in Florida. In each state, the initiative amended the state's constitution and prevented the state legislature from making any law that diminished or ignored the role of English as the state official language.

Most of the existing research on Official English has focused on individual-level attitudes, and mostly among voters in one state, California.[12] The present discussion summarizes the research, but then considers whether and how racial/ethnic contexts may shape county-level voting patterns; it also assesses the issues across a broader range of governmental jurisdictions. Reconsidering the issue of Official English at the county level from the social diversity perspective suggests that voter support for this and later policies, such as illegal immigration (discussed below) and antiaffirmative action measures in the 1990s, has social underpinnings. Examining this issue in three states permits comparison of how the composition of minority populations within and across states affects voting (see discussion of 50-state analysis in chapter 6).

Citrin et al. and Smith argue that there have been two major conceptions of American nationality.[13,14] The first, liberal conception has been associated with ideas of democracy, liberty, equality (of opportunity), and individual achievement. The second, ethnocultural conception is a "rival though not mutually exclusive conception of American identity" that developed in the nineteenth century, partly in response to white ethnic immigration. "At the core of the ethnocultural conception of American identity is the belief in ascriptive criteria for citizenship, the idea that only some races, religions, or cultures are 'truly' American."[15] In a 1988 study of Anglo (white) Californian attitudes Citrin et al. found a "pervasive attachment . . . to a conception of American identity that incorporates both exclusionary and liberal elements."[16] Thus, Citrin et al. and others have examined conceptions of nationality relative to individual-level traits. But context may also influence those conceptions.

Evidence developed below strongly suggests that the presence and the tensions in the two conceptions of American nationalism—the liberal and the ethnocultural—may be affected by ethnic/racial contexts in voting on the ballot initiative concerning Official English. By examining voting patterns on initiatives, by analyzing at the county (contextual) level, and by comparing counties in three states, the potential theoretical importance of racial/ethnic diversity is illuminated and extended.

Social Composition in California, Colorado, and Florida

Based on their large minority population and relatively small white ethnic populations, California, Colorado, and Florida may be thought of as relatively bifurcated states compared with other states in the United States (see chapter 1). Although each state has a diverse population, all three have white (nonethnic) majorities and relatively large minority, primarily Latino, populations. Within each state, racial/ethnic composition varies by region. In California, the southern and south-central part of the state have the most bifurcated racial/ethnic composition, with large Latino and large white (nonethnic) populations. The central and coastal regions of the state are more heterogeneous, and the extreme northern part of the state is relatively homogeneous.

In Florida, the southern part of the state has a bifurcated, heterogeneous composition with large Latino (Cuban) and black populations, while the northern part of the state is relatively homogeneous. A similar dispersion of groups is found in Colorado; the southern region and southern "rim" areas of the state have a Latino/white bifurcated social structure, while much of the rest of the state is more homogeneous.

California's 1990 population (the closest census count to the vote on Official English) is the most complex, including 57 percent whites, 26 percent Latinos, 9.5 percent Asian Americans, and 7.5 percent African Americans. Thus, minority groups constitute 43 percent of the state's population. But Latinos and Asians constitute a much smaller proportion of the *voting* population for several reasons, such as noncitizenship, a younger population, language, and low socioeconomic status. Ten of California's 58 counties have a sizable Latino population of between 30 and 66 percent of the population. Latinos constitute between 20 and 29 percent of the population in 12 counties and an additional 10 counties have between 11 and 20 percent Latino population. Thus 55 percent ($n = 32$) of the counties in California have a Latino population over 10 percent. Counties with the largest Latino populations include Los Angeles (33 percent) and Imperial County (66 percent).

Florida's 1990 population includes 73 percent whites, 13.6 percent African Americans, 12.2 percent Latinos, and 1.2 percent Asian Americans. Colorado's 1990 population is 88 percent white, 13 percent Latino, 4 percent blacks, and less than 2 percent Asians. Twelve of Florida's 67 counties have a sizable Latino, heavily Cuban, population of between 15 and 50 percent. Two counties, Dade (Miami) and an adjoining county (Collier), have near majority Latino populations. Finally, 11 of Colorado's 63 counties have large Latino populations, of between 25 and 77 percent of the population; Latinos constitute between 9 and 24 percent of the population in an additional 13 Colorado counties.

Public opinion polls conducted after the 1986 election in California and 1988 elections in Florida and Colorado showed that Official English initiatives polarized the electorate along ethnic lines, with strong support among white voters and lower levels of support among other ethnic groups. In California, whites voted almost 2 to 1 in support of Official English (72 percent approval rate). Blacks also supported the measure, but by a smaller margin. Latinos, in contrast, opposed the measure 61 to 39 percent.[17]

Exploring the Impact of Context in California

As noted, most studies of voting patterns focus on the individual level. Thus, first considered here is whether an individual's race significantly affects one's vote on Official English. Various analyses indicated that whites strongly supported the measure in California, while Latinos strongly opposed the initiative. Republican partisanship was also associated with support for Official English.

To probe for contextual effects, the actual county-level vote for Official English was compared with an estimated county-level vote based on an extrapolation from individual-level voting preferences. The estimated individual-level pattern was consistent with the earlier findings. One would expect homogeneous, heavily white populated counties to vote for Official English at higher levels than counties with large minority populations because whites are most supportive of the measure (according to the individual-level data). However, the actual county-level patterns suggested a somewhat different, more complex story.

The county vote for Official English was higher at every level of percent of white population compared to the estimate, and furthermore, the gap between the two increases as the size of the minority population increases. An estimation of county-level voting patterns based on individual-level patterns alone was unable to account for higher support among whites in bifurcated counties than in homogeneous counties (indicated in the actual vote). In the most homogeneous county, the actual vote was 22 percent higher than collectively predicted by the individual-level measures. In the most bifurcated county, the difference between the actual and the expected was even greater—the gap was almost 50 percent. Two counties that were exceptions to this pattern are two rather heterogeneous counties. The social diversity view suggests that there are county-level (contextual) effects; accounting for the racial/ethnic context may help explain the differential voting pattern in counties with large minority populations.[18]

To assess these observations further, other analysis was undertaken.[19] That examination produced findings that are also consistent with the earlier analyses. It indicated that the percent of Latino population in a county leads to a significant ($p = .05$), additional impact on the vote for Official English, beyond that associated with percent of racial /ethnic group population, partisanship, and unemployment levels. The greater the Latino population, the greater the vote for the initiative. This further suggests that a context of a larger Latino population has an independent and additive impact on the vote for Official English.

Other evidence also suggested such a pattern. Citrin et al. studied responses to ethnic change using individual level data in a 1988 survey.[20] In one instance, they examined the impact of percent of Hispanic in county of residence on general assessments of Hispanics and found that, among Anglos, as the percent of Hispanics in one's county increased, so did negative assessments of Hispanics. This was one of only three statistically significant relationships, of 12 variables examined in that study.

Counties in the Three States

Next, the analysis considered the impact of racial/ethnic diversity on county-level voting for Official English across the three states located in different regions of the United States. California and Florida are the first and fourth largest states, together accounting for about 15 percent of the total U.S. population; both states have substantial minority populations and are the two largest states with the initiative process. And California and Colorado have been characterized as among the most liberal states in terms of their public opinion and public policies;[21] they are also seen as relatively moralistic[22] or progressive states. While Latinos are the largest minority in each state, they all have low parity scores in terms of the number and percentage of Latino elected officials relative to the state population.[23] In California and Colorado, the Latino population is primarily of Mexican-American background (although the native versus foreign-born percentage is much higher in the latter than in the former). In Florida, Cubans constitute the bulk of the Latino population. In both California and Florida, there are also substantial populations of other Latinos, particularly Central and South American.[24]

Each of the three states adopted Official English initiatives within the two-year period between 1986 and 1988. In all three, Official English measures were expected to be strongly supported in counties where there were large concentrations of Latinos and/or Asians, because this makes language a salient issue and generates responses among English speaking people. Context may be critical beyond individual-level factors because the social context shapes individual perspectives on politics and policy.[25] To measure this context, census data were used for California's 58 counties, Colorado's 63 counties, and Florida's 67 counties on the percent of Latino, black, Asian, and white population. (These indicators of county social composition are similar to the state-level measures examined in the previous chapters; see especially chapter 1.)

Counties are powerful governmental entities and the direct implementors of major state social services,[26] including voting materials and bilingual education. There was a wide range in the county level vote for each measure. In California, the vote for the ballot measure ranged from a low of 53 percent in San Francisco County to a high of almost 90 percent. In Colorado, the vote ranged from a low of 20 percent in Costilla County (predominantly Latino) to a high of 85 percent in some far-north counties. Similarly, in Florida, the vote ranged from a low of roughly 60 percent in Dade County (Miami) to a high of 95 percent in some of the state's northernmost counties.

First examined is the relationship between race/ethnicity and the county-level vote for Official English. For each state, a county-level index of minority diversity was created (similar to the state-level analyses in earlier chapters). The patterns (see figures 7.1, 7.2, and 7.3) suggest a strong relationship between the size of the minority population and support for Official English. In all three states there is an inverse relationship between minority diversity and the vote for Official English; as the size of the minority population increased, the county-level vote for Official English decreased. This is consistent with individual-level data showing that minority groups were less supportive of Official English than were white voters.

Across states, there is substantial similarity in the dispersion of the vote for the ballot initiative in relation to minority populations. In all three states the vote for Official English was highest in homogeneous counties. Homogeneous counties with a predominantly white (nonminority) and small minority populations (below their state average) are concentrated in the upper-left-hand quadrant of each graph. In all three states, counties below the state mean for minority diversity (i.e., more homogeneous) tend to be above the aggregate county-level mean vote for Official English. Indeed, such

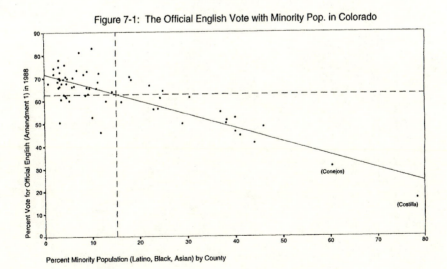

Figure 7-1: The Official English Vote with Minority Pop. in Colorado

Percent Vote for Official English (Amendment 1) in 1988

Percent Minority Population (Latino, Black, Asian) by County

(Conejos)

(Costilla)

Figure 7.1 The Official English Vote with Minority Pop. in Colorado

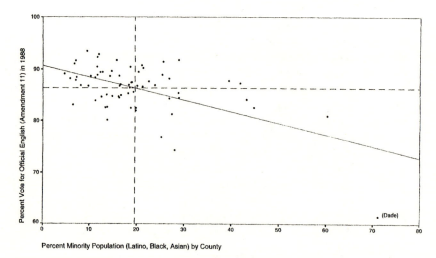

Figure 7.2 The Official English Vote with Minority Pop. in Florida

counties account for over 40 percent of the total counties within each state. This suggests that the immediate presence of Latinos or Asians is not necessary for whites to be concerned with minority populations and to exhibit what appear to be enthocultural values.[27] On the other hand, the lowest levels of voter support occurred in heterogeneous counties—those with moderately large minority populations. Notable in itself, this is also consistent with other findings on social diversity delineated earlier,[28] and does not seem to just result from aggregation effects.

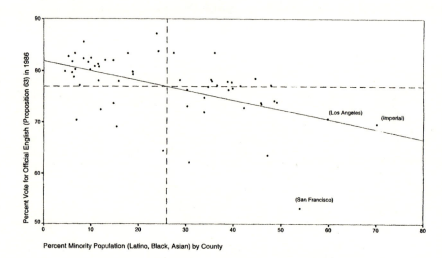

Figure 7.3 The Official English Vote with Minority Pop. in California

The strongest (bivariate) relationship between minority diversity and the vote for Official English was in Colorado (explaining 67 percent of the statistical variance). Latinos (Mexican Americans) constitute virtually all of Colorado's minority group population. In two counties with overwhelmingly large Latino populations (Conejos and Costilla), the vote for Official English was between 20 and 30 percent. In contrast, county-level approval rates in Colorado's more homogeneous counties, with minority populations below 10 percent, ranged from 65 to 85 percent.

A similar voting pattern was found in Florida, where there was also a strong inverse relationship between the vote for Official English and the minority population (see figure 7.2). The greatest opposition to the initiative was in Dade County (Miami area), with a majority Latino population. In Florida's homogeneous counties (with minority populations well below the state mean), the county-level vote for the ballot initiative was very high, ranging from 87 to 95 percent.

Voting patterns on Official English in California were similar to the patterns for Colorado and Florida. The strongest support for Official English in California was in the more homogeneous counties (with minority populations below the state average). The least support was in heterogeneous counties, with San Francisco County being the clearest example. The vote for Official English was also below the mean in the bifurcated counties of Los Angeles and Imperial, which have large Latino populations; but even in these counties the initiative was still approved by 70 percent of voters. In Imperial and Los Angeles Counties, whites account for a majority of the electorate, unlike Dade County in Florida or two of Colorado's Latino majority counties. Individual-level data showed that Latinos in California opposed the measure by a 2-to-1 margin. Thus, white voters in California's bifurcated counties with large Latino populations *and* in homogeneous counties with quite small minority (and Latino) population strongly approved of an official language. This state variation in voting patterns may also be the result of differences in the composition of the Latino population: Florida's Cuban population tends to have lower poverty rates and very high political participation rates compared to California's Mexican Americans.[29]

To examine the impact of race/ethnicity on county-level support for Official English in each state, further analyses were undertaken. In each instance, the relationship of racial/ethnic population with the county-level vote for Official English was the issue examined. Analysis (bivariate regression) indicated that larger Latino, black, and Asian populations were inversely related to support for Official English in each state; as the size of the Latino, black, and Asian populations rose in a county, the vote for the language proposal decreased. As expected, the size of the white population was positively related to the vote for this policy in each state.[30]

The impact of race on the vote for Official English was estimated, controlling for the percent Latinos in each of the three states. This control was used because the initiatives were widely perceived to target Latinos, who represent the largest linguistic minority in the United States. Controlling for the percent Latino does not change the strong inverse relationship between higher black and Asian populations and lower approval levels. In each state, the size of the white population was positively associated with higher approval levels of the ballot initiative; as the size of the white population increased, so did the vote for Official English.

Across the three states, white voters in counties with quite small minority (and Latino) populations appeared to have strongly approved of a language amendment to the state's constitution. In California, after accounting for the white population, the percent of Latino is positively related to the vote for Official English. As discussed earlier, this suggests (although it does not show conclusively) that white voters in California's bifurcated counties with large Latino populations and in homogeneous counties with a quite small minority (and Latino) population strongly approved of the language amendment. This finding is similar to other research on white voting patterns in heavily minority areas.[31]

Historically, economic conditions have been an important factor in white responses to immigration and ethnic groups. Competition for jobs is a central part of that concern.[32] The analysis was extended to control for county unemployment rates and political party affiliation patterns.[33] Both of these variables, along with social diversity, have an impact on support for an official language. In California, poorer economic conditions were associated with the vote for the ballot initiative; as the county unemployment rate increased, so did the vote for the language initiative. However, the indicators of racial/ethnic composition remain strong and statistically significant, suggesting that economic conditions and the social diversity context both had an impact on support for the official language initiative, especially among white voters in California. In Florida and Colorado, economic conditions have little impact on voting patterns. The relationship between unemployment rates and the Latino population is also weaker, reflecting the lower poverty rates for Latinos in Florida and Colorado than in California.[34]

Also examined was the impact of political party (measured by the percent of registered Republicans per county in California [1986] and Colorado and Florida [1988]). In each state, Republican Party leaders tended to be more supportive of Official English, although many Republican leaders called the measure unnecessary and said that it could arouse resentment among minority groups. State Democratic Party leaders generally opposed the measure.[35] Higher Republican Party affiliation was related to a vote for the language proposal, especially in California and Colorado. In Florida, party affiliation is less important, probably reflecting that Democratic Party identifiers there are more conservative than in the other two states[36] and that Cubans voted overwhelmingly against Official English and tend to be Republicans. For California and Colorado, the variables accounted for a great deal of the variation in the county-level vote for Official English (between 63 and 71 percent). In Florida, the explained variance is lower.

A Combined Analysis

As states, California, Colorado, and Florida all have racial/ethnic compositions that are somewhat bifurcated relative to national patterns. Hence, it is useful and appropriate to combine the counties for each state into one data set (188 cases). This permits an assessment of the impact of diversity on voting patterns across jurisdictions and is consistent with the social diversity interpretation that posits a general significance of social diversity in American politics.

The size of the Latino population accounted for at least a moderate portion of the variance in the county-level vote for Official English across the three states (31 percent). The percent of Republican voters was associated with higher approval of Official English, as found in the individual state analysis. Larger white populations were strongly related to support for Official English. Also, when unemployment rates were accounted for, the findings indicated that unemployment and political party were important, but that these factors alone were not sufficient to explain voting patterns on Official English. Diversity remains significant.

Conclusions Regarding Official English

The significance of ethnic/racial diversity for understanding subnational politics illustrated here parallels and reinforces the findings of previous analyses, further suggesting the importance of context in politics and policy. Overall, support for Official English was very strong within and across the three states, consistent with the diversity interpretation. The highest support for the measure was in homogeneous counties, those with small minority populations, and it appears that homogeneity had an additive effect on voting. Much of the previous research on public policy in the states does not anticipate or explain the dynamics of race/ethnicity in homogeneous contexts. In California, support for Official English was also strong in bifurcated counties where minorities constitute a large portion but not a majority of the voter population. The greatest opposition to the measures occurred in heterogeneous counties. These patterns were consistent with the state-level findings examining the impact of diversity on various policy outcomes (refer to chapters 5 and 6).

In broader terms, this evidence also indicates that while both the liberal and ethnocultural conceptions of American identity may co-exist, the ethnocultural view of American identity appears most prominent in homogeneous environments and is dominant regarding Official English.[37] The liberal conception seems more evident in heterogeneous contexts. Heterogeneity may thus be understood as a form of social pluralism that appears to foster greater, if incomplete, political pluralism in the sense described by Dahl.[38]

Interesting in themselves, these findings on Official English (in the mid- to late-1980s) may have broader implications in foreshadowing later developments in American politics. County-level voting patterns on California's illegal immigration initiative in 1994 (Proposition 187) were strikingly similar to those found here;[39] in fact, the relationship between county-level voting on the Official English and that on the illegal immigration initiatives is very strong (Pearson r correlation = .82). County-level voting on the illegal immigration initiative is examined next.

Illegal Immigration

Voting patterns on California's 1994 illegal immigration initiative, Proposition 187, also are consistent with the social diversity interpretation. Analysis has found that racial/ethnic diversity shows a strong relationship to county-level support for Proposition 187.[40]

California voters supported Proposition 187 by a 59 to 41 percent overall margin. The ballot initiative denied social services, nonemergency health care, and education to illegal immigrants and required public agencies to report suspected illegal immigrants to state and federal authorities. Although federal courts placed an injunction on implementation of parts of the measure days after the election, this policy has important implications for both national and subnational politics. Proposition 187 is not necessarily unique in the history of California. Other policies relevant to minority groups adopted by ballot initiative in California include the repeal of fair housing legislation in 1965, along with Official English in 1986 (discussed earlier in this chapter) and the antiaffirmative action initiative of 1996.[41]

Analysis

Proposition 187 was commonly referred to as the "Save our State" (SOS) initiative. Supporters argued that California could not afford the cost of serving a large and growing illegal immigrant population. The ballot measure was devised as a means to save billions of dollars in state tax dollars and to "send a message to Washington" about the economic and social problems posed by the estimated 1.6 million illegal immigrants in the state.

Opponents argued that the proposition bordered on being racist and its passage would create a two-tiered society if implemented. They argued that the proposal did nothing to strengthen border enforcement or prevent employers from hiring illegal immigrants. Opponents also argued that the measure would foster a police-state mentality in which legal residents would be questioned simply because of their accent and/or skin color.

A *Los Angeles Times* exit poll found that the illegal immigration initiative polarized the electorate along racial lines, with broad support among white voters while losing among other ethnic groups. Whites voted almost 2 to 1 in support of Proposition 187. Latinos, in contrast, opposed the measure 77 to 23 percent. The poll also showed that 53 percent of black and Asian voters opposed the measure, suggesting that the measure may have been broadly conceived as antiminority and/or anti-Latino (and/or illegal alien).

Again, note that the measure was referred to as "Save our State," framing the issue as one of statewide importance. It also implies that the immediate presence of Latinos (or illegal immigrants) is not necessary for whites to be concerned with growing minority populations.[42]

A series of analyses (regression equations) were used to estimate the impact of race and ethnicity on county-level support for Proposition 187. Analysis (bivariate regression) indicated that larger black and Asian populations were inversely related to support for Proposition 187; as the size of the black and Asian population rose in a county, the vote for the immigration proposal decreased. As expected, the size of the white population is positively correlated with the vote for this policy.

The impact of race on the vote for Proposition 187 was examined controlling for the percent Latino (this control was used because the initiative was widely perceived to target Latinos, who represent the majority of illegal aliens in the state). The size of both the Latino and the white populations were positively related to the vote of the proposition at the county level. As the size of the Latino population increased and/or as the size of the white population increased, so did the vote for the initiative. But individual-level data make clear that Latinos strongly opposed the measure. Thus, white voters in counties with large Latino populations and in counties with quite small minority (and Latino) populations strongly approved of immigration control. Controlling for the percent of Latinos does not change the inverse relationship between higher black and Asian populations and lower approval levels.

Economic conditions also appear to have had an impact on support for Proposition 187. Thus, it is necessary to account for county unemployment rates, historically an important factor in responses to high immigration;[43] county-level data on the percent unemployed of the civilian workforce is from the *City and County Data Book* (1990). In each of the analyses, as the unemployment rate increased, so did the county-level vote for the statewide initiative. But the relationship of racial/ethnic composition remained strong and statistically significant. These findings suggest that economic conditions and racial/ethnic context had a combined impact on support for the illegal immigration initiative, especially among white voters.

The impact of economic conditions and political party were also controlled. Party was measured by the percent registered Republicans per county in 1994.[44] California's Republican Party leaders, including incumbent Republican Governor Pete Wilson, were vocal advocates of Proposition 187, while the state's Democratic Party leaders, including assembly Speaker Willie Brown, generally opposed the measure. The percent of Republicans in counties was strongly associated with the vote for the immigration proposal.

Controlling for political party and economic conditions further clarified the relationship between race/ethnicity and county-level voting patterns. The findings indicate that when these factors are controlled, the percent Latino is inversely related to the vote for the ballot measure. Controlling for party and unemployment rates statistically eliminated the effect of the high vote for Proposition 187 in counties with large Latino populations because these counties had the highest unemployment and registered Republicans. The remaining (homogeneous) counties showed a slight negative relationship. Similarly, controlling for percent white statistically eliminated the effect of high support for the measure in counties with very low Latino populations because these counties had the largest white populations. The remaining (bifurcated) counties indicated a positive relationship.

Both sets of findings seem correct; counties with both high and very low Latino populations strongly supported the measure. Thus, while unemployment and political party may be important, these factors alone are not sufficient to explain the voting patterns on Proposition 187. Race/ethnicity remain critical.

Counties with moderately large Asian populations opposed the measure, even controlling for party and economic conditions. When party and unemployment are accounted for, however, larger black populations are associated with higher levels of support for the initiative. This suggests that interminority competition may exist between Latinos and blacks for employment and even governmental social services. Previous studies support this finding. McClain, for example, found evidence for competition among blacks and Latinos for municipal employment.[45]

Proposition 187 and the Wilson Gubernatorial Campaign

Proposition 187 was related to several candidate-based races in California, especially that for governor.[46] In 1993, public opinion of incumbent Governor Pete Wilson (Republican) reached record lows in the face of recession, tax increases, and defense cutbacks that weakened the California economy. In the early stages of the campaign, Democratic candidate Kathleen Brown was leading Wilson in the opinion polls by as much as 23 percent. Wilson made illegal immigration the central issue of his reelection campaign. In contrast, the Democratic candidate linked her campaign closely to opposition to Proposition 187.

Since Wilson allied his reelection campaign closely with his support for Proposition 187, it is not surprising that race and ethnicity played a central role in the 1994 vote for Governor.[47] The county-level vote for Wilson and for Proposition 187 were strongly related ($r = .72, p = .0001$) in California's 58 counties. A *Los Angeles Times* exit poll indicated that 61 percent of whites voted for the Republican incumbent candidate and 35 percent for the Democratic candidate. Seventy-two percent of Latinos voted for Brown and 23 percent for Wilson. Blacks strongly supported the Democratic candidate (77 percent to 20 percent), while Asian Americans split their vote evenly between the Republican and Democratic gubernatorial candidates. This suggests that issue elections (ballot initiatives), including those where ethnic/racial issues are salient, may spill over into candidate-based elections.

Conclusion Regarding Proposition 187

Proposition 187 appears to be one of a series of policies adopted through the initiative process in bifurcated racial/ethnic contexts. These findings parallel those of state-level analysis of racial/ethnic diversity. Although voter approval was expected to increase with the size of the Latino population, the relationship was more complex. Support for the proposition was high in bifurcated counties, with above-average Latino populations and a dominant white population. Support for the policy was also very strong in homogeneous counties with very small minority populations.[48] The lowest support occurred in racially heterogeneous counties with sizable black and Asian populations. These several patterns are consistent with other findings.

Economic conditions (unemployment) and party (registered Republicans) also played a role in county-level voting patterns. But the analysis shows that racial/ethnic diversity was important in shaping voting patterns, even when these other factors are accounted for.

Social Diversity's Impact on Candidate Voting at the County Level

A major study has produced findings supportive of social diversity's relevance at the substate level. Gimpel examined the political party voting in 10 states in different regions of the country—New York, New Jersey, Ohio, Pennsylvania, New Mexico, Arizona, California, Washington, Oregon, and Idaho.[49] His analysis includes county-level voting patterns and indicates that the minority or racial composition of counties has consistently affected partisan voting in presidential, gubernatorial, and senatorial elections. And it has done so for a number of years, dating back to the 1960s. Gimpel found that race significantly affects partisan electoral outcomes in such states as New York, California, and New Mexico.[50] That may not be surprising. But that race also has some impact in such homogeneous contexts as Washington state, Oregon, and Idaho suggests a noteworthy breadth of importance.[51] Thus, social diversity appears to have an impact on candidate voting as well as initiative voting, along with its implications for various political attitudes. Moreover, its influence is evident across a variety of states with different racial/ethnic contexts.

Local Government Structures

The impact of social diversity is evident in institutional aspects of substate politics. Here, I discuss the ostensible importance and legacy of ethnicity/race on one dimension of local governments in the United States.

The basic institutional structures of local governments still manifest the ideas and concerns of the urban reform movement of the early 1900s, itself

ethnic diversity. The *consequences* of those diversity-influenced reforms also have significantly affected minority groups in the recent past and in the present.

Conclusion

This chapter has shown that social diversity has various political manifestations and implications at the substate, including the individual, level—not just at the state level. A number of studies over time have indicated that the presence of large minority populations (bifurcation) affects individual political attitudes and behaviors. Perhaps more notable are other studies that have shown racial isolation (homogeneity) related to negative racial attitudes among individuals.[57] On the whole, the findings are consistent with and supportive of the contextual and institutional findings described in chapters 3 through 6.

The analyses of two major ballot initiatives (Official English and illegal immigration) strongly suggest that social diversity helps explain voting patterns within and across several states. Finally, historical discussions indicate that social diversity concerns have had a significant part in shaping the structures of urban governmental institutions. Those structures have, in turn, had clear consequences for the ability of some groups, especially minority groups, to gain access to urban government.

Overall, the evidence demonstrates that social diversity's implications are not confined to the state level; they are quite apparent in various dimensions of substate processes and politics as well. Given the important legal and political linkages among state and local processes and politics, this is probably not surprising. Importantly, however, the evidence adds further support to the social diversity interpretation of state and national politics, in that national politics in the U.S. federal system is shaped by and is an aggregation of state/local politics and policy.

8

The Social Diversity
Interpretation of State
Politics and Policy
in Perspective

This study has developed, and provided evidence regarding a social diversity interpretation on state politics and policy. And because of the critical role states play in U.S. politics and policy, that interpretation has broader implications. The argument and evidence suggest that racial/ethnic diversity is, and has been, a major thread in the states', and thus American, political and social fabric. The core claim is that social diversity is a significant aspect of state politics—one that is substantially greater, more pervasive, and more institutional in its importance than has previously been acknowledged or understood. Social diversity can be thought of as an analytical construct, not simply just another variable, and as a phenomenon embedded in the states, and hence the United States, political systems. Thus, social diversity deserves consideration as a distinct perspective on state and U.S. politics.

Social diversity is significant for understanding aggregate-level patterns of state politics and policies—issues commonly studied. The evidence presented in earlier chapters has indicated that state political patterns manifest effects associated with levels and types of social diversity. Furthermore, social diversity contexts appear critical to understanding other aspects of state public policies pertaining to distributive justice, especially the differential dimensions. Questions pertaining to these other aspects of inequality are seldom studied in state politics research.

Social diversity patterns form different contexts, and social diversity's significance is evident across contexts but in different forms—the particular forms are influenced by specific racial/ethnic contexts. That this is also evident to the extent and in the way that it is in homogeneous (moralistic) settings is an especially interesting finding.

Much data were collected and statistical analysis undertaken and summarized in chapters 3 to 7. But the overarching goal has been to bring a different focus and understanding to the study of state politics and policy; the data and statistical analyses were means to those ends, not ends in themselves. I have sought to present a contextual perspective, grounded in a social diversity view. That view is rooted in broadly familiar aspects of state and U.S. history and tradition. But the aspects have not been incorporated systematically into theory and research. At the same time, I have sought to focus theoretical attention on the pervasive and complex influence of racial and ethnic factors generally, and as modified by context. The argument underscores that there are indeed multiple normative theoretical traditions in U.S. political practice,[1] but that they have seldom been adequately acknowledged or systematically integrated into the states politics research.

The study has shown that race and ethnicity, associated with the theoretical tradition of ascriptive hierarchy, is evident in numerous ways and in various contexts; those ways include political processes and public policies and, to a lesser degree, formal institutions. Differential policy outcomes tend to be especially low for ethnic/racial minorities in all states, an apparent legacy of the hierarchical tradition (as was developed in chapters 5 and 6). Furthermore, the way in which different racial/ethnic configurations shape or mediate political and policy patterns suggests the complex nature of that tradition in the United States. The social diversity perspective thus helps explain a variety of political phenomena in the states. As such, it provides something of a unifying contextual theory along the lines called for by Brace and others.[2] Let's retrace the thesis and evidence.

Reviewing the Argument and Findings

Chapter 1 laid out the broad argument of social diversity and suggested how patterns might be summarized into three broad contexts—homogeneous, heterogeneous, and bifurcated. It also specified that the concept of social diversity should be disaggregated into minority diversity and white ethnic diversity (and homogeneity) and, in turn, how those concepts were to be operationalized. Also suggested was that a major interpretation of state politics and policy—political culture—might well be rooted in social diversity, but that this possibility had been generally ignored.

The first chapter also offered that the social diversity contexts are related to general traits of state political systems, including several forms of political pluralism, called consensual, competitive, and hierarchical, and that these are, in turn, linked to several social systems or structures (review table 1.3). Furthermore, it was suggested that those social settings create a tendency toward different orientations to social order—community, contract/market, and hierarchy. This suggestion is not entirely new;[3] importantly, however, the ideas were expressly linked to racial/ethnic diversity, which *is* a novel assertion. Chapter 1 also outlined a number of broad expectations or hypotheses about each of the types of states relative to a host of state politics questions; those were explored in chapters 3 through 7.

Chapter 2 reviewed other approaches to the study of state politics, indicating their main points and suggesting some of their limitations. At the same time, certain parallels between social diversity and other perspectives, especially political culture, were noted. However, the chapter emphasized that the social diversity perspective typically views social and political phenomena differently from the political culture perspective, and that the central focus, understanding, and conclusions of social diversity are quite distinct from, and often directly challenge, those of political culture, as well as of other approaches.

Chapter 3 began applying the social diversity interpretation, while also considering the impact of socioeconomic traits of states—specifically education, per capita income, and urbanization. Those traits were used as control variables, but they can also be seen as representing an alternative interpretation in that the socioeconomic perspective has long been a major one in the state politics and policy literature. First assessed were political processes, which might also be viewed as political institutions, such as electoral patterns, party systems (and a number of aspects thereof), and the strength of interest group systems. The analysis indicated that minority diversity and/or white ethnic diversity show significant relationships with a number of the processes or political institutions (see summary in table 3.1, compare to table 1.3). Furthermore, social diversity provides new insights into several of these processes. For example, social diversity seems to help reconcile an ostensible but often overlooked tension between high levels of political party competition and the commonwealth or consensual orientation, which are alleged to co-exist in certain (homogeneous or moralistic) settings. Also, state ideological patterns have been said to have major impacts on state policies, but scholarship has had difficulty explaining the underlying sources or bases of state ideology.[4] Social diversity helps account for patterns of ideological self-identification in the states, specifically moderate identification ideologically and independent identification regarding partisanship.

A number of the processes and institutions that were examined are themselves often seen as important in explaining state public policies. Social diversity is instrumental in explaining these processes and appears logically prior to them. That is, it seems more plausible to say that race/ethnicity explains ideology than to say that ideology explains racial/ethnic background. Because of the significant relationship of social diversity to those processes, social diversity is an important dimension of state politics. But social diversity also was linked to broader patterns of state processes.

It seems that social diversity contexts and political patterns in the states parallel an explanatory framework developed by James Q. Wilson that focuses on the costs and benefits of public policies for groups and general populations. For example, I suggested that the homogeneous context was often associated with a "majoritarian" pattern or regime. Homogeneous states are also said to have commonwealth, or "communitarian," orientations (see chapter 1 and Elazar). While majoritarian and commonwealth are somewhat different concepts, when considered relative to social context—that is, a context of racial/ethnic homogeneity—the two may substantially converge.

In chapter 4, relationships between social diversity and two aspects of state formal or governmental institutions—their basic structure and/or strength, and issues concerning descriptive representation—were explored. Specific expectations were put forth and then examined. The expectations concerning the structural features of institutions were not especially well supported by the actual patterns. Social diversity showed some relationship to legislative professionalism, but not necessarily in the way expected; and social diversity had no consistent impact on governors' powers. For several states, the aggregate strength of these two institutions was consistent with the anticipated patterns, but the overall patterns are less clear. However, social diversity showed some relationship to judicial selection methods. Furthermore, historians argue that the presence or absence of another state institution, the initiative, is at least partly explicable in terms of social diversity.

Social diversity's relationship to descriptive representation within state legislatures and state bureaucracies is quite strong. An especially interesting finding was that several of the most homogeneous (moralistic) states have the largest underrepresentation of minorities within their state bureaucracies (review figure 4.4). Possible explanations, other than social diversity, for the findings were explored, but they do not seem readily explicable by several of the other leading interpretations of state politics.

Chapter 5 examined social diversity relative to three major policy responsibilities of the states—education, welfare, and health. First, the findings of previous research on some of these questions were summarized. That research, drawing on evidence from the early to mid-1980s, had found that social diversity is related to education (graduation and student suspensions) and to health (infant mortality) policies. Especially notable was that social diversity often had an impact on *both* general or aggregate patterns and differential or disaggregated patterns—that is, outcomes for minority populations relative to overall outcomes.[5] These and other related policies were then reassessed with evidence from the 1990s. To a substantial degree, the further assessment supported the earlier findings relative to policy outcomes, and other notable findings emerged.

The evidence indicated that higher minority diversity is related to greater education effort, a somewhat unexpected finding. Also, greater minority diversity was related to better minority graduation and to better minority suspension ratios, and some of the worst relative outcomes are found in homogeneous (moralistic) states. These findings are by and large consistent with the previous ones. Social diversity did not have an impact on several indicators of state welfare financial effort, and, with exceptions, has little impact on financial effort concerning health policy. Previous research by other scholars actually has provided stronger evidence that race is important in these areas than was found here (see chapter 5).

Minority diversity has a significant impact on both overall infant mortality rates, positively, and on minority versus overall rates, negatively. That is, more minority diversity is related to higher overall infant mortality rates but also to better differential ratios. Again, these relationships echo those found in the earlier studies, suggesting that social diversity has significant implications for these issues and that this has been the case for some time.

Social diversity was examined relative to an array of other policies in chapter 6. Perhaps most significant, minority diversity was strongly related to a major criminal justice issue—incarceration rates—for the 1980s and the early 1990s. More minority diversity is related to less disparate incarceration rates for minorities; and some of the more homogeneous states, such as Minnesota and Iowa, have the most disparate outcomes. Again, the patterns are consistent with findings from the early 1980s, and thus not a temporally isolated finding.

Research (also discussed in chapter 6) has found that social diversity, particularly minority diversity, was related to the adoption of Official English policies in the states during the late 1980s.[6] More recent adoptions of that policy in the mid-1990s in several homogeneous states follows a pattern found a number of times in this study—that is, that the homogeneous and bifurcated settings stand out in terms of various policy outcomes, although in different ways. While social diversity did not appear to have an impact on certain other policies, increases in social diversity appear to have affected the adoption of several governance policies in the last decade or so. Overall, social diversity seems to significantly shape public policies, especially certain aspects of education, health, and criminal justice.

Perhaps the most important general conclusion of the two major chapters on public policies (chapters 5 and 6)—and one of the most important findings of this study—is that each type of diversity (homogeneity, heterogeneity, bifurcation) seems associated with different patterns of inequality. The pattern of the policy outcomes, delineated most extensively in chapters 5 and 6, is broadly summarized in figure 8.1.

The figure implies that most state politics and policy research focuses primarily, or solely, on aggregate indicators, on the levels, the quantity or quality of state policies. This may be thought of as the first face of politics. But there are other faces—concerning the *distributive consequences* of state policy—which are typically overlooked or overshadowed in most mainstream research. Here, the policy patterns are often rather different than in the first. And the heterogeneous setting, often mid-range of the two axes, is also somewhat unique. These other dimensions are no less substantively important than the first dimension, but are too often ignored.

The social diversity interpretation not only brings attention to these other dimensions, it also helps explain them as the analysis in chapters 5 and 6, especially, underscores. In addition, the findings suggest that if we think of policies as institutions in some respects—as I think we should—social diversity is a particularly important social force in state polities, with major implications for U.S. politics generally.

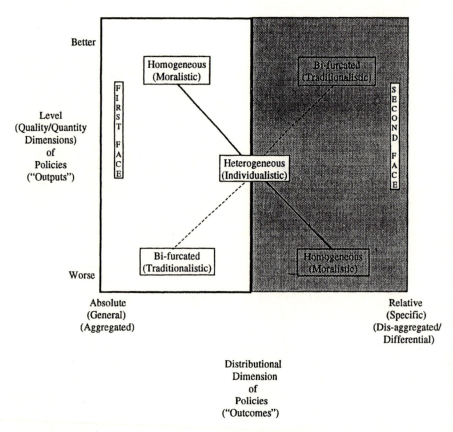

Figure 8.1 Social Diversity Contexts and State Governments' Policy Patterns Summary

In chapter 7, social diversity's relevance at the substate level was explored concerning political attitudes and voting patterns on several questions, as well as substate institutions. First, several studies that have considered social context's implications for individual political attitudes were discussed. Some research has shown that both racial threat and racial isolation may be related to negative attitudes toward minorities; in a sense, it appears that insulation may beget insularity. This is generally consistent with the broad patterns shown in earlier chapters of this study (especially chapters 5 and 6). Second, studies of county-level voting patterns on ballot initiatives suggest that social diversity has an impact, and that its influence seems clearest in bifurcated and in homogeneous contexts—again, not unlike patterns found in earlier analyses.[7] Third, studies of county-level voting patterns in state candidate–based elections and over extended periods of time indicate the importance of counties' racial or minority composition across a number of states.[8] Finally, the importance of social diversity for understanding the structures of urban governmental institutions was developed. Taken individually and collectively, the evidence strongly points to the importance of social diversity at the substate level.

Alternative Interpretations

While many political and policy phenomena were examined relative to social diversity, those phenomena were not examined relative to that construct only. Rather, a number of alternative, interpretations were also considered in this study. Overall, it appears that social diversity not only helps explain a host of the phenomena but also commonly does so better than other interpretations. Social diversity showed significant relationships with various political processes that are, themselves, seen as important in the policy research, such as aspects of party competition, mass and party elite political ideology, and interest group influence, (see chapter 3). To the extent that such processes influence government and policies in the states, which is often the case, social diversity may have an indirect, along with a direct, relevance for state politics and policies.

Concerning public policies more directly, social diversity's impact was quite consistently strong relative to other interpretations. Three socioeconomic variables—income, education, and urbanization—were used as control variables in conjunction with diversity throughout the analysis of policies. At the same time, because those variables are commonly viewed as central to the socioeconomic interpretation of state politics, the analysis in effect examined that as an alternative interpretation.

Like racial/ethnic diversity, socioeconomic variables often influence the political and policy (especially the aggregate policy), issues examined in this study. However, the impacts of the socioeconomic variables are not always especially strong and not always consistent with the expected direction of impact. Nor are they always consistent with each other regarding the directions of impact. For example, in a number of instances one might expect that income and education would have similar impacts—that is, both positive or both negative. But often that is not the case. Moreover, the meaning of the impacts of the socioeconomic variables is ambiguous. How a variable such as education is (directly) related to or causes particular policy outcome, for example, is not always clear. In several respects, then, my findings and questions about the utility of the socioeconomic school of state politics are similar to the reservations noted by Erikson, Wright, and McIver.[9]

Furthermore, social diversity typically was substantially more important than socioeconomic variables regarding the differential policy indicators. In three instances—the differential policy outcomes for minorities concerning school suspension ratios, infant mortality rates, and incarceration ratios—the impact of an additional socioeconomic variable, relative poverty rates, was another variable examined. In all three instances, the importance of minority diversity remained, with this additional (and the several other) socioeconomic variable accounted for. In short, social diversity holds up rather well in explaining important state politics questions relative to the socioeconomic interpretation. The patterns for differential policies thus do not appear attributable to broad economic or social-class factors; social diversity seems most critical.

The political culture argument was also examined extensively.[10] Indeed, a considerable part of chapter 1 and other places in the discussion developed the case that political culture may largely be an artifact of social diversity. A great deal of evidence suggested that political culture, as typically considered in the literature, is rather seldom significantly related to policies when social diversity is also considered, further supporting the claim that political culture is an outgrowth of social diversity. For these and other reasons, I argued that political culture has not been adequately attentive to underlying social diversity issues. Moreover, social diversity's relationship to the differential policies is consistently stronger than that of political culture. Seldom is political culture significant at all for these policy indicators in the way that culture would ostensibly predict. In short, a substantial portion of evidence developed in this study calls into question the political culture view.

In addition to helping explain various aspects of state mass and elite political ideology in the first place (see chapter 3), social diversity appears to be related as or more strongly to the aggregate policy indicators as is ideology. Furthermore, ideology provides little insight into the differential policy indicators; minority diversity's relationship to such measures tends to be quite strong, even when ideology is examined simultaneously.

Party competition was also examined, along with social diversity and the socioeconomic variables, regarding a number of policies. Party competition does have significant impacts on several expenditure indicators of policy, such as education and welfare spending, as well as for composite policy liberalism; several times its impact is greater than that of social diversity. However, on a number of other indicators party competition does not add much to what social diversity offers when considered together; this is especially so for the differential policy measures, where diversity is most telling.

Other alternative interpretations considered were that certain traits of formal institutions, especially legislative professionalism and/or governors' formal powers, are central to explaining policy patterns. Such measures have some importance for some of the social policies, particularly spending efforts on Medicaid, where legislative professionalism is especially important (see chapter 5). However, they show no impact on education policies or on infant mortality rates.

This study has been somewhat unique in considering numerous alternative interpretations to the core argument. Other studies generally take one of several approaches. A common approach is to consider most or all variables that are plausibly associated with a policy or other phenomena (dependent variable) in a statistical (regression) analysis, and ascertain which ones appear most important. A second approach is to examine a policy or phenomena with a specific (independent) variable and to control for a few other, typically socioeconomic, variables, but not to consider alternative interpretations beyond that. The present study has thus been different in several important respects.

First, it has sought to develop a distinct and new interpretation. Second, it has examined that interpretation with regard to a variety of state political, institutional, and policy issues. In the process, it is one of the first to bring attention to and find important implications concerning several differential policies. Third, it not only controlled for socioeconomic factors but also considered a number of alternative interpretations, along with social diversity. Often, social diversity was significantly related to the phenomena of interest, including certain political processes and institutions and formal institutions. And social diversity was typically the only or major factor that helped explain the differential public policies. While much of the analysis indicated the importance of social diversity for collective or institutional outcomes—for example, for broad political processes such as party competition, the presence or absence of direct democracy, and various policies— other evidence (see chapter 7) suggests that its significance is also apparent at individual and/or substate levels of politics.

Social diversity suggests that distinct historical experiences of various groups have shaped U.S. politics including and, perhaps especially, state politics because of particular population configurations. The implication is that the historical experience of the white/Anglo population has been different from that of the white ethnic immigrants, which in turn differed from that of racial/ethnic minorities. And when the various groups are present or absent within states to varying degrees, the different contexts lead to different political and policy dynamics. Despite nationalization or the impact of modernization in U.S. politics, important differences—differences associated with social diversity contexts—remain.[11]

While those differences were evident in numerous aspects of state politics and policy, perhaps the most striking had to do with policies as they affect minorities. This is not surprising, for several reasons. Almost by definition, the historical experience of minorities is particularly distinct within United States, and state politics. The black or African-American experience has been viewed as being at the heart of the "American dilemma." This dilemma has been confronted in a number of important ways, such as the civil rights and voting rights legislation of the 1960s and 70s. However, the dilemma has also become more subtle or complex and has taken different forms, including second-generation discrimination and two-tiered pluralism.[12]. The issues have become more complex with the emergence of other groups, such as Latinos. This study has delineated and helped explain some of that complexity. But while Latinos and other groups may have only recently emerged as political forces, some, especially African Americans and Mexican Americans, have had a rather longstanding presence in American society. That they have emerged only recently says more about unique historical experiences than sheer chronological longevity or presence in U.S. society.

In this study I have often referred to the "American dilemma." A formal definition of *dilemma* is "a situation involving choice[s] between unsatisfactory alternatives." In virtually all states, inequality for minorities is evident in some form—relatively, absolutely, or some of both. Hence, the political alternatives for minorities are problematic—a dilemma. Some observers might dismiss the evidence in this study, claiming that the U.S. political system is, and should be, one of "equality of opportunity," not "equality of outcome." However, another assumption of U.S. liberal democratic values is that equality of opportunity will or should produce outcomes that are not disproportionately associated with race or ethnicity. But the evidence provided in this study hardly supports such an assumption or assertion. The analysis also examined another, presumably related basis by which policy outcomes might be explained—social "class," including state income and education profiles, and the relative poverty levels of minorities compared to nonminorities. Consideration of those factors did not alter several differential or distributional outcomes that were related to minority diversity.

In any case, some proponents of the political culture interpretation have argued that the moralistic culture, with its alleged focus on commonwealth and/or community, is indeed concerned with "equality of *result* in policy-making,"[13] not just equality of opportunity. That the research findings presented here indicate that results are often the most negatively skewed for minorities in moralistic or homogeneous settings thus seems especially telling. And that Minnesota is an obvious "outlier" regarding several differential policies is likewise interesting, in that that state has been referred to as the "heartland" of the moralistic culture.[14]

Some criticisms of the evidence presented in this book might include that the focus on policy outcomes is inappropriate, in that those outcomes are at least in part attributable to factors outside the control of state governments. There is only limited merit to this criticism. First, if for the sake of argument one concedes that there is something to that criticism, we would expect that the policy outcomes would be equally and/or randomly outside the control of state governments, thus suggesting no specific pattern to the differential outcomes. But even conceding something to the criticism still does not explain why the outcomes take on the particular ethnic/racial patterns relative to state contexts that they do.

Second, the differential policies examined *are*, to a substantial degree, within the authority of state and local governments. Indeed, it is probably no accident that the most notable findings regarding differential policies were associated with certain types of policies. Education is provided through public schools and student suspension decisions are within their authority. And incarceration decisions are made by law enforcement agencies. Such public bureaucracies are quintessential street-level bureaucracies[15] and are known to have considerable discretion. Implementation, the major function of these bureaucracies, is a central part of policies and that is likely an important part of what explains the policy outcomes.[16] Moreover, evidence presented earlier (chapter 4) indicated that minority presence or representation in state bureaucracies tends to be disproportionately low in homogeneous (moralistic) settings.

Part of the problem with other research, as noted above, is that it focuses primarily, and often only, on policy outputs or what might also be thought of as potential policies. That is, attention is given to whether a law has been enacted by states, the scope of the policy and/or the expenditure levels. Such policy indicators are limited in that they do not address distributional questions or implications or the possibility that policies may have largely or only symbolic, but marginal substantive, consequence. This is not to suggest that symbolic policy is not important, but it is to suggest that its importance can be overstated or at least should be kept in perspective. Moreover, policy outputs may take on more or less substantive significance relative to context. For instance, several states that were early adopters of civil rights policies were relatively homogeneous states. While the adoption of such a policy is not unimportant, its particular impact is somewhat limited given the nature of the diversity context. Part of the reason that the policy is adopted is that it may be attractive in the abstract and, at the same time, of little direct consequence substantively.

Certainly, more needs to be known about the specific processes associated with diversity contexts that lead to the political and policy patterns delineated in the empirical analysis chapters. (However, much the same can be said about most other interpretations of state politics and policies.) An underlying assumption of this book's argument has been that different group historical experiences continue to manifest themselves in politics, institutions, and policies. Different patterns of state politics, including democratization, party competition, ideology, and interest group systems, were shown to be shaped by diversity. Similarly, the social composition, if not always the structural characteristics, of institutions, especially bureaucracies and legislatures, major policymaking and implementing institutions, is influenced by racial/ethnic context. Finally, policies, including or especially differential policy outcomes, are linked to social diversity. The implication I draw is that these various political, institutional, and policy patterns are connected to each other and a central connecting factor is ethnic/racial context.

State racial/ethnic diversity patterns are complex. That is why evidence was delineated into three types of diversity—white/Anglo, white ethnic, and minority. But I also discussed the states as being more or less homogeneous, heterogeneous (simple or complex) and bifurcated, although probably no state entirely fits those categories; thus the efforts to measure the types of diversity were important. Some general conclusions about the various contexts may be offered, most of which were shown to be related to social diversity.

The homogenous (moralistic) settings tend to do rather well in terms of procedural democracy, with, for instance, relatively high levels of voter turnout, party competition, and weak interest group systems. Regarding the traits or strength of formal government institutions, these states tend to have relatively weak legislatures and governors—weaker than I expected. Despite high levels of procedural democracy, homogenous states tend to fall well short of parity in descriptive representation in their state bureaucracies. Policy outputs, in terms of the level of policies, in these settings are moderately high; that the outputs are not higher may be due to a relative lack of need in such settings. However, the homogeneous context often shows a pattern in another face of policy—distributive or differential outcomes—that is not consistent with what other theories suggest (when those theories think about the issue at all). Thus, homogeneous (moralistic) states may be majoritarian or oriented to a commonwealth (see chapter 3). But that characterization seems based on conditions applying to the majority population—that is, white/Anglo (nonethnic) majority. And in these states, that is indeed a large proportion of the population. However, when the differential policy side or relative equality of policy is considered, the homogeneous or moralistic states are not the bastions of social democracy implied in some other perspectives, at least not pertaining to minority group circumstances.

States that are heterogeneous are notable for having relatively large white ethnic populations. Some have rather small minority populations, a situation referred to as simple heterogeneity, while others have a larger minority group presence, referred to as complex heterogeneity. In such contexts, group competition characterizes the political setting, although all groups do not compete to the same degree or with equal effectiveness. In most of these states, especially those with moderate to large populations, governmental institutions are relatively strong and minority descriptive representation in state legislatures and bureaucracies falls short of parity. Policy patterns, both aggregate and differential, tend to be in the middle range relative to other types of states. These states thus have another pattern of inequality.

Bifurcated states, with large minority populations, tend to have low levels of procedural democracy and, relatedly, a hierarchical form of political pluralism. Their aggregate policy outcomes tend to be low. However, such states often have more relative equality in public policy outcomes than has previously been noted. But, again, that relative equality typically occurs at a low absolute level. Hence, this sort of diversity is associated with yet another aspect of inequality.

Previous state politics research has often implied that the major context of inequality in the United States is the Old South, the more traditionalistic or bifurcated settings. It is not unusual to find studies that differentiate the South from the non-South (using 1, 0 in regressional analyses). The implication is that the individualistic or heterogeneous setting have less, and that the moralistic or homogeneous have very little, inequality. But the reality—the evidence developed here suggests—is that political inequality is substantially more complex and more pervasive than commonly assumed. It appears in all types of settings and states, but again it takes different forms in different contexts.

Scholars have come to agree that there have been several major theoretical traditions in U.S. political thinking. Liberalism and individualism is seen as one tradition. Others argue that a republican tradition has long existed.

More recently, a number of scholars have conceded that ascriptive hierarchical views have long been influential.[17] Elazar's work implies, though the specific political culture argument does not really develop, that the liberal tradition may be most associated with individualistic patterns, republican traditions with moralism, and ascriptive hierarchy with traditionalistic political cultures. The present work agrees with the broad patterns delineated. However, social diversity argues that the patterns are more related to context than has previously been acknowledged, and do not necessarily arise from the factors Elazar would suggest. Moreover, and probably more important, the social diversity perspective indicates that outcomes consistent with ascriptive hierarchy are evident in *all* types of states and are not confined to the bifurcated or traditionalistic contexts. To repeat, racial/ethnic inequality is an *American* dilemma.

Further Comments on the Social Diversity Interpretation

While social diversity appears to be a central, even a defining feature of state politics, the presentation of the argument oversimplifies the issues somewhat. This was done with the goal of putting forth the argument forcefully and directly and for the sake of clarity and parsimony. This approach was not unusual, in that virtually all statements of new theoretical frameworks tend to make simplifying assumptions. Some assumptions and questions about them are worth noting here.

Three major groups were delineated in this study (white/Anglo, white ethnics, and minorities) on the assumption that, to a substantial degree, there is and has been enough group commonality to warrant such aggregation. As noted earlier, previous research has made similar delineations, and I feel that these are, by and large, appropriate. Nonetheless, social diversity is obviously more complex than this.

There are a great many intragroup and intergroup differences, group competition, and so on that is not emphasized in the diversity interpretation, or other interpretations for that matter. Several examples of that greater complexity can be given readily. To take one minority group, Latinos or Hispanics include at least three major national origin groups (Mexican Americans, Puerto Ricans, and Cuban Americans), each of which has had somewhat different historical experiences, is concentrated in different regions or states, has different levels of socioeconomic well-being, and so on. And Latinos may as often compete as cooperate with other minority groups, such as blacks or Asian Americans.[18] Also, white ethnics include a variety of groups, each with somewhat distinct characteristics, histories, and other unique attributes. Moreover, whites/Anglos are not monolithic, either. Thus, this complexity, the circumstances under which group competition is more or less likely, and a host of related considerations should be addressed as the social diversity interpretation is extended.

Another issue concerns the conceptualization of social diversity. The size or extent of a state's diversity was measured here as the percentage or proportion of groups in a state's population, which seems plausible and quite defensible. However, it may be the case that a group's size might also be considered in terms of raw numbers.[19] For example, while 3 percent minority population is considered small, the raw numbers would be quite different in a state with a population of 5 million versus one with 500 thousand (150 thousand versus 15 thousand). Such differences might lead to different political and social dynamics and political or policy implications. On the one hand, the smaller population might be less visible, or bring less attention. However, the small number might also make political mobilization more difficult because a numerical critical mass may be harder to achieve. On the other hand, the larger numbers might make the group more visible and more likely to be threatening and/or singled out. But because the numbers are larger, there may be greater ability to act in defense of group concerns.

A related issue about social diversity, especially minority diversity, has to do with population concentrations. It is possible, indeed likely, that as groups are more geographically concentrated within a state, they may be more visible and be seen as more threatening than if they are more dispersed. Also, the recent arrival of a group in a state, the rate of change, and the presence in large numbers are important. These are potentially important points. They only qualify but likely do not seriously undermine the basic arguments of the social diversity interpretation. Social diversity remains a central factor, and these other considerations only modify the basic relationships between social diversity and politics.

Another issue is changing diversity; that itself has several dimensions. The states have been and are changing at different rates and with respect to different groups. For instance, much of the change in minority diversity that took place during the 1980s was the result of increasing Latino populations in a number of states. By comparison, the growth of the African-American population has been slower. Thus, states that had the largest minority populations in 1990 are often states where Latinos are the largest minority group (e.g., California, Texas, New Mexico). Most of the states of the Old South have changed relatively less because their black populations have been stable and they have not experienced a major influx of other minority populations. The nature and rates of changing minority diversity will make social diversity, and the understanding of that diversity, more complex.

Other, new groups are becoming established within states—for example, substantial Arab populations are now common in parts of the United States. In addition, increasingly persons view themselves as multiracial, or "other." But much of the understanding and theorizing about U.S. politics has focused on the three broad categories used in this study. Developments suggest that group diversity may have to be reconsidered.

The very concept and meaning of the term *diversity* is complex and dynamic. *Diversity* once had a rather innocuous, descriptive meaning in popular and political discourse, but it has come to be associated, and praised and criticized, with various loaded meanings. Similarly, while the term "African American" is now often used, one can recall times when "black," "Negro," or "colored" were used. This indicates that the concept of diversity and the status of various groups are socially constructed. But that construction is an ongoing political process in and of itself. Studying and understanding that process is an ongoing scholarly enterprise. However, the assumption of the present study is that the basic parameters and outcomes of political processes have been sufficiently stable in U.S. history, at least for the last generation, so that social diversity as utilized here maintains its theoretical significance.

Conclusion

The writings of Tocqueville in the 19th century, of DuBois, Myrdal, and Key over a century after Tocqueville, and a host of recent writers[20] all underscore the historical and continuing significance of racial/ethnic issues in the United States. Others have discussed new dimensions to the issues and implications for other groups.[21] And much evidence presented in early chapters of this study indicates the continued importance of race and ethnicity in state politics. Hence, while race or ethnicity is a dynamic concept, its impact has historically been and continues to be manifest in U.S. politics, including state politics. This book has, I believe, shown that rather convincingly. It has also shown that the particular forms of racial and ethnic inequality varies, however. And these forms seem to vary relative to particular social contexts or configurations. Those social diversity contexts seem to significantly shape many important political policies and processes commonly understood to be central to state political systems. And the states are, of course, central to politics in the United States. Therefore, as the social diversity interpretation helps better understand state politics and policy, it is of major significance.

Notes

Preface

1. Jody L. Fitzpatrick and Rodney E. Hero (1988), "Political Culture and Political Characteristics of the American States: A Consideration of Some Old and New Questions," *Western Political Quarterly* 41, 1 (March); also see Virginia Gray (1990), "The Socioeconomic and Political Context of States," in Virginia Gray, Herbert Jacob and Robert B. Albritton, eds., *Politics in the American States*, 5th ed. (Glenview, IL: Scott, Foresman): 3–37; and Virginia Gray (1996), "The Socioeconomic and Political Context of States," in Virginia Gray and Herbert Jacob, eds., *Politics in the American States* 6th ed. (Washington, DC: Congressional Quarterly Press): 1–34.

2. Gary King, Robert O. Keohane, and Sidney Verba (1994), *Designing Social Inquiry* (Princeton, NJ: Princeton University Press).

Chapter I

1. Daniel J. Elazar (1984), *American Federalism: A View from the States*, 3rd ed. (New York: Harper and Row); Theodore Lowi and Benjamin Ginsberg (1990), *American Government: Freedom and Power* (New York: W. W. Norton): 70–78.

2. Rodney E. Hero (1992), *Latinos and the U.S. Political System: Two-tiered Pluralism* (Philadelphia: Temple University Press), esp. ch. 11; cf. Kenneth Meier and Joseph Stewart Jr. (1991), *The Politics of Hispanic Education* (Albany, NY: State University of New York Press); Kenneth Meier, Joseph Stewart Jr., and Robert England (1989), *Race, Class, and Education: The Politics of Second Generation Discrimination* (Madison: University of Wisconsin Press).

3. Virginia Gray (1996), "The Socioeconomic and Political Context of States," in Virginia Gray and Herbert Jacob, eds., *Politics in the American States*, 6th ed. (Washington, DC: Congressional Quarterly Press); Virginia Gray (1990), "The Socioeconomic and Political Context of States," in Virginia Gray, Herbert

Jacob and Robert B. Albritton, eds., *Politics in the American States*, 5th ed. (Scott, Foresman). 3–37.

4. Robert S. Erikson, Gerald C. Wright, John P. McIver (1993), *Statehouse Democracy* (New York: Cambridge University Press): 72.

5. Paul Brace and Aubrey Jewett (1995), "Field Essay: The State of the State Politics Research," *Political Research Quarterly* 48, 3 (September): 643–682.

6. Jody L. Fitzpatrick and Rodney E. Hero (1988), "Political Culture and Political Characteristics of the American States: A Consideration of Some Old and New Questions," *Western Political Quarterly* 41, 1 (March): 145–153.

7. Peter F. Nardulli (1990), "Political Subcultures in the American States: An Empirical Examination of Elazar's Formulation," *American Politics Quarterly* 18: 287–315.

8. Hero (1992), 112–114.

9. Brace (1995), p. 663.

10. Brace (1995), p. 666.

11. V. O. Key (1949), *Southern Politics in State and Nation* (New York: Alfred A. Knopf).

12. Walter Dean Burnham (1974), "The United States: The Politics of Heterogeneity" in Richard Rose, ed., *Electoral Behavior: A Comparative Handbook* (New York: Free Press): 653–726.

13. Cf. Edward G. Carmines and James A. Stimson (1989), *Issue Evolution: Race and the Transformation of American Politics* (Princeton, NJ: Princeton University Press.).

14. Burnham (1974).

15. Brace and Jewett (1995).

16. Gray (1990); Joel Lieske (1993), "Regional Subcultures of the United States," *Journal of Politics* 55, 4 (November): 86–113; John L. Sullivan (1973), "Political Correlates of Social, Economic and Religious Diversity in the American States," *Journal of Politics* 35, 1 (February); Norman Luttbeg (1992), *Comparing the States and Communities* (New York: HarperCollins).

17. Robert C. Lieberman (1993), "The Structural Politics of Race: Toward a New Approach to the Study of Race and Politics," paper delivered at the annual meeting of the American Political Association, Washington, D.C., September 2–5.

18. Rogers M. Smith (1993), "Beyond Tocqueville, Myrdal, and Hartz: The Multiple Traditions in America," *American Political Science Review* 87, 3 (September): 549–566.

19. Patricia Nelson Limerick (1987), *Legacy of Conquest: The Unbroken Past of the American West* (New York: W. W. Norton); Richard M. Merelman (1994), "Racial Conflict and Cultural Politics in the United States," *Journal of Politics* 56, 1 (February): 1–20.

20. For exceptions, see Kim Q. Hill and Jan E. Leighley (1996), "Racial Diversity and Voter Mobilization in the U.S.," paper presented at the Annual Meeting of the Western Political Science Association, San Francisco, CA; Benjamin Radcliff and Martin Saiz (1995), "Race, Turnout, and Public Policy in the American States," *Political Research Quarterly* 48, 4 (December): 775–794; Meier and Stewart (1991).

21. Gray (1990,1996).

22. Edward Carmines (1974), "The Mediating Influence of State Legislatures

on the Linkage Between Interparty Competition and Welfare Policies," *American Political Science Review* 68, 3 (September); Thomas R. Dye (1981), *Understanding Public Policy*, 4th ed., (Englewood Cliffs, NJ: Prentice-Hall), 334; Michael Lewis-Beck (1977), "The Relative Importance of Socioeconomic and Political Variables in Public Policy," *American Political Science Review* 71, 3 (June); Robert D. Plotnick and Richard F. Winters (1985), "A Politico-Economic Theory of Income Redistribution," *American Political Science Review* 79, 2 (June).

23. See, e.g., Erikson, Wright, and McIver (1993).

24. Cf. Gray (1996); Rodney E. Hero and Caroline J. Tolbert (1996), "A Racial/Ethnic Diversity Interpretation of Politics and Policy in the States of the U.S." *American Journal of Political Science* 40, 3 (August).

25. Fitzpatrick and Hero (1988), 150; Thomas R. Dye (1969), "Inequality and Civil Rights Policy in the States," *Journal of Politics* 31 (November).

26. Burnham (1974); Jennifer Hochschild (1984), *The New American Dilemma: Liberal Democracy and School Desegregation* (New Haven, CT: Yale University Press); Limerick(1987); Gunnar Myrdal (1944), *An American Dilemma: The Negro Problem and Modern Democracy* (New York: Harper and Brothers); Alexis de Tocqueville (1958), *Democracy in America*, Richard D. Heffner, ed.,(New York: New American Library); Hanes Walton (1985), *Invisible Politics: Black Political Behavior* (Albany, NY: State University of New York Press).

27. These assertions should not be taken to suggest political correctness nor interpreted in any similar way that trivializes or diminishes the argument. I am simply suggesting that theories of state politics need to acknowledge and incorporate the racial/ethnic diversity that clearly exists in the United States, at present and historically. Other scholars have made similar points—Smith (1993); Key (1949), Lieske (1993)—although they have not developed a broad interpretation of state politics that seeks to be applicable across the states and that is centered in racial/ethnic configurations, as I do here.

28. Steven P. Erie (1985), "Rainbow's End: From the Old to the New Urban Ethnic Politics," in Joan Moore and Lionel Maldonado, eds., *Urban Ethnicity in the United States* (Urban Affairs Annual Reviews, Beverly Hills: Sage); Raymond Wolfinger (1974), *The Politics of Progress* (Englewood Cliffs, NJ: Prentice-Hall).

29. See Hero (1992).

30. Cf. Elazar (1984); Daniel J. Elazar (1994) *The American Mosaic* (Boulder, CO: Westview Press); Lieske (1993).

31. Cf. Lieske (1993).

32. Daniel J. Elazar (1966), *American Federalism: A View from the States*, 1st ed. (New York: Crowell); Daniel J. Elazar (1970), *Cities of the Prairie* (New York: Basic Books); Daniel J. Elazar (1972), *American Federalism: A View from the States*, 2nd ed. (New York: Crowell); Elazar (1984, 1994); cf. Lieske (1993): 889.

33. Cf. Gray (1996); Nardulli (1990); Lieske (1993); also see chapter 2.

34. see Elazar (1984, 1994); Lieske (1993).

35. cf. Michael Thompson, Richard Ellis, and Aaron Wildavsky (1990); *Cultural Theory* (Boulder, CO: Westview Press); Lieske (1993).

36. cf. Lieberman (1993).

37. Elazar (1984); cf. Mark I. Lichbach (1997), "Social Theory and Comparative Politics," in Mark I. Lichbach and Alan. S. Zuckerman, editors, *Com-

parative Politics: Rationality, Culture and Structure (New York: Cambridge University Press).

38. Key (1949); Hubert M. Blalock (1970), *Toward a Theory of Minority-group Relations* (New York: Capricorn Books); Burnham (1974); Michael W. Giles and Arthur S. Evans (1986), "The Power Approach to Intergroup Hostility," *Journal of Conflict Resolution* 30 (September): 469–486; Lichbach (1997).

39. At least in part; David R. Morgan and Sheilah S. Watson (1991), "Political Culture, Political System Characteristics, and Public Policies Among the American States," *Publius* 21, 2 (Spring): 31–45.

40. Elazar (1994), 283–284.

41. Elazar (1994), 200–220; cf. (1984) [index] 263–270; Lieske (1993).

42. Key (1949); Bruce Cain (1992), "Voting Rights and Democratic Theory: Toward a Colorblind Society?" in Bernard Grofman and Chandler Davidson, eds., *Controversies in Minority Voting Rights* (Washington, DC: Brookings); Jack Citrin, Ernst B. Haas, Christopher Muster, and Beth Reingold (1994), "Is American Nationalism Changing? Implications for Foreign Policy," *International Studies Quarterly* 38, 1: 1–31.

43. The states also differ significantly in their degree of heterogeneity, particularly concerning the extent of minority populations; compare, e.g., Rhode Island and New York in figure. At present, however, I maintain the focus on the three major categorizations, although I modify it by indicating that heterogeneity may be simpler or more complex. Because these are interval-level variables, the data need not be conceptualized as a "two by two" table. In any case, note that the majority of states fall into the homogeneous or bifurcated sectors of the scatterplot (figure 1.1), and are evenly distributed across the index of minority diversity. In contrast, relatively few cases are high on the white ethnic diversity measure. Indeed, the smaller variation with respect to white ethnic diversity is why much of the discussion describes the index as simply a high-low categorization, while the index of minority diversity is described in terms of several levels or divisions. As is emphasized later, some of the most surprising substantive findings are associated with the homogeneous and bifurcated states. Also, while many, indeed most, Latinos consider themselves white, socially and politically they are considered part of a minority group (protected class), as indicated in numerous laws and in several court decisions. The census provides for and many Latinos list themselves as such (i.e., Hispanic). Asians are also included as minorities, although by some measures of social well-being this may be questionable. Because Native Americas have tribal governments and interact primarily with the federal government, their impact on state politics is limited; also, their population size is very small.

44. An index of state minority diversity, adapted from Sullivan (1973), was created from 1990 and 1980 census data on the percent Hispanic, black, white, and Asian in the states. To measure diversity, the index is a measure of a state's minority populations relative to the "white" population. The index was computed with the following formula:

Minority diversity $= 1 - [($Latino population$)^2 + ($black population$)^2 + ($white population$)^2 + ($Asian population$)^2]$.

The index of a state's white ethnic diversity was created by adding the percent Greek, Hungarian, Italian, Polish, Portuguese, Russian, and Irish reported in the

1990 and 1980 census. Ethnic affiliation is a self-reported category and the percent identifying with any particular nationality is quite small. This index of white ethnic diversity indicated little variation across states. When total percentages identifying with these ethnic groups were considered, higher variation was found.

45. Hero (1992).

46. Data from the 1990 and 1980 census were used to create both indices. This census year is nearest in time to the most recent extended discussion of political culture (Elazar [1984]) and the specific policy measures. The analyses in this and later chapters draw on these measures of diversity; the 1990 data versus the 1980 data are used as appropriate. (Also see note 43 above.)

47. Lieske (1993), 910.

48. cf. James Q. Wilson and Edward Banfield (1964), "Public Regardingness as a Value Premise in Voting Behavior," *American Political Science Review* 58, 4 (December): 876–887; James Q. Wilson and Edward Banfield (1971), "Political Ethos Revisited," *American Political Science Review* 65, 4 (December): 876–887.

49. The measures of racial/ethnic diversity used here differ from previous studies focusing primarily on a state's black population. While there is a positive correlation between the index of state minority diversity and percent black and Latino populations, they are distinct measures. The Pearson (r) correlation between the index of minority diversity and percent black 1980 is .69. The correlation between the index of minority diversity and percent Latino 1980 is .50. Neither percent black or Latino populations is even moderately correlated with the index of white ethnic diversity.

50. This part of the discussion of social diversity and political culture is based on the diversity patterns for 1980. This is because Elazar's most recent direct statement and classification of states appeared in 1984, thus the 1980 data are closer in time and more appropriate for comparison.

51. Elazar (1984), 135–137.

52. Elazar (1984), 135–137.

53. Here Elazar's categories are treated as a continuum, as Elazar has sometimes referred to them although on other occasions Elazar has claimed that they are not on a continuum. Elazar has also said that it is a "forced continuum that actually has elements of circularity" (1984: 136); cf. Lieske [1993]: 889 and 909.

54. Again, this is based on diversity data for 1980. When 1990 data are considered, the explained variance is .25; this suggests an increasing divergence between the political culture categorization and social diversity. I suspect that it results from the static nature of Elazar's political culture categories and their related inattention to minority group presence and growth.

55. see Elazar (1984), 134–135. Indeed, a recent analysis that sought to extend Elazar's own framework claims that he *mis*classifies 46 percent of the states; Morgan and Watson (1991); cf. Nardulli (1990).

56. Elazar (1984, 1994).

57. Brace (1995).

58. Elazar (1984).

59. Elazar (1984), 112, emphasis added.

60. see Hero and Tolbert (1996).

61. cf. Erikson, Wright, and McIver (1993), 115–117.

62. Hero (1992); Kim Q. Hill (1994), *Democracy in the Fifty States*. (Lincoln, Nebraska: University of Nebraska Press); Key (1949); Meier, Stewart, and England (1989); Myrdal (1944); Meier and Stewart (1991); Smith (1993).

63. Elazar (1984); Thomas R. Dye (1984), "Party and Policy in the States," *Journal of Politics* 46 (November): 1067–1116.

64. cf. Thompson, Ellis, and Wildavsky (1990).

65. Elazar (1984), 150–152, emphases added.

66. Elazar (1984), 151, emphasis added.

67. see Hero (1992), ch. 11.

68. see Clarence N. Stone (1989), *Regime Politics: Governing Atlanta, 1946–1988*, (Lawrence, KS: University Press of Kansas).

69. Lichbach (1997).

70. Louis Hartz (1995), *The Liberal Tradition in America; an interpretation of American political thought since the revolution*. (New York: Harcourt-Brace); Lowi and Ginsberg (1990).

71. Also see Russell L. Hanson (1994), "Liberalism and the Course of American Social Welfare Policy," in Lawrence C. Dodd and Calvin Jillson, eds., *The Dynamics of American Politics* (Boulder, Co.: Westview Press): 132–159.

72. cf. Elazar (1984).

73. Robert A. Dahl (1996) "Equality versus Inequality," *PS: Political Science*, 29, 4 (December): 462.

74. e.g., Thompson, Ellis, and Wildavsky (1990).

75. see Elazar (1984); Thompson, Ellis, and Wildavsky (1990).

76. Thompson, Ellis, and Wildavsky (1990); cf. Erikson, Wright, and McIver (1993).

77. cf. Elazar (1984).

78. Hero and Tolbert (1996).

79. Hero and Tolbert (1996).

80. Meier, Stewart, and England (1989); Cain (1992).

81. cf. Brace and Jewett (1995).

82. John B. Bibby, Cornelius P. Cotter, James L. Gibson, and Robert J. Huckshorn (1990), "Parties in State Politics," in Virginia Gray, Herbert Jacob, and Robert Albritton, eds., *Politics in the American States*, 5th ed., Glenview, IL: Scott, Foresman/Little, Brown): 85–122; John B. Bibby and Thomas M. Holbrook (1996), "Parties and Elections," in Virginia Gray and Herbert Jacob, eds., *Politics in the American States*, 6th ed. (Washington DC: Congressional Quarterly Press); Dye (1984).

83. Erikson, Wright, and McIver (1993).

84. Virginia Gray and David Lowery (1993), "The Diversity of State Interest Group Systems," *Political Research Quarterly* 46: 81–97; David Lowery and Virginia Gray (1993), "The Density of State Interest Group Systems," *Journal of Politics* 55, 1: 191–206; Virginia Gray and David Lowery (1996), *The Population Ecology of Interest Group Representation: Lobbying Communities in the American States*. (Ann Arbor: The University of Michigan Press); Clive S. Thomas and Ronald J. Hrebenar (1996), "Interest Groups in the States," in Virginia Gray and Herbert Jacob, eds., *Politics in the American States*, 6th ed. (Washington, DC: Congressional Quarterly Press): 122–158.

85. cf. Erikson, Wright, and McIver (1993); Elazar (1984).

86. see, e.g., Thad L. Beyle (1990). "Governors," in Virginia Gray, Herbert Jacob, and Robert Albritton, eds., *Politics in the American States*, 5th edtn.,

(Glenview, IL: Scott, Foresman/Little, Brown): 201–251; Peverill Squire (1992), "Legislative Professionalization and Membership Diversity in State Legislatures," *Legislative Studies Quarterly*, 17, 1 (February): 69–80.

87. Hero (1992).

Chapter 2

1. Paul Brace and Aubrey Jewett (1995), "Field Essay: The State of the State Politics Research," *Political Research Quarterly* 48, 3 (September).

2. Virginia Gray (1996), "The Socioeconomic and Political Context of States," in Virginia Gray and Herbert Jacob, eds., *Politics in the American States*, 6th ed. (Washington, DC: Congressional Quarterly Press), ch. 1; (1990), ch. 1.

3. It seems that much, probably the vast majority, of the state-politics research has appeared in scholarly journals rather than books. Thus, Brace and Jewett's focus on journals probably includes much of the research. However, that the state-politics research is so heavily journal oriented is itself interesting.

4. Brace may use an overly broad definition of state politics research. He appears to include virtually all research where state governments are considered. However, my sense is that a number of articles that Brace includes are not really looking at states as such; instead, states may just be the place where a phenomenon of interest occurs. For instance, some studies examine elections and, of course, all elections take place in states in some way. But the real object of interest in many articles is elections, not states per se.

5. Brace and Jewett (1995).

6. Virginia Gray and Herbert Jacob (1996), *Politics in the American States*, 6th ed. (Washington, DC: Congressional Quarterly Press).; also see Gray (1990).

7. Gray and Jacob (1996); Gray (1990).

8. Gray and Jacob (1996); Gray (1990).

9. Brace and Jewett (1995); see chapter 1 this book; Malcom E. Jewell (1982), "The Neglected World of State Politics," *Journal of Politics*, 44, 3: 638–658.

10. Daniel J. Elazar (1984), *American Federalism: A View from the States*, 3rd ed. (New York: Harper and Row).

11. Joel Lieske (1993), "Regional Subcultures of the United States," *Journal of Politics* 55, 4 (November): 86–113; Peter F. Nardulli (1990), "Political Subcultures in the American States: An Empirical Examination of Elazar's Formulation," *American Politics Quarterly* 18: 287–315.

12. On the surface, political culture as a concept certainly appears inherently, perhaps entirely, contextual. However, as suggested in chapter 1 and as implied in much of my discussion of the concept, as it has developed in the state politics research (Elazar, 1984), political culture is only somewhat contextual. Its emphasis on predominant groups, and that it often (though not always) tends to minimize relations between or among groups, lessens its contextualness. Similarly, other writings would suggest that Elazar's cultural approach is a subjective rather than an intersubjective cultural approach (see Lichbach (1997).

13. Virginia Gray (1996), "The Socioeconomic and Political Context of States," in Virginia Gray and Herbert Jacob, eds., *Politics in the American States*, 6th ed. (Washington, DC: Congressional Quarterly Press).

14. Gray (1996), 6–11.

15. Gray (1996), 11–15.

37. Hero and Tolbert (1996) note and discuss this as well.

38. Lieske (1993), 889–890.

39. Lieske (1993), 896–897.

40. Lieske (1993), 903.

41. Lieske (1993), 904–905, emphases added.

42. Lieske (1993), 902–905, emphases added.

43. Lieske (1993), 910.

44. Erikson, Wright, and McIver (1993).

45. Erikson, Wright, and McIver (1993), 51.

46. Erikson, Wright, and McIver (1993), 50.

47. Erikson, Wright, and McIver (1993), 52.

48. Erikson, Wright, and McIver (1993), 69, 53.

49. Erikson, Wright, and McIver (1993), 68–69, emphasis added.

50. Erikson, Wright, and McIver (1993), 69, emphasis added.

51. Erikson, Wright, and McIver (1993), 72, emphasis added.

52. Gray (1996), 31, emphasis added. This specific assertion is highly questionable, in my view. It confuses moralistic egalitarianism or generosity with homogeneity. Social diversity suggests that if there indeed is more willingness to support redistributive programs in moralistic states, it is because of who—i.e., what types of people—are the potential or real beneficiaries of the redistribution. Because they are similar to one's own group in racial/ethnic terms (versus those who might be different, such as minorities), there may be more willingness to support programs. In moralistic, or homogeneous, states there are very few minorities. These issues are developed later in chapters 5 and 6. For the moment, the central point is the link between what Gray calls socioeconomic and political context variables, here "political culture."

53. I do not "test" these hypotheses here, but that might be interesting and useful.

54. Erikson, Wright, and McIver (1993), 70.

55. Kim Q. Hill, (1994). *Democracy in the Fifty States*. (Lincoln, NE: University of Nebraska Press): xiv.

56. Brace (1995).

Chapter 3

1. cf. Virginia Gray, Herbert Jacob, and Robert B. Albritton (1990), *Politics in the American States* 5th ed., (Glenview, IL: Scott, Foresman).

2. V. O. Key (1949). *Southern Politics in State and Nation* (New York: Alfred A. Knopf).

3. E. E. Schattschneider (1960, 1975). *The Semisovereign People* (Hinsdale, IL: Dryden Press).

4. John B. Bibby and Thomas M. Holbrook (1996). "Parties and Elections," in Virginia Gray and Herbert Jacob, eds., *Politics in the American States*, 6th edtn (Washington, DC: Congressional Quarterly Press): 78–121.

5. Bibby and Holbrook (1996).

6. Kim Q. Hill (1994) *Democracy in the Fifty States* (Lincoln, NE: University of Nebraska Press). Robert L. Lineberry and Ira Sharkansky (1978), *Urban Politics and Public Policy* (New York: Harper and Row).

7. Clive S. Thomas and Ronald J. Hrebenar (1996) "Interest Groups in the States," in Virginia Gray and Herbert Jacob, eds., *Politics in the American States*

6th edtn., (Washington, D.C.: Congressional Quarterly Press): 122–158. Clive S. Thomas and Ronald J. Hrebenar (1990), "Interest groups in the States," in Virginia Gray, Herbert Jacob, and Robert B. Albritton, eds., *Politics in the American States*, 5th ed. (Glenview, IL: Scott, Foresman): 123–158.

8. Caroline J. Tolbert (1996). *The New Populism: Direct Democracy and Governance Policy*. A Doctoral Thesis submitted to the Graduate School of the University of Colorado at Boulder.

9. Hill (1994).

10. Hill (1994), 31.

11. Hill (1994), 38.

12. Hill (1994).

13. cf. Joel Lieske "Regional Subcultures of the United States," *Journal of Politics* 55, 4 (November): 86–113 (1993), 908; Daniel J. Elazar (1984). *American Federalism: A View from the States* 3rd edtn. (New York: Harper and Row).

14. Kim Q. Hill and Jan E. Leighley (1996). "Racial Diversity and Voter Mobilization in the U.S." Paper presented at the Annual Meeting of the Western Political Science Association, San Francisco.

15. cf. Robert S. Erikson, Gerald C. Wright, and John P. McIver (1993). *Statehouse Democracy* (New York: Cambridge University Press).

16. also see Benjamin Radcliff and Martin Saiz (1995). "Race, Turnout, and Public Policy in the American States" *Political Research Quarterly* 48, 4 (December): 775–794.

17. Hill (1994).

18. It is not clear why these findings differ from Hill and Leighley's (1986), but several factors may contribute to this. First, their diversity measure differs somewhat from mine. Also, their time period, 1980 and 1982, differs from the time frame I use, 1980 to 1986; see Hill (1994). And they divide the data on a South/non-South basis while I do not.

19. Bibby and Holbrook (1996).

20. Holbrook and Van Dunk (1993), "Electoral Competition in the American States," *American Political Science Review* 87, 4: 955–962.

21. Diana Dwyre, Mark O'Gorman, Jeffrey M. Stonecash, and Rosalie Young (1994), "Disorganized Politics and the Have-Nots: Politics and Taxes in New York and California," *Polity* 27, 1: 25–48.

22. While there are various measures of party organizational strength, I do not examine those here because, those measures focus mostly on the strength of parties as electoral mechanisms. While that is important, my interest in this section, similar to Dwyre et al. (1994), has more to do with the strength of parties *in government*. But for parties in government, I mean their organization and cohesion (cf. Dwyre et al. 1994), not merely the number or percent holding office; there are few or no good indicators that address this, to my knowledge.

23. As measured by Cornelius P. Cotter, James L. Gibson, John B. Bibby, and Robert J. Huckshorn (1984), *Party Organizations in American Politics* (New York: Praeger); Bibby and Holbrook (1996): 78–121 (1984) indicator.

24. Dwyre et al. (1994); cf. Erikson, Wright, and McIver (1993).

25. Hill (1994).

26. Hill (1994), 96–98.

27. Cf. Rodney E. Hero (1992), *Latinos and the U.S. Political System: Two-tiered Pluralism* (Philadelphia: Temple University Press).

28. cf. Dwyre et al. (1994), see above.

29. Robert D. Brown (1995), "Party Cleavages and Welfare Effort in the American States," *American Political Science Review* 89, 1 (March): 23–33.

30. Brown (1995), 24, emphasis in original.

31. Brown (1995) p. 27.

32. Or the absence of data on certain groups; cf. Hill's (1994) analysis.

33. Brown (1995), 27–28.

34. David Lawrence (1995), *California: The Politics of Diversity* (St. Paul, MN: West Publishing Company).

35. Dwyre et al. (1994).

36. Michael W. Giles and Kaenan Hertz (1994), "Racial Threat and Partisan Identification," *American Political Science Review* 88, 2 (June): 317–326.

37. Also see Caroline J. Tolbert and Rodney E. Hero (1996), "Race/Ethnicity and Direct Democracy: An Analysis of California's Illegal Immigration Initiative," *Journal of Politics* 58, 3: 806–818; and discussion in chapter 7.

38. James M. Glaser (1994), "Back to the Black Belt: Racial Environment and White Racial Attitudes in the South," *Journal of Politics*, 56, 1: 21–41.

39. Erikson, Wright, and McIver (1993), 14.

40. While Erikson, Wright, and McIver consider and/or control for a number of variables, including some that parallel social diversity, it is not clear whether they directly consider diversity as defined and measured here. In their efforts to account for state effects they note that when the impact of "the South" is put aside, or accounted for, the source of state effects is difficult to pinpoint. The present analysis does not, of course, "set aside" the South for several reasons—among them is that race and ethnicity (white ethnics) are expected to be important in different ways and to different degrees across the states.

41. cf. Erikson, Wright, and McIver (1993), 15, 62–72.

42. Brown's analysis (1995), discussed just above.

43. Erikson, Wright, and McIver (1993), 15, 62–72; cf. Brown (1995).

44. Erikson, Wright, and McIver (1993), 16.

45. They use the three, rather than the eight categories, with their "in-between" designations—e.g., I-M, "as is." They do not challenge its assumptions or specific state classifications. See chapters 1 and 2 for comment and critique of Elazar's framework and classifications.

46. Erikson, Wright, and McIver (1993), 161–164.

47. Elazar (1984); Erikson, Wright, and McIver (1993).

48. Erikson, Wright, and McIver (1993): 16.

49. cf. Erikson, Wright, and McIver (1993); Elazar (1984).

50. Also see Elazar (1984): 150 and discussion in chapter 1.

51. From Erikson, Wright, and McIver (1993): 103.

52. Cf. Erikson, Wright, and McIver (1993).

53. Cf. figure 1.4.

54. Cf. Erikson, Wright, and McIver (1993).

55. Cf. James Kuklinski, Michael Cobb, and Martin Gilens (1996), "Racial Attitudes and the 'New South,'" *Journal of Politics* (May) 59, 2: 323–349.

56. Erikson, Wright, and McIver (1993).

57. Erikson, Wright, and McIver (1993): 115–119.

58. Erikson, Wright, and McIver (1993).

59. Elazar (1984).

60. Cf. data in Erikson, Wright, and McIver (1993).

61. Cf. Elazar (1984), 121.

62. E.g., Elazar (1984); Erikson, Wright and McIver (1993).

63. Robert D. Brown, (1995), "Party Cleavages and Welfare Effort in the American States," *American Political Science Review* 89, 1 (March): 23–33; Robert C. Lieberman, (1993), "The Structural Politics of Race: Toward a New Approach to the Study of Race and Politics." Paper presented at the annual meeting of the American Political Association, Washington, DC, September 2–5.

64. Virginia Gray and David Lowery (1996), *The Population Ecology of Interest Group Representation: Lobbying Communities in the American States.* (Ann Arbor: The University of Michigan Press).; Virginia Gray and David Lowery (1993), "The Diversity of State Interest Group Systems." *Political Research Quarterly* 46, 81–97.

65. Thomas and Hrebenar (1996, 1990).

66. Thomas and Hrebenar (1996).

67. See Thomas and Hrebenar (1996, 1990).

68. Cf. Thomas and Hrebenar (1990, 1996).

69. Cf. Bibby and Holbrook (1996); Bibby, Cotter, Gibson, and Huckshorn (1990).

70. Jack Citrin (1996), "Who's the Boss? Direct Democracy and Popular Control of Government," in Stephen C. Craig, ed., *Broken Contract? Changing Relationship Between Americans and Their Government* (Boulder, CO: Westview Press): 268–294; Barbara S. Gamble (1997), "Putting Civil Rights to a Popular Vote," *American Journal of Political Science* 4, 1: 245–269; David Magleby (1984), *Direct Legislation: Voting on Ballot Propositions in the U.S.* (Baltimore: Johns Hopkins University Press).

71. Rodney E. Hero (1996), "An Essential Vote: Latinos and the 1992 Elections in Colorado," in Rodolfo O. de la Garza and Louis DeSipio, eds., *Ethnic Ironies: Latino Politics in the 1992 Elections* (Boulder, CO: Westview Press): 75–94.

72. Tolbert (1996).

73. Gamble (1997).

74. James Q. Wilson (1980), "The Politics of Regulation," in James Q. Wilson, ed., *The Politics of Regulation* (New York: Basic Books): 357–394.

75. Hill (1994).

76. Hill and Leighley (1996).

77. Brown (1995)

78. Giles and Hertz (1994).

79. Glaser (1994).

Chapter 4

1. Paul Brace and Aubrey Jewett (1995), "Field Essay: The State of the State Politics Research," *Political Research Quarterly* 48, 3 (September): 643–682.

2. Thad L. Beyle, (1990), "Governors," in *Politics in the American States,* 5th ed., Virginia Gray, Herbert Jacob, and Robert Albritton, eds., (Glenview, Ill.: Scott, Foresman/Little, Brown): 201–251.

3. Daniel J. Elazar (1984), *American Federalism: A View from the States,* 3rd ed. (New York: Harper and Row).

4. Jody L. Fitzpatrick and Rodney E. Hero (1988), "Political Culture and Political Characteristics of the American States: A Consideration of Some Old and New Questions," *Western Political Quarterly* 41, 1 (March). 145–153.

5. Bruce Cain (1992), "Voting Rights and Democratic Theory: Toward a Colorblind Society?" in Bernard Grofman and Chandler Davidson, eds., *Controversies in Minority Voting Rights* (Washington, DC: Brookings).

6. Cf. Elazar (1984). One might add, however, that a limited set of governmental institutions may be relatively strong in this context—those structures that directly or indirectly support stratification.

7. Citizens' Conference on State Legislatures (1973), *The Sometimes Governments* (Kansass City, MO: Citizens Conference on State Legislatures).

8. Edward Carmines (1974), "The Mediating Influence of State Legislatures on the Linkage Between Interparty Competition and Welfare Policies," *American Political Science Review* 68, 3 (September): 1118–1124.

9. Cf. Citizens' Conference on State Legislatures (1973).

10. Peverill Squire (1992), Legislative Professionalization and Membership Diversity in State Legislatures," *Legislative Studies Quarterly* 17, 1 (February): 69–80

11. Caroline J. Tolbert (1996). "The New Populism: Direct Democracy and Governance Policy." A thesis submitted to the Graduate School of the University of Colorado at Boulder.

12. Cf. Beyle (1996): 228–238; Beyle (1990).

13. Beyle (1996): 221–228.

14. See, e.g., Beyle (1996, 1990).

15. See John J. Harrigan (1994), *Politics and Policy in States and Communities*, 5th ed. (New York: Harper Collins): 274.

16. Beyle (1990).

17. Clive S. Thomas and Ronald J. Hrebenar (1990), "Interest Groups in the States," in V. Gray, H. Jacob, and R. Albritton, eds., *Politics in the American States*, 5th edtn., (Scott, Foresman): 123–158.

18. Virginia Gray, Herbert Jacob, and Robert B. Albritton (1990). *Politics in the American States*, 5th edtn., (Scott, Foresman).

19. Herbert Jacob (1990), "Courts," in Virginia Gray, Herbert Jacob and Robert B. Albritton, eds., *Politics in the American States* 5th edth., (Glenview, Ill: Scott, Foresman) 252–286.

20. Jacob (1990): 267 and 281.

21. Cf. Jacob (1990).

22. Lee Sigelman and N. Joseph Cayer (1986), "Minorities, Women, and Public Sector Jobs: A Status Report," in Michael W. Combs and John Gruhl, eds., *Affirmative Action: Theory, Analysis and Prospects* (Jefferson, NC: McFarland and Company): 91–111.

23. Charles Barrilleaux, Richard Feiock, and Robert E. Crew, Jr. (1992), "Measuring and Comparing American States' Administrative Characteristics," *State and Local Government Review* (Winter): 12–18, see especially p. 17.

24. Cf. Elazar (1984); Fitzpatrick and Hero (1988).

25. David Schmidt (1989), *Citizen Lawmakers: The Ballot Initiative Revolution* (Philadelphia: Temple University Press).

26. Schmidt (1989), emphasis added.

27. Schmidt (1989): 13, emphasis added.

28. Schmidt (1989): 13, emphasis added.

29. Patricia Nelson Limerick (1987), *Legacy of Conquest: The Unbroken Past of the American West* (New York: W.W. Norton).

30. The parity measure is calculated with the subtraction method (rather than the ratio or division method). Thus, the group as a percent of those in the legislature (black or Latino) is subtracted from the percent of the group in the state's general population. For example, if 10 percent of a state's legislators were black and 20 percent of the state's general population is black, the parity score with the subtractive method would be -10 (i.e., $10 - 20 = -10$). The subtraction method is used because it is a better indicator when states have no black and/or Latino members. With the subtraction method, negative scores may better differentiate between states with different sizes of minority populations. The ratio method does not differentiate between two states with no minority members of the legislature, although one state may have a very large minority population while the other may have a small minority population. Both would receive a 0 with the ratio method; yet the real underrepresentation is much greater in the former than in the latter.

31. California also appears to have very extensive underrepresentation. Some observers, however, might well dispute whether California's score is actually this low because the score does not account for the large noncitizen Latino population. This and similar questions might be raised for other states and/or other minority populations. The questions are legitimate ones. Yet even if appropriate adjustments were made for California, it might still have considerable underrepresentation. Similarly, if other adjustments were made for other states or groups, the overall patterns would be modified somewhat but likely remain.

32. The EEOC provides only full-time employment information categorized by salary range. This makes it difficult to differentiate between job types for minorities and whites. Therefore, the parity measure is a ratio of minority to white total employment controlled by population; U.S. Equal Employment Opportunity Commission (1990), *Job Patterns for Minorities and Women in State and Local Government* (Washington, DC: U.S. Government Printing Office).

33. It is important to note that for bureaucracies, the ratio or division method of calculation is used, unlike the subtraction measure used for legislatures (see note 30). This is because all state bureaucracies have some minorities, while some state legislatures have none. Thus, the ratio method seems more appropriate to assessing bureaucratic descriptive representation. If the subtraction measure were used, it would have little impact on the basic findings.

34. Cf. Rufus P. Browning, Dale Rogers Marshall, and David H. Tabb (1984), *Protest Is Not Enough: The Struggle of Blacks and Hispanics for Equality in Urban Politics* (Berkeley: University of California Press).

35. Donald R. Kinder and Tali Mendelberg (1995), "Cracks in American Apartheid: The Political Impact of Prejudice among Desegregated Whites," *Journal of Politics* 57, 2: 402–424; J. Milton Yinger (1985), "Assimilation in the United States: The Mexican-Americans," in Walker Connor, ed., *Mexican-Americans in Comparative Perspective* (Washington, DC: Urban Institute Press): 29–55.

36. Whatever the case may be, the findings do not seem to support a political culture interpretation of state politics, especially if one views the moralistic (homogeneous) context as one stressing basic procedural equality and a commonwealth orientation.

37. Richard C. Elling (1996), "Bureaucracy: Maligned yet Essential," in Virginia Gray and Herbert Jacob, eds., *Politics in the American States*, 6th ed. (Washington, DC: Congressional Quarterly Press.): 301, emphasis added.

38. See, e.g., Rodney E. Hero (1992), *Latinos and the U.S. Political System: Two-tiered Pluralism* (Philadelphia: Temple University Press): 142.

39. Elling (1996): 300.

Chapter 5

1. Rodney E. Hero and Caroline J. Tolbert (1996), "A Racial/Ethnic Diversity Interpretation of Politics and Policy in the State of the U.S." *American Journal of Political Science* 40, 3 (August). 851–871; Caroline J. Tolbert, and Rodney E. Hero (1996), "Race/Ethnicity and Direct Democracy: An Analysis of California's Illegal Immigration Initiative," *Journal of Politics* 58, 3: 806–818.

2. Virginia Gray and Herbert Jacob, eds. (1996), *Politics in the American States*, 6th ed. (Washington, DC: Congressional Quarterly Press).

3. Hero and Tolbert (1996).

4. Helen Ingram and Anne L. Schneider (1995), "Social Reconstruction (continued)," *American Political Science Review* 89, 2 (June) 441–446.

5. Cf. Hero and Tolbert (1996).

6. Robert S. Erikson, Gerald C. Wright and John P. McIver (1993), *Statehouse Democracy* (New York: Cambridge University Press).

7. Frederick Wirt (1990), "Education," in Virginia Gray, Herbert Jacob and Robert B. Albritton, eds., *Politics in the American States*, 5th ed., (Glenview, Ill.: Scott, Foresman): 447–478.

8. Kenneth Meier, Joseph Stewart, Jr. and Robert England (1989), *Race, Class, and Education: The Politics of Second Generation Discrimination* (Madison: University of Wisconsin Press). Kenneth Meier and Joseph Stewart, Jr. (1991), *The Politics of Hispanic Education* (Albany: State University of New York Press).

9. Robert Albritton (1990), "Social Services: Welfare and Health," in Virginia Gray, Herbert Jacob, and Robert B. Albritton, eds., *Politics in the American States*, 5th ed. (Glenview, IL: Scott, Foresman): 426–427.

10. Erikson, Wright, and McIver (1993): 75.

11. Meier and Stewart (1991).

12. Wirt (1990).

13. Hero and Tolbert (1996).

14. Wirt (1990): 447; Hero and Tolbert (1996).

15. It is very important to note here, and is emphasized later, several important differences between the Hero and Tolbert study (1996) discussed immediately below and the new research on differential education outcomes presented later in this chapter. The new research presented later includes evidence on two sets of states, all 50 states, and a subset of 41 states. The reasons for this are delineated later in this chapter. The earlier research (Hero and Tolbert, 1996) assessed only states with certain population thresholds, and school districts rather than states were the unit of analysis. Here, states and all states are the units of analysis because the underlying theory and its development would seem to require such an analysis. However, because the distribution of states on several dependent variables presents problems for statistical analysis,

a subset ($n = 41$) is also examined separately. In some contrast, the Hero and Tolbert study (1996) focused on education outcomes for blacks based on districts with at least 15,000 students and with black populations of at least 5 percent; these were then aggregated to the state level. Graduation and suspension rates were the average for years 1976, 1978, 1980, 1982, and 1986 measures as a ratio of blacks to all students The measures were odds ratios; the probability that a black student will be assigned to the category. Thus, any differences between the findings of the new and earlier research (Hero and Tolbert, 1996) may be due to the differences in the set of states and related factors.

16. Hero and Tolbert (1996); Meier, Stewart, and England (1989).

17. Cf. Meier, Stewart, and England (1989).

18. Rodney E. Hero (1992), *Latinos and the U.S. Political System: Two-tiered Pluralism* (Philadelphia: Temple University Press).

19. Meier, Stewart, and England (1989).

20. Cf. Daniel J. Elazar, (1984), *American Federalism: A View from the States*, 3rd ed. (New York: Harper and Row).

21. Hero and Tolbert (1996).

22. Hero and Tolbert (1996).

23. Michael Thompson, Richard Ellis, and Aaron Wildavsky (1990), *Cultural Theory*. (Boulder Colo.: Westview Press).

24. States were excluded from the analysis if the percent or proportion of their minority population was one standard deviation or more below the (50-state) mean. The nine states excluded are thus, by definition, among the lowest on minority diversity (black, Latino, Asian, etc.). They are Iowa, Kentucky, Maine, Minnesota, Nebraska, New Hampshire, North Dakota, Vermont, and West Virginia.

25. Wirt (1990): 452.

26. Ingram and Schneider (1995).

27. Cf. Hero and Tolbert (1996).

28. Cf. Hero and Tolbert (1996).

29. Cf. Hero and Tolbert (1996).

30. Theodore J. Lowi (1964), "American Business, Public Policy, Case-Studies and Political Theory," *World Politics* 16: 677–715.

31. Albritton (1990).

32. E.g., Erikson, Wright, and McIver (1993).

33. Robert D. Brown (1995), "Party Cleavages and Welfare Effort in the American States," *American Political Science Review* 89, 1 (March): 23–33.

34. Benjamin Radcliff and Martin Saiz, (1994), "Race, Turnout, and Public Policy in the American States," *Political Research Quarterly* 48, 4(December): 775–794.

35. Drawn from Mark Rom (1996), "Health and Welfare in the American States: Politics and Policies," in Virginia Gray and Herbert Jacob, eds., *Politics in the American States*, 6th ed. (Washington, DC: Congressional Quarterly Press): 414.

36. Cf. Rom (1996): 415–416.

37. Just noted; Rom (1996): 415–416.

38. Colleen M. Grogan (1994), "Political-Economic Factors Influencing State Medicaid Policy," *Political Research Quarterly* 47, 3 (September): 565–588.

39. Hero and Tolbert (1996).

40. Robert D. Plotnick and Richard F. Winters (1985), "A Politico-

Economic Theory of Income Redistribution," *American Political Science Review* 79, 2 (June): 458–473.

41. Grogan (1994).

42. Hero and Tolbert (1996).

43. Cf. Albritton (1990): 441.

44. Hero and Tolbert 1996; cf. Albritton (1990): 441.

45. See various works of Giles and co-authors noted in this book and elsewhere; Elazar (1984).

46. Grogan (1994).

47. Cf. Erikson, Wright, and McIver (1993).

48. Albritton attributes some of the pattern of Medicaid spending to another factor. He argues that Medicaid spending may be especially high in some states, such as New York, where the cost of medical care is, simply, substantially higher than other states.

49. Grogan (1994).

50. Grogan (1994); cf. Hero and Tolbert (1996).

51. Albritton (1990).

52. Cf. Hero and Tolbert (1996).

53. Hero and Tolbert (1996); Grogan (1994).

54. Daniel J. Elazar (1984). *American Federalism: A View from the States*, 3rd ed. (New York: Harper and Row). Russell L. Hanson (1994). "Liberalism and the Course of American Social Welfare Policy," in Lawrence C. Dodd and Calvin Jillson, eds., *The Dynamics of American Politics* (Boulder, Colo.: Westview Press): 132–159.

55. Elazar (1984).

56. Erikson, Wright, and McIver (1993).

57. Thomas M. Holbrook and Emily Van Dunk (1993), "Electoral Competition in the American States," *American Political Science Review* 87, 4: 955–962,

58. Peverill Squire (1992). Legislative Professionalization and Membership Diversity in State Legislatures," *Legislative Studies Quarterly* 17, 1 (February): 69–80

59. Thad L. Beyle (1990). "Governors." In *Politics in the American States*, 5th ed., Virginia Gray, Herbert Jacob, and Robert Albritton, eds. (Glenview, Ill.: Scott, Foresman/Little, Brown): 201–251.

60. Erikson, Wright, and McIver found that ideology had a significant impact on per pupil expenditures. Thus, the measure they used in their study differed from the one used here; this, along with the inclusion of a different group of control variables, may account for what appear to be inconsistent findings.

61. Hero and Tolbert (1996).

Chapter 6

1. Wesley G. Skogan (1996), "Crime and Punishment," in Virginia Gray and Herbert Jacob, eds., *Politics in the American States*, 6th ed. (Washington, DC: Congressional Quarterly Press): 397.

2. Skogan (1996): 394–395.

3. U.S. Department of Justice, Bureau of Justice Statistics (Washington, DC: (1992).

4. Jack Citrin, Beth Reingold, Evelyn Walters, and Donald P. Green (1990),

"The 'Official English' Movement and the Symbolic Politics of Language in the United States," *Western Political Quarterly* 43, 3 (September): 535–560.

5. Supporters of official English have asserted this, and been quoted, to that effect.

6. Citrin et al. (1990), "The Official English": 539.

7. Citrin et al. (1990), "The Official English."

8. Citrin et al. (1990), "The Official English": 549.

9. Citrin et al. (1990), "The Official English": 540.

10. Citrin et al. (1990), "The Official English": 540.

11. Citrin et al. (1990), "The Official English": 540–541.

12. Hero and Tolbert (1996).

13. Citrin et al. (1990), "The Official English": 541–544.

14. Susan Welch, Sue Thomas, and Margery M. Ambrosius (1996), "The Politics of Family Policy," In Virginia Gray and Herbert Jacob, eds., *Politics in the American States*, 6th ed. (Washington, DC: Congressional Quarterly Press): 549–587.

15. Welch et al. (1996).

16. Welch et al. (1996): 568–570.

17. Welch et al. (1996): 572.

18. Welch et al. (1996): 565.

19. From another study, Glen A. Halva-Neubauer (1990), "Abortion Politics in the Post-Webster Age," *Publius*, 20, 32: 27–44.

20. Welch et al. (1996): 565.

21. Winters (1996): 333.

22. Russell L. Hanson (1994), "Liberalism and the Course of American Social Welfare Policy," in Lawrence C. Dodd and Calvin Jillson, eds., *The Dynamics of American Politics* (Boulder, Colo.: Westview Press): 132–159. Daniel J. Elazar (1984), *American Federalism: A View from the States*, 3rd edtn. (New York: Harper and Row).

23. See, e.g., Rodney E. Hero (1992): *Latinos and the U.S. Political System: Two-tiered Pluralism* (Philadelphia: Temple University Press): 53 and 104–105.

24. Susan E. Clarke and Martin Saiz (1996), "Economic Development and Infrastructure Policy," in Virginia Gray and Herbert Jacob, eds., *Politics in the American States*, 6th ed. (Washington, DC: Congressional Quarterly Press): 516–548, 521; Peter Eisinger (1988), *The Rise of the Entrepreneurial State: State and Local Economic Development Policy in the United States* (Madison: University of Wisconsin Press).

25. Clarke and Saiz (1996): 531.

26. Clarke and Saiz (1996), 532.

27. Susan E. Clarke and Martin Saiz (1996), quoting from Peter Eisinger (1988), *The Rise of the Entrepreneurial State: State and Local Economic Development Policy in the United States* (Madison: University of Wisconsin Press): 230.

28. Robert S. Erikson, Gerald C. Wright, and John P. McIver (1993). *Statehouse Democracy* (New York: Cambridge University Press).

29. Several of these policies parallel some also examined in the present study. Importantly, however, Erikson, Wright, and McIver define and measure the policies somewhat differently than is done here.

30. Erikson, Wright, and McIver (1993): ch. 4.

31. Erikson, Wright, and McIver (1993).

32. Most of this discussion of governance policies draws directly and extensively from Caroline J. Tolbert, (1996), "The New Populism: Direct Democracy and Governance Policy." A thesis submitted to the Graduate School of the University of Colorado at Boulder: ch. 6.

33. Bruce Cain (1992), "Voting Rights and Democratic Theory: Toward a Colorblind Society?" in Bernard Grofman and Chandler Davidson, eds., *Controversies in Minority Voting Rights* (Washington, DC: Brookings).

34. Tolbert (1996).

35. Lonna Rae Atkeson, James A. McCann, Ronald B. Rapoport, and Walter J. Stone (1994), "Citizens for Perot: Activists and Voters in the 1992 Presidential Campaign," in Stephen C. Craig, ed., *Broken Contract? Changing Relationships between Citizens and their Government in the United States* (Boulder, CO: Westview Press).

36. Elazar (1984).

37. Erikson, Wright, and McIver (1993).

38. Holbrook and Van Dunk (1993).

39. Squire (1992).

40. Beyle (1990).

41. Elazar (1984).

42. Cf. Elazar (1984); Erikson, Wright, and McIver (1993): 79.

Chapter 7

1. V. O. Key (1949), *Southern Politics in State and Nation* (New York: Alfred A. Knopf).

2. Michael W. Giles (1977), "Percent Black and Racial Hostility: An Old Assumption Reexamined," *Social Science Quarterly* 58: 848–865; Michael W. Giles and Melanie A. Buckner (1993), "David Duke and Black Threat: An Old Hypothesis Revisted," *Journal of Politics*, 55, 3 (August): 702–713; Michael W. Giles, and Kaenan Hertz (1994), "Racial Threat and Partisan Identification," *American Political Science Review* Vol. 88, No. 2 (June): 317–326.

3. James M. Glaser (1994), "Back to the Black Belt: Racial Environment and White Racial Attitudes in the South." *Journal of Politics*, 56, 1: 21–41.

4. Also see Martin Gilens (1995), "Racial Attitudes and Opposition to Welfare," *Journal of Politics* 57, 4 (November): 994–1014; cf. Thomas M. Carsey (1995), "The Contextual Effects of Race on White Voters Behavior: The 1989 New York City Mayoral Election," *Journal of Politics* 57, 1 (February): 221–228.

5. Michael W. Link and Robert W. Oldendick (1996), "Social Construction and White Attitude toward Equal Opportunity and Multiculturalism," *Journal of Politics* 58, 1: 149–168.

6. Link and Oldendick (1996).

7. Link and Oldendick (1996).

8. Donald R. Kinder and Tali Mendelberg (1995), "Cracks in American Apartheid: The Political Impact of Prejudice among Desegregated Whites," *Journal of Politics* 57, 2: 402–424.

9. Kinder and Mendelberg (1995): 420, emphases added.

10. Rodney E. Hero, Caroline J. Tolbert, and Robert R. Lopez (1996), "Ra-

cial/Ethnic Context and Direct Democracy: Reexamining 'Official English' and its Implications," paper presented at the annual meeting of the American Political Science Association, San Francisco.

11. Bruce Cain, (1992), "Voting Rights and Democratic Theory: Toward a Colorblind Society?" in Bernard Grofman and Chandler Davidson, eds., *Controversies in Minority Voting Rights* (Washington, DC: Brookings).

12. Jack Citrin, Beth Reingold, Evelyn Walters and Donald P. Green (1990), "The 'Official English' Movement and the Symbolic Politics of Language in the United States," *Western Political Quarterly* 43, 3 (September): 535–560. Jack Citrin, Beth Reingold, and Donald P. Green (1990), "American Identity and the Politics of Ethnic Change," *Journal of Politics* 52, 4: 1124–1154; Raymond Tatalovich (1995); *Nativism Reborn?* (Lexington: The University Press of Kentucky); Rodney E. Hero (1992). *Latinos and the U.S. Political System: Two-tiered Pluralism* (Philadelphia: Temple University Press).

13. Citrin et al. (1990), "American Identity."

14. Rogers M. Smith (1988), "The 'American Creed' and American Identity: The Limits of Liberal Citizenship in the United States," *Western Political Quarterly* 41: 225–251.

15. Citrin et al. (1990), "American Identity": 1129.

16. Citrin et al. (1990), "American Identity": 1134; Citrin et al. (1990), "The Official English."

17. Citrin et al. (1990), "The Official English." Jack Citrin, Ernst B. Haas, Christopher Muster and Beth Reingold (1994), "Is American Nationalism Changing? Implications for Foreign Policy," *International Studies Quarterly* 38, 1: 1–31; cf. Hero (1992).

18. Hero, Tolbert, and Lopez (1996) discuss this fully.

19. Hero, Tolbert, and Lopez (1996).

20. Citrin et al. (1990), "American Identity": 1140.

21. Robert S. Erikson, Gerald C. Wright, John P. McIver (1993), *Statehouse Democracy* (New York: Cambridge University Press).

22. Daniel J. Elazar (1984), *American Federalism: A View from the States*, 3rd ed. (New York: Harper and Row); but see Rodney E. Hero and Caroline J. Tolbert (1996), "A Racial/Ethnic Diversity Interpretation of Politics and Policy in the States of the U.S." *American Journal of Political Science* 40, 3 (August): 851–871.

23. National Association of Latino Elected and Appointed Officials (Washington, DC). (1993).

24. Hero (1992).

25. Cf. Key (1949); Michael W. Giles and Arthur S. Evans (1986), "The Power Approach to Intergroup Hostility," *Journal of Conflict Resolution* 30 (September). 469–486; Paul Brace, and Aubrey Jewett (1995), "Field Essay: The State of the State Politics Research," *Political Research Quarterly* 48, 3 (September): 643–682.

26. Cf. Joel Lieske (1993), "Regional Subcultures of the United States," *Journal of Politics* 55, 4 (November): 86–113.

27. Cf. Key (1949); Giles and Evans (1986); Citrin et al. (1994).

28. Cf. Citrin et al. (1990), "The Official English."

29. Hero (1992).

30. Cf. Citrin et al. (1990), "The Official English."

31. Cf. Key (1949): Giles and Buckner (1993).

32. Richard Hofstadter (1955), *The Age of Reform: From Bryan to F.D.R.* (New York: Vintage Books).

33. Cf. Citrin et al. (1990), "The Official English."; County and City Databook (1986) (Washington, DC: U.S. Government Printing Office). (1986) California, and (1988) Colorado and Florida.

34. Hero (1992).

35. Hero, Tolbert, and Lopez (1996).

36. Cf. Erikson, Wright, and McIver (1993).

37. Cf. Link and Oldendick (1995); Kinder and Mendelberg (1995); also see Citrin et al. (1994).

38. Cf. however, Hero (1992): ch. 11; Jennifer Hochschild (1984), *The New American Dilemma: Liberal Democracy and School Desegregation* (New Haven: Yale University Press).

39. Caroline J. Tolbert and Rodney E. Hero (1996), "Race/Ethnicity and Direct Democracy: An Analysis of California's Illegal Immigration Initiative," *Journal of Politics* 58, 3: 806–818.

40. Hero and Tolbert (1996); cf. Raymond E. Wolfinger and Fred I. Greenstein (1968), "The Repeal of Fair Housing in California: An Analysis of Referendum Voting," *American Political Science Review* 62: 753–769.

41. Wolfinger and Greenstein (1968); Citrin et al. (1990), "The Official English."; Cain (1992); Citrin et al. (1990), "American Identity."

42. Cf. Key (1949); Giles and Buckner (1993).

43. Hofstadter (1955).

44. Data from California Secretary of State's Office.

45. Paula D. McClain (1993), "The Changing Dynamics of Urban Politics: Black and Hispanic Municipal Employment—Is There Competition?" *Journal of Politics* 55, 2: 399–414.

46. While not discussed in this book, the 1996 California Civil Rights Institute, or anti-affirmative action also can be partly explained in racial/ethnic terms.

47. David Magleby (1984), *Direct Legislation: Voting on Ballot Propositions in the U.S.* (Baltimore: Johns Hopkins University Press).

48. Cf. Kinder and Mendelberg (1995).

49. James Gimpel (1996), *National Elections and the Autonomy of American State Party Systems* (Pittsburgh: University of Pittsburgh Press).

50. See Gimpel (1996): 47, 51, 113, 146, 152.

51. Gimpel (1996): 167, 182, 195, 198.

52. Robert L. Lineberry and Ira Sharkansky (1978), *Urban Politics and Public Policy.* (New and Row): 118–119; Clarence N. Stone, Robert K. Whelan, and William J. Murin (1986), *Urban Policy and Politics in a Bureaucratic Age*, 2nd ed. (Englewood Cliffs, NJ: Prentice-Hall): 91–99; Wolfinger (1974): ch. 2.

53. Robert L. Lineberry and Edmund P. Fowler (1967), "Reformism and Public Policy in American Cities," *American Political Science Review* 61: 701–716; William Lyons (1978), "Reform and Response in American Cities: Structure and Policy Reconsidered," *Social Science Quarterly* 59: 118–132; Stephen L. Elkin (1987), *City and Regime in the American Republic* (Chicago: University of Chicago Press).

54. Lineberry and Sharkansky (1978): 95–96 and 124–127.

55. Susan Welch (1990), "The Impact of At-Large Elections on the Representation of Blacks and Hispanics," *Journal of Politics* 52, 4: 1050–1076; Albert Karnig and Susan Welch (1982), "Electoral Structure and Black Representa-

tion," *Social Science Quarterly* 63 (March): 99–114; Richard Engstrom and Michael McDonald (1981), "The Underrepresentation of Blacks on City Councils," *American Political Science Review* 75 (June): 344–355; Chandler Davidson and George Korbel (1981), "At Large Elections and Minority Group Representation: A Re-Examination of Historical and Contemporary Evidence," *Journal of Politics* 43, 4: 982–1005; Theodore Robinson and Robert England (1981), "Black Representation on Central City School Boards Revisited," *Social Science Quarterly* 62: 495–501; Stone, Whelan, and Murin (1986); Theodore Robinson and Thomas Dye (1978), "Reformism and Representation on City Councils," *Social Science Quarterly* 59 (June): 133–141.

56. Kenneth Meier, Joseph Stewart, Jr. and Robert England (1989), *Race, Class, and Education: The Politics of Second Generation Discrimination* (Madison: University of Wisconsin Press); Kenneth Meier and Joseph Stewart, Jr. (1991), *The Politics of Hispanic Education* (Albany: State University of New York Press).

57. Kinder and Mendelberg (1995).

Chapter 8

1. Rogers M. Smith (1993), "Beyond Tocqueville, Myrdal, and Hartz: The Multiple Traditions in America," *American Political Science Review* 87, 3 (September): 549–566.

2. Paul Brace and Aubrey Jewett (1995), "Field Essay: The State of the State Politics Research," *Political Research Quarterly* 48, 3 (September): 643–682; Malcolm E. Jewel (1982), "The Neglected World of State Politics," *Journal of Politics* 44, 3: 638–658.

3. Cf. Daniel J. Elazar (1984), *American Federalism: A View from the States*, 3rd edtn. (New York: Harper and Row); Michael Thompson, Richard Ellis, and Aaron Wildavsky (1990), *Cultural Theory.* (Boulder, Colo.: Westview Press).

4. Robert S. Erikson, Gerald C. Wright, John P. McIver (1993), *Statehouse Democracy* (New York: Cambridge University Press).

5. Rodney E. Hero and Caroline J. Tolbert (1996), "A Racial/Ethnic Diversity Interpretation of Politics and Policy in the States of the U.S." *American Journal of Political Science* 40, 3 (August). 851–871.

6. Hero and Tolbert (1996); Jack Citrin, Beth Reingold, Evelyn Walters and Donald P. Green (1990), "The 'Official English' Movement and the Symbolic Politics of Language in the United States," *Western Political Quarterly* 43, 3 (September): 535–560.

7. Cf. Tolbert and Hero (1996); Rodney E. Hero, Caroline J. Tolbert and Robert R. Lopez (1996), "Racial/Ethnic Context and Direct Democracy: Reexamining "Official English" and its Implications." Paper presented at the Annual Meeting of the Western Political Science Association, San Francisco.

8. James Gimpel (1996), *National Elections and the Autonomy of American State Party Systems* (Pittsburgh: University of Pittsburgh Press).

9. Erikson, Wright, and McIver (1993); also see Jennifer Hochschild (1988), "The Double-edged Sword of Equal Opportunity," in Ian Shapiro and Grant Reeher, eds., *Power, Inequality and Democratic Politics* (Boulder, CO.: Westview Press).

10. Elazar (1966).

11. Cf. Gimpel (1996): 23.

12. Cf. Kenneth Meier and Joseph Stewart, Jr. (1991), *The Politics of His-*

panic Education (Albany: State University of New York Press); Kenneth Meier, Joseph Stewart, Jr. and Robert England (1989), *Race, Class, and Education: The Politics of Second Generation Discrimination* (Madison: University of Wisconsin Press); Hero (1992): ch. 11.

13. Russell L. Hanson (1994), "Liberalism and the Course of American Social Welfare Policy," in Lawrence C. Dodd and Calvin Jillson, eds., *The Dynamics of American Politics* (Boulder, Colo.: Westview Press): 132-159.

14. Elazar (1984).

15. Michael Lipsky (1980), *Street-Level Bureaucracy* (New York: Russell Sage).

16. Lipsky (1980); Meier, Stewart, and England (1989); Meier and Stewart (1991).

17. Smith (1993); Richard J. Ellis (1993), *American Political Culture* (New York City: Oxford University Press).

18. Paula D. McClain and Albert K. Karnig (1990), "Black and Hispanic Socioeconomic and Political Competition," *American Political Science Review* 84, 2 (June): 535-545.

19. Cf. Rufus P. Browning, Dale Rogers Marshall, and David H. Tabb (1984), *Protest Is Not Enough: The Struggle of Blacks and Hispanics for Equality in Urban Politics* (Berkeley: University of California Press).

20. Hanes Walton (1985). *Invisible Politics: Black Political Behavior* (Albany: State University of New York Press); Jennifer Hochschild (1984), *The New American Dilemma: Liberal Democracy and School Desegregation* (New Haven: Yale University Press).

21. Hero (1992); Hero and Tolbert (1996); Meier, Stewart, and England (1989); Meier and Stewart (1991); Mario Barrera (1979), *Race and Class in the Southwest: A Theory of Racial Inequality* (Notre Dame, IN: University of Notre Dame Press).

References

Albritton, Robert (1990). "Social Services: Welfare and Health," in Virginia Gray, Herbert Jacob and Robert B. Albritton, eds., *Politics in the American States* 5th ed., (Glenview, IL: Scott, Foresman/Little Brown): 411–416.

Atkeson, Lonna Rae, James A. McCann, Ronald B. Rapoport, and Walter J. Stone (1994). "Citizens for Perot: Activists and Voters in the 1992 Presidential Campaign," in Stephen C. Craig, ed., *Broken Contract? Changing Relationships between Citizens and their Government in the United States* (Boulder, CO: Westview Press.)

Barker, Lucius J. and Jesse J. McCorry, Jr. (1980). *Black Americans and the Political System* (Cambridge, MA: Winthrop).

Barrilleaux, Charles, Richard Feiock, and Robert E. Crew, Jr. (1992). "Measuring and Comparing American States' Administrative Characteristics," *State and Local Government Review* (Winter): 12–18.

Beyle, Thad L. (1990). "Governors," in Virginia Gray, Herbert Jacob, and Robert B. Albritton, eds., *Politics in the American States*, 5th ed., (Glenview, IL.: Scott, Foresman/Little, Brown): 201–251

Beyle, Thad L. (1996) "Governors" in Virginia Gray and Herbert Jacob, eds., *Politics in the American States* 6th ed. (Washington, DC: Congressional Quarterly Press): 207–252.

Bibby, John B., and Thomas M. Holbrook (1996). "Parties and Election," in Virginia Gray and Herbert Jacob, eds., *Politics in the American States*, 6th ed. (Washington, DC: Congressional Quarterly Press): 78–121.

Bibby, John B., Cornelius P. Cotter, James L. Gibson, and Robert J. Huckshorn. (1990). "Parties in State Politics," in Virginia Gray, Herbert Jacob, and Robert Albritton, eds., *Politics in the American States*, 5th ed., (Glenview, IL: Scott, Foresman/Little, Brown): 85–122

Blalock, Hubert M. (1970). *Toward a Theory of Minority-group Relations* (New York: Capricorn Books).

Brace, Paul and Aubrey Jewett (1995). "Field Essay: The State of the State Politics Research," *Political Research Quarterly* 48, 3 (September): 643–682.

Brown, Robert D. (1995). "Party Cleavages and Welfare Effort in the American States," *American Political Science Review* 89, 1 (March): 23–33.

Browning, Rufus P., Dale Rogers Marshall, and David H. Tabb (1984). *Protest Is Not Enough: The Struggle of Blacks and Hispanics for Equality in Urban Politics* (Berkeley: University of California Press).

Burnham, Walter Dean. (1974) "The United States: The Politics of Heterogeneity," in Richard Rose, ed., *Electoral Behavior: A Comparative Handbook* (New York: Free Press): 653–726.

Cain, Bruce (1992). "Voting Rights and Democratic Theory: Toward a Colorblind Society?" in Bernard Grofman and Chandler Davidson, eds., *Controversies in Minority Voting Rights* (Washington, DC: Brookings Institution).

Carmines, Edward (1974). "The Mediating Influence of State Legislatures on the Linkage Between Interparty Competition and Welfare Policies," *American Political Science Review* 68, 3 (September): 1118–1124.

Carmines, Edward G. and James A. Stimson (1989), *Issue Evolution: Race and the Transformation of American Politics.* (Princeton, NJ: Princeton University Press.)

Carsey, Thomas M. (1995). "The Contextual Effects of Race on White Voters Behavior: The 1989 New York City Mayoral Election," *Journal of Politics* 57, 1 (February): 221–228.

Citizens Conference on State Legislatures (1973). *The Sometimes Governments* (Kansas City, MO: Citizens Conference on State Legislatures).

Citrin, Jack (1996). "Who's the Boss? Direct Democracy and Popular Control of Government," in Stephen C. Craig, ed., *Broken Contract? Changing Relationships between Citizens and their Government in the United States* (Boulder, CO: Westview Press): 268–294.

Citrin, Jack, Beth Reingold, and Donald P. Green (1990). "American Identity and the Politics of Ethnic Change," *Journal of Politics* 52, 4: 1124–1154.

Citrin, Jack, Beth Reingold, Evelyn Walters, and Donald P. Green (1990). "The 'Official English' Movement and the Symbolic Politics of Language in the United States," *Western Political Quarterly* 43, 3 (September): 535–560.

Citrin, Jack, Ernst B. Haas, Christopher Muster, and Beth Reingold (1994). "Is American Nationalism Changing? Implications for Foreign Policy," *International Studies Quarterly* 38, 1: 1–31.

Clarke, Susan E (1987). "More Autonomous Policy Orientations: An Analytic Framework," in Clarence N. Stone and Heywood T. Sanders, eds., *The Politics of Urban Development* (Lawrence: University Press of Kansas): 105–124.

Clarke, Susan E. and Martin Saiz (1996). "Economic Development and Infrastructure Policy," in Virginia Gray and Herbert Jacob, eds., *Politics in the American States*, 6th ed. (Washington DC: Congressional Quarterly Press): 516–548.

Cotter, Cornelius P., James L. Gibson, John B. Bibby, and Robert J. Huckshorn. (1984). *Party Organizations in American Politics* (New York: Praeger).

Dahl, Robert A. (1996). "Equality versus Inequality," *PS: Political Science*, 29, 4, (December): 462.

Davidson, Chandler and George Korbel (1981). "At Large Elections and Minority Group Representation: A Re-Examination of Historical and Contemporary Evidence." *Journal of Politics* 43, 4: 982–1005.

Dwyre, Diana et al. (1994). "Disorganized Politics and the Have-Nots: Politics and Taxes in New York and California," *Polity* 27, 1: 25–48.

Dye, Thomas R. (1966). *Politics, Economics, and the Public* (Chicago: Rand McNally).

Dye, Thomas R. (1969). "Inequality and Civil Rights Policy in the States," *Journal of Politics* 31 (November): 1080–1097.

Dye, Thomas R. (1981). *Understanding Public Policy*, 4th ed., (New York: Prentice-Hall).

Dye, Thomas R. (1984). "Party and Policy in the States," *Journal of Politics* 46 (November): 1097–1116.

Eisinger, Peter (1980). *The Politics of Displacement: Racial and Ethnic Transition in Three American Cities* (New York: Academic Press).

Eisinger, Peter (1988). *The Rise of the Entrepreneurial State: State and Local Economic Development Policy in the United States.* (Madison: University of Wisconsin Press).

Elazar, Daniel J. (1966). *American Federalism: A View from the States* 1st ed. (New York: Crowell).

Elazar, Daniel J. (1970). *Cities of the Prairie* (New York: Basic Books).

Elazar, Daniel J. (1972). *American Federalism: A View from the States*, 2nd ed. (New York: Crowell).

Elazar, Daniel J. (1984). *American Federalism: A View from the States*, 3rd ed. (New York: Harper and Row).

Elazar, Daniel J. (1994) *The American Mosaic* (Boulder, CO: Westview Press).

Elkin, Stephen L. (1987). *City and Regime in the American Republic* (Chicago: University of Chicago Press).

Elling, Richard C. (1996). "Bureaucracy: Maligned Yet Essential," in Virginia Gray and Herbert Jacob, eds., *Politics in the American States* 6th ed. (Washington, DC: Congressional Quarterly Press): 286–318.

Ellis, Richard J. (1993). *American Political Culture* (New York: Oxford University Press).

Engstrom, Richard and Michael McDonald (1981). "The Underrepresentation of Blacks on City Councils." *American Political Science Review* 75 (June): 344–55.

Erie, Steven P. (1985). "Rainbow's End: From the Old to the New Urban Ethnic Politics," in Joan Moore and Lionel Maldonado, eds., *Urban Ethnicity in the United States* (Urban Affairs Annual Reviews, Sage).

Erikson, Robert S., Gerald C. Wright, John P. McIver (1993). *Statehouse Democracy* (New York: Cambridge University Press).

Fitzpatrick, Jody L. and Rodney E. Hero (1988). "Political Culture and Political Characteristics of the American States: A Consideration of Some Old and New Questions," *Western Political Quarterly* 41, 1 (March): 145–153.

Gamble, Barbara S. (1997). "Putting Civil Rights to a Popular Vote," *American Journal of Political Science* 4, 1: 245–269.

Gilens, Martin (1995). "Racial Attitudes and Opposition to Welfare," *Journal of Politics* 57, 4 (November): 994–1014.

Giles, Micheal W. (1977). "Percent Black and Racial Hostility: an Old Assumption Reexamined," *Social Science Quarterly* 58: 848–865.

Giles, Michael W. and Arthur S. Evans (1986). "The Power Approach to Inter-group Hostility," *Journal of Conflict Resolution* 30 (September).

Giles, Michael W. and Kaenan Hertz (1994). "Racial Threat and Partisan Identification," *American Political Science Review* 88, 2 (June): 317–326.

Giles, Michael W. and Melaine A. Buckner (1993). "David Duke and Black Threat: An Old Hypothesis Revisted," *Journal of Politics*, 55, 3 (August): 702–713

Gimpel, James (1996). *National Elections and the Autonomy of American State Party Systems* (Pittsburgh: University of Pittsburgh Press).

Glaser, James M. (1994). "Back to the Black Belt: Racial Environment and White Racial Attitudes in the South," *Journal of Politics*, 56, 1: 21–41.

Gray, Virginia (1990). "The Socioeconomic and Political Context of States," in Virginia Gray, Herbert Jacob, and Robert B. Albritton, eds., *Politics in the American States*, 5th ed., (Glenview, IL: Scott, Foresman): 3–37.

Gray, Virginia (1996). "The Socioeconomic and Political Context of States," in Virginia Gray and Herbert Jacob, eds., *Politics in the American States*, 6th ed. (Washington, DC: Congressional Quarterly Press): 1–34.

Gray, Virginia and David Lowery (1993). "The Diversity of State Interest Group Systems." *Political Research Quarterly* 46: 81–97.

Gray, Virginia and David Lowery (1996). *The Population Ecology of Interest Group Representation: Lobbying Communities in the American States* (Ann Arbor: University of Michigan Press).

Gray, Virginia and Herbert Jacob, eds. (1996). *Politics in the American States*, 6th ed. (Washington DC: Congressional Quarterly Press).

Gray, Virginia, Herbert Jacob, and Robert B. Albritton, eds. (1990). *Politics in the American States*, 5th ed. (Glenview, IL Scott, Foresman).

Grogan, Colleen M. (1994). "Political-Economic Factors Influencing State Medicaid Policy," *Political Research Quarterly* 47, 3 (September): 565–588.

Halva-Neubauer, Glen A. (1990). "Abortion Politics in the Post-Webster Age." *Publius*, 20, 32: 27–44

Hanson, Russel L. (1994). "Liberalism and the Course of American Social Welfare Policy," in Lawrence C. Dodd and Calvin Jillson, eds., *The Dynamics of American Politics* (Boulder, CO: Westview Press): 132–159.

Harrigan, John J. (1994). *Politics and Policy in States and Communities*, 5th ed. (New York: HarperCollins).

Hartz, Louis (1955). *The Liberal Tradition in America: An interpretation of American political thought since the revolution* (New York: Harcourt-Brace).

Hero, Rodney E. (1992). *Latinos and the U.S. Political System: Two-Tiered Pluralism* (Philadelphia: Temple University Press).

Hero, Rodney E. (1996). "An Essential Vote: Latinos and the 1992 Elections in Colorado," in Rodolfo O. de la Garza and Louis DeSipio, eds., *Ethnic Ironies: Latino Politics in the 1992 Elections* (Boulder, CO: Westview Press) 75–94.

Hero, Rodney E. and Caroline J. Tolbert (1996). "A Racial/Ethnic Diversity Interpretation of Politics and Policy in the State of the U.S." *American Journal of Political Science* 40, 3 (August): 851–871

Hero, Rodney E. Caroline J. Tolbert and Robert R. Lopez (1996). "Racial/Ethnic Context and Direct Democracy: Reexamining 'Official English' and Its Implications." Paper presented at the Annual Meeting of the Western Political Science Association, San Francisco.

Hietala, Thomas R. (1985). *Manifest Design: Anxious Aggrandizement in Late Jacksonian America* (Ithaca, NY: Cornell University Press).

Hill, Kim Q. (1994). *Democracy in the Fifty States* (Lincoln, NE: University of Nebraska Press).

Hill, Kim Q. and Jan E. Leighley (1996) "Racial Diversity and Voter Mobilization in the U.S." Paper presented at the Annual Meeting of the Western Political Science Association. San Francisco.

Hochschild, Jennifer (1984). *The New American Dilemma: Liberal Democracy and School Desegregation* (New Haven, CT: Yale University Press).

Hochschild, Jennifer (1988). "The Double-edged Sword of Equal Opportunity" in Ian Shapiro and Grant Reeher, eds., *Power, Inequality and Democratic Politics* (Boulder, CO: Westview Press): 168–200.

Hofstadter, Richard (1955). *The Age of Reform: From Bryan to F.D.R.* (New York: Vintage Books).

Holbrook, Thomas M. and Emily Van Dunk (1993). "Electoral Competition in the American States," *American Political Science Review* 87 4: 955–962,

Jacob, Herbert (1996). "Courts: The Least Visible Branch," in Virginia Gray and Herbert Jacob, eds. *Politics in the American States*, 6th ed. (Washington, DC: Congressional Quarterly Press): 253–285.

Jewell, Malcom E. (1982). "The Neglected World of State Politics." *Journal of Politics*, 44, 3: 638–658.

Karnig, Albert and Susan Welch (1982). "Electoral Structure and Black Representation," *Social Science Quarterly* 63 (March): 99–114;

Key, V. O. (1949). *Southern Politics in State and Nation* (New York: Alfred A. Knopf).

Kinder, Donald R. and Tali Mendelberg (1995). "Cracks in American Apartheid: The Political Impact of Prejudice among Desegregated Whites," *Journal of Politics* 57, 2: 402–424.

King, Gary, Robert O. Keohane, and Sidney Verba (1994). *Designing Social Inquiry* (Princeton, NJ: Princeton University Press).

Kuklinski, James, Michael Cobb, and Martin Gilens (1996). "Racial attitudes and the 'New South,'" *Journal of Politics* 59, 2 (May): 323–349.

Lawrence, David (1995). *California: The Politics of Diversity* (St. Paul, MN: West Publishing Company).

Lewis-Beck, Michael (1977). "The Relative Importance of Socioeconomic and Political Variables in Public Policy," *American Political Science Review* 71, 3 (June): 559–566.

Lichbach, Mark I. (1997) "Social Theory and Comparative Politics," in Mark I Lichbach and Alan. S. Zuckerman, eds., *Comparative Politics: Rationality, Culture and Structure* (New York: Cambridge University Press)

Lieberman, Robert C. (1993). "The Structural Politics of Race: Toward a New Approach to the Study of Race and Politics." Paper delivered at the annual meeting of the American Political Association, Washington, D.C., September 2–5.

Lieberman, Robert; Helen Ingram and Anne L. Schneider (1995). "Social Construction" (continued), *American Political Science Review* 89, 2: 437–446.

Lieske, Joel (1993). "Regional Subcultures of the United States," *Journal of Politics* 55, 4 (November): 86–113

Limerick, Patricia Nelson (1987). *Legacy of Conquest: The Unbroken Past of the American West* (New York: Norton).

Lineberry, Robert L. and Edmund P. Fowler (1967). "Reformism and Public Policy in American Cities," *American Political Science Review* 61: 701–716.

Lineberry, Robert L. and Ira Sharkansky (1978). *Urban Politics and Public Policy*. (New York: Harper and Row).

Link, Michael W. and Robert W. Oldendick (1996). "Social Construction and White Attitudes toward Equal Opportunity and Multiculturalism," *Journal of Politics* 58, 1: 149–168.

Lipsky, Michael (1980). *Street-Level Bureaucracy* (New York: Russell Sage).

Lowery, David and Virginia Gray (1993). "The Density of State Interest Group Systems," *Journal of Politics* 55, 1: 191–206.

Lowi, Theodore (1967). "Machine Politics: Old and New," *The Public Interest* 9 (Fall): 83–92

Lowi, Theodore (1979). *The End of Liberalism*, 2nd ed. (New York: Norton).

Lowi, Theodore J. (1964). "American Business, Public Policy, Case-Studies, and Political Theory," *World Politics* 16: 677–715.

Lowi, Theodore J. and Benjamin Ginsberg (1990). *American Government: Freedom and Power* (New York: Norton).

Luttbeg, Norman (1992). *Comparing the States and Communities* (New York: HarperCollins).

Lyons, William (1978). "Reform and Response in American Cities: Structure and Policy Reconsidered," *Social Science Quarterly* 59: 118–132.

Magleby, David (1984). *Direct Legislation: Voting on Ballot Propositions in the U.S.* (Baltimore: Johns Hopkins University Press).

McClain, Paula D. (1993). "The Changing Dynamics of Urban Politics: Black and Hispanic Municipal Employment—Is There Competition?" *Journal of Politics* 55, 2: 399–414.

McClain, Paula and Albert K. Karnig (1990). "Black and Hispanic Socioeconomic and Political Competition," *American Political Science Review* 84, 2 (June): 535–545.

Meier, Kenneth and Joseph Stewart, Jr. (1991). *The Politics of Hispanic Education* (Albany: State University of New York Press).

Meier, Kenneth, Joseph Stewart, Jr. and Robert England (1989). *Race, Class, and Education: The Politics of Second Generation Discrimination* (Madison: University of Wisconsin Press).

Merelman, Richard M. (1994). "Racial Conflict and Cultural Politics in the United States," *Journal of Politics* 56, 1 (February): 1–20.

Moore, Joan and Harry Pachon (1985). *Hispanics in the United States* (Englewood Cliffs, NJ: Prentice Hall).

Morgan, David R. and Sheilah S. Watson (1991). "Political Culture, Political System Characteristics, and Public Policies among the American States," *Publius* 21, 2 (Spring): 31–45.

Myrdal, Gunnar (1944). An American Dilemma: The Negro Problem and Modern Democracy (New York: Harper and Brothers).

Nardulli, Peter F. (1990). "Political Subcultures in the American States: An Empirical Examination of Elazar's Formulation," *American Politics Quarterly* 18: 287–315.

Omi, Michael and Howard Winant (1986). *Racial Formation in the United States: From the 1960s to the 1980s* (New York: Routledge & Kegan Paul).

Peterson, Paul (1981). *City Limits* (Chicago: University of Chicago Press).

Plotnick, Robert D. and Richard F. Winters (1985). "A Politico-Economic Theory of Income Redistribution," *American Political Science Review* 79, 2 (June): 458–473.

Radcliff, Benjamin and Martin Saiz, (1995). "Race, Turnout, and Public Policy in the American States," *Political Research Quarterly* 48, 4 (December): 775–794.

Robinson, Theodore and Robert England (1981). "Black Representation on Central City School Boards Revisited," *Social Science Quarterly* 62: 495–501

Robinson, Theodore and Thomas Dye (1978). "Reformism and Representation on City Councils," *Social Science Quarterly* 59 (June): 133–41.

Rom, Mark (1996). "Health and Welfare in the American States: Politics and Policies," in Virginia Gray and Herbert Jacob, eds., *Politics in the American States*, 6th ed. (Washington DC: Congressional Quarterly Press): 399–437.

Rosenthal, Alan (1990). *Governors and Legislatures: Contending Powers* (Washington, DC: Congressional Quarterly Press).

Schattschneider, E. E. (1960, 1975). *The Semisovereign People* (Hinsdale, IL: Dryden Press).

Schmidt, David (1989). *Citizen Lawmakers: The Ballot Initiative Revolution* (Philadelphia: Temple University Press).

Shapiro, Michael J. (1981). *Language and Political Understanding: The Politics of Discursive Practices* (New Haven, CT: Yale University Press).

Sigelman, Lee and N. Joseph Cayer (1986). "Minorities, Women, and Public Sector Jobs: A Status Report," in Michael W. Combs and John Gruhl, eds., *Affirmative Action: Theory, Analysis and Prospects* (Jefferson, NC: McFarland and Company): 91–111.

Skogan, Wesley G. (1996). "Crime and Punishment," in Virginia Gray and Herbert Jacob, eds., *Politics in the American States*, 6th ed. (Washington, DC: Congressional Quarterly Press): 361–398.

Smith, Rogers M. (1988). "The 'American Creed' and American Identity: The Limits of Liberal Citizenship in the United States," *Western Political Quarterly* 41: 225–251.

Smith, Rogers M. (1993). "Beyond Tocqueville, Myrdal, and Hartz: The Multiple Traditions in America," *American Political Science Review* 87, 3 (September): 549–566.

Squire, Peverill (1992). Legislative Professionalization and Membership Diversity in State Legislatures," *Legislative Studies Quarterly* 17, 1 (February): 69–80

Stone, Clarence N. (1980). "Systemic Power in Community Decision Making: A Restatement of Stratification Theory," *American Political Science Review* 74 (December): 978–990.

Stone, Clarence N. (1989). *Regime Politics: Governing Atlanta, 1946–1988.* (Lawrence: University Press of Kansas.)

Sullivan, John L. (1973). "Political Correlates of Social, Economic and Religious Diversity in the American States," *Journal of Politics* 35, 1 (February).

Tatalovich, Raymond (1995). *Nativism Reborn?* (Lexington: The University Press of Kentucky).

Thomas, Clive S. and Ronald J. Hrebenar (1990). "Interest Groups in the States," in Virginia Gray, Herbert Jacob, and Robert Albritton, eds., *Politics in the American States*, 5th ed. (Glenview, IL Scott, Foresman): 123–158.

Thomas, Clive S. and Ronald J. Hrebenar (1996). "Interest Groups in the

States," in Virginia Gray and Herbert Jacob, eds., *Politics in the American States* 6th ed., (Washington, DC: Congressional Quarterly Press): 122–158.

Thompson, Michael, Richard Ellis, and Aaron Wildavsky (1990). *Cultural Theory.* (Boulder, CO: Westview Press).

Tocqueville, Alexis de (1958). *Democracy in America*, Richard D. Heffner, ed., (New York: New American Library).

Tolbert, Caroline J. (1996). "The New Populism: Direct Democracy and Governance Policy." A thesis submitted to the Graduate School of the University of Colorado at Boulder.

Tolbert, Caroline J. and Rodney E. Hero (1996). "Race/Ethnicity and Direct Democracy: An Analysis of California's Illegal Immigration Initiative," *Journal of Politics* 58, 3: 806–818.

U.S. Department of Commerce, Bureau of the Census 1993. *Statistical Abstract of the United States* 113th ed. (Washington, DC: U.S. Government Printing Office).

U.S. Department of Commerce, Bureau of the Census (1986, 1988, 1990). *County and City Data Book* (Washington D.C: U.S. Government Printing Office).

U.S. Department of Education, Office of Civil Rights (1990). *Elementary and Secondary School Civil Rights Survey* (Washington, DC: U.S. Government Printing Office).

U.S. Department of Justice, Office of Justice Programs, Bureau of Justice Statistics (1992). *Bureau of Justice Statistics Statistical Programs* (Washington D.C.: U.S. Government Printing Office).

U.S. Equal Employment Opportunity Commission (1990). *Job Patterns for Minorities and Women in State and Local Government* (Washington, DC: U.S. Government Printing Office).

Verba, Sidney and Norma Nie (1972). *Participation in America: Political Democracy and Social Equality* (New York: Harper and Row).

Walton, Hanes (1985). *Invisible Politics: Black Political Behavior* (Albany: State University of New York Press).

Welch, Susan (1990). "The Impact of At-Large Elections on the Representation of Blacks and Hispanics," *Journal of Politics* 52, 4: 1050–1076.

Welch, Susan, Sue Thomas, and Margery M. Ambrosius (1996). "The Politics of Family Policy," in Virginia Gray and Herbert Jacob, eds. *Politics in the American States*, 6th ed. (Washington DC: Congressional Quarterly Press): 549–587.

Wilson, James Q. (1980). "The Politics of Regulation," in James Q. Wilson, ed., *The Politics of Regulation* (New York: Basic Books): 357–394.

Wilson, James Q. and Edward Banfield (1964). "Public Regardingness as a Value Premise in Voting Behavior," *American Political Science Review* 58, 4 (December): 876–887.

Wilson, James Q. and Edward Banfield (1971). "Political Ethos Revisited," *American Political Science Review* 65, 4 (December): 1048–1062.

Winters, Richard F. (1996). "The Politics of Taxing and Spending," in Virginia Gray and Herbert Jacob, eds., *Politics in the American States*, 6th ed. (Washington DC: Congressional Quarterly Press): 319–360.

Wirt, Frederick (1990). "Education," in Virginia Gray, Herbert Jacob and Robert B. Albritton, eds, *Politics in the American States*, 5th ed. (Glenview, IL Scott, Foresman): 447–478.

Index

Printed in the United States
49891LVS00006B/167

9 780195 137880